Contemporary reflections on the medieval
Christian tradition

Contemporary reflections on the medieval Christian tradition

Essays in honor of Ray C. Petry

edited by GEORGE H. SHRIVER

Duke University Press   Durham, N.C.   1974

© 1974, Duke University Press

L.C.C. card no. 73–77639

I.S.B.N. 0–8223–0304–3

Printed in the United States of
America by Heritage Printers, Inc.

Contents

Part V. Teaching in the great tradition

Preface

Essays in this *Festschrift* range from one by a former mentor of Professor Petry at the University of Chicago to one by Professor Petry's last graduate student at Duke University. The others are written by those whose graduate work at Duke University was directed by Professor Petry during his long tenure. The sole exception is the essay written by the present bishop in the United Methodist Church, the Atlanta Area, former dean and medievalist at Candler School of Theology. In every case, the choice of essay is related to the study of medieval Christianity and to Ray C. Petry's special interest in and contribution to this discipline. The five themes in the volume are those around which the teaching and writing career of Professor Petry has nucleated. The essay in appreciation is sensitively written by one who has been a close personal friend and colleague in the discipline of church history. The direct traces of Ray C. Petry himself are found in the selections from religious affirmations which he shared through the years in York Chapel and elsewhere.

Appreciation is expressed to those who gave early and enthusiastic encouragement to the production of such a volume. Robert E. Cushman, then Dean of the Divinity School of Duke University and Stuart C. Henry, Professor of American Christianity in the Divinity School of Duke University, were the first to endorse such a project and at later stages shared wise counsel and advice toward its completion. Thomas A. Langford, Dean of the Divinity School of Duke University, gave his positive support during the final stages of preparation. Ashbel G. Brice, Director and Editor, Duke University Press, was especially helpful in every phase of the project. The support and subsidy of the Divinity School and the Duke University Press assured publication.

Acknowledgement and appreciation is expressed to the editors of *Church History* for permission to revise and enlarge "A Summary of Images of Catharism and the Historian's Task," 40 (March, 1971), pp. 48–54 and to St. Mary's College, Notre Dame, Indiana, where on January 25, 1971 an abbreviated version of Dr. McNeill's essay "Perspectives on Celtic Church History" was delivered. Appreciation is also expressed to the editor of *Outlook* for permission to use Dr. Petry's article, "The Historic University," which appeared in that publication in July–August, 1971.

Finally, each writer is warmly thanked. The response in participation and the conscientious spirit in relation to deadline have been beyond the call of duty and illustrative of the dedication in friendship and love for Ray C. Petry.

There are many others whose names do not appear here but who in some way played a role in the appearance of this *Festschrift*. May they be well aware of the sincere and deep appreciation for those things they have done which have been so necessary to the whole project.

Lastly, it is hoped that this volume will both honor Ray C. Petry and give him genuine pleasure.

G. H. S.

Ray C. Petry: an appreciation

STUART C. HENRY

Nothing quite affects us as does conversation with another, whose person defies ordinary analysis, even while shutting off any escape from the challenge to attempt it. We are never the same after such encounters. Doubtless many of Ray Petry's students, and all of his friends, have more than once parted company with him, and—preoccupied with the baffling essence of the man—have unexpectedly discovered something hitherto unknown about themselves which the meeting with Dr. Petry, whether accidental or planned, had brought to light. The maieutic quality is but one aspect of his personality, though surely reason enough to explain why the responsibility of expressing appreciation for his genius in the present form is not confidently attempted. Yet a word must be recorded about him concerning whom "to tell but the tenth part would tax my wits."

No one would condone less than the scholar-historian Ray Petry himself the misapplication or superficial use of quotation (least of all quotation from his much admired Nicholas of Cusa). There is, however, in the effort to suggest what manner of man Dr. Petry is—some justification for beginning with reference to the cardinal's treatise *On Learned Ignorance*:

> It is clear, therefore, that we know nothing concerning the true except that we know it to be incomprehensible precisely as it is . . . . And the more we shall be profoundly learned in this ignorance, the more we shall approach truth itself . . . . And when we try to perceive . . . with the intellectual eye, we fall down in the fog, knowing only that this fog hides us from the mountain, on which only those may live who flourish in understanding . . . . with internal hearing we perceive the voices, the thunder, and the terrible signs of the majesty of God, . . . believers . . . are carried up to intellectuality in its simplicity, passing beyond all sensible things, as if from sleep to waking, from hearing to sight, where those things are seen which cannot be revealed, because they are beyond all hearing and the teaching of the voice.

It is precisely this ability to hear what is not said, to see what is not written, which characterizes Ray Petry's grasp of human affairs about him and of history. It is manifest in his peculiar genius of communication without and in spite of words, and his intensely vital relationship to others. His perception of the dimension of the historical problem manifests itself (along with other ways) in ready willingness to admit that history cannot be known exhaustively; it appears in his acknowledgment that in spite of the inability of any man to see clearly into the depths of another's soul, history bespeaks a thirst for such communion. These traits assist him in the pursuit of history through his understanding of human nature, and in enriching the community of his residence through astringent comment upon the present or poignant reference to the past. There is no intent to prove the foregoing estimate, nor even to present it in systematic and complete case. Rather the purpose is to offer witness to the character and person of the man, whose qualities the writer has observed both as a former student and a privileged colleague. Let one thing, however, be remembered: each one who speaks of Dr. Petry introduces another perspective from which to read the man. An anecdote may illustrate.

Not too many years ago, during one of his classroom lectures, Ray Petry was holding forth, as only he can do, recreating an era with seemingly spontaneous, but actually carefully chosen selection of detail, throwing away casual reference to esoteric bibliography, correcting immature impression and prejudice in graphic distillation of years of reflection, and (as often happens in his classes) frustrating, even infuriating, those who at the particular moment were unwilling to be pushed, and too earth-bound to be pulled. One student was busily taking notes, trying to keep pace with his teacher by racing along in a combination of shorthand and hieroglyphics, nodding his head and smiling, or frowning, but plainly responding to the lecture. His seatmate was frozen in immobility, pencil posed but note pages blank, although uncomfortably aware of the industrious scribe by his side. When the class was dismissed he confronted his colleague: "How *could* you reduce what we heard to systematic notes?" The answer is illuminating: "I didn't. Nobody could. I just wrote down what I was learning about myself."

There is a temptation to think of Ray Petry as, primarily, or even only, a historian, but the classification is not sufficient. He is a historian. That much is certain; but it is neither the first nor foremost category which applies to him. He is ever this, never less, though usually a great deal more. It is true, however, that many folk think of him first as a historian, and there is cogency, therefore, in considering him as such.

No student crosses Dr. Petry's path without thereafter feeling for original sources a respect both compelling and enduring. The unsophisticate who arrives in his class, innocent of the techniques in research and canons of documentation, does not leave even the initial session without having seen, in a way which makes it impossible for him to ever un-see it again, that history is concerned with documents. The fledgling historian does not progress very far in his novitiate, though, before grasping the insight that nothing, in Dr. Petry's opinion, is so unworthy of the historian as juggling the sources, beginning the endeavor with conclusions in hand, or examining data in the interest of substantiating a prejudice. Primary sources may be slanted or fragmentary; they may be unimportant or misleading; they may, paradoxically, even be fabricated; but they may not be forgotten or discarded without being studied and assessed. Yet Dr. Petry, as a historian, has little sympathy, or, more correctly, much compassion for those who would endeavor to make history a science, and who even boast that they are in the process of doing so. Fond of reminding students that writers of history frequently overlook the losers, and never unmindful of the great streams of mortal dust which bear the heroes along in the avalanche of human events, Ray Petry will not settle for the precision which results from the application of caliper or the reverence for tape measure and microscope. His are the pronouncements which take due regard of the dreams of the nameless actors of the past and, though unable to discover their identity, never forget that measure of vitality which they enjoyed. With learned ignorance, Dr. Petry often concludes no more than that it is neither just nor wise to rule out the possibility that thus and such might possibly have been the case.

As he himself has said: The true historian "recognizes the great danger of fabricating the story of the past out of the wishes of the present . . . . and knows that history which ignores minds, meanings, and values is hardly real history; that pure facts divorced from interpretation are something of a mirage; and that past experiences which have any meaning for the present necessarily undergo some valuative interpretation . . . ." History which is written from such a perspective

definitely commits itself to an interest which extends beyond episodes and events. It is unashamedly curious about the meaning of these facts in relation to ordinary people. Human environment, attitudes, motivations, doings, ideas, and ideals are as definitely the concern of history as they are beyond the sheerly quantitative measurement of pure science. The historical process is rightly seen to include not only the more material elements such as geography and economics but also the psychic factors, without consideration of which the record of living men cannot be even approximately known. History thus abandons atomistic and isolated approaches for a critically interpretative survey which gladly employs the finding of cooperative research in sociology, anthropology, psychology, art, archeology, and other related fields. Scientific methodology wherever applicable is in no way compromised. However, the concern of history with man's individual and social integrity, with his mental as well as his physical activity, goes beyond the findings of pure science into the realm of applications and values as well.

The distinction which Dr. Petry claims as a historian lies, obviously, not in his awareness of the New History, or his acceptance of demanding standards, but with the remarkable degree to which he has achieved conformity to the canons which he acknowledges. Being introduced by him to such study of history is a simple matter. Not only is he accessible to all, but the sense of community with the past continually emanates from him. The consciousness of more worlds than can be numbered lies behind all that he says, and attends him like a nimbus wherever he goes. The face of truth which he wears, however, is easier to recognize than to describe. His statement can be as cryptic and as sparse as the motifs of the arts which he continually employs in fascinating way with telling effect.

As he has studied and taught history, so he has written it, preserving in his publications that same respect for the reader's personality and right to discover for himself, which he exhibits in his honest and imaginative use of documents. This is only to recognize that for Ray Petry problems of history and gathered data are windows through which to see a little more clearly into the nature of truth, or to learn a little more surely of ignorance. Sometimes he tells the reader this. On occasion, however, he allows the reader to be dazzled, even temporarily blinded, by the light which research discovers so that he has no recourse save to look inward, which is exactly what Dr. Petry has intended all the time. Thus, Ray Petry's *Francis of Assisi* presents the

Poverello as a prism through which to examine a whole complex of circumstance and data, all of which reduce to the possibility and necessity of inquiring into the nature of truth as exampled by a man before God.

In this volume, to quote W. E. Garrison of *The Christian Century,* Dr. Petry "penetrates . . . much more deeply into the spiritual life of Francis . . . than either the Protestant panegyrists of a romanticized Francis, or the deflaters . . . or the Catholic writers who have sought to capitalize his prestige for the benefit of the church or . . . have used him as a club with which to beat heretics." Typically, Dr. Petry offers original perspective from which to view a familiar figure. "Nothing published [on the seventh hundred anniversary of Francis] . . . or since," concludes the critic, "has thrown more light upon this perennially interesting character than Dr. Petry's sympathetic and critical study."

Widely commended for the research and preparation which went into the work, *Christian Eschatology and Social Thought* offers extended example of the meticulous attention to detail and the authenticity of data which combine to effect the opening of unexpected vistas. It is a tribute to writer and mentor that John T. McNeill in reviewing the study of eschatology says of his former student and close friend, "Dr. Petry has undertaken this informing work in a spirit of inquiry rather than of dogmatism." The book, incidentally, is an affirmation of this world, paradoxically, because it renounces the world as it is, and any willingness to accept it thus, in the interest of affirming the world as it might be, will be, and, finally, must be, because any outcome otherwise would be intolerable. Just so, all of Dr. Petry's historical writings are part of a quest, a search for community which he was seeking long before reference to it became a cliché among seminarians.

His sensitive and beautiful *History of Christianity* appears on initial examination to say, "Remember how lovely the Christian tradition is. See the exquisite plates. Consider the fugitive documents, so thoughtfully gathered, so carefully edited." In the end, though, the reader is awed by the perplexing vitality and variety of the tradition as were the fathers confronted by the dilemma at Chalcedon. The idiom is not inapposite. For what the man does again and again, in his study, in his teaching, in his writing, is to say, "Reflect on the facts, read the documents. The pattern is not clear. There may, indeed, be no pattern; but there is life, and it is the life of community watched over by a cloud of many witnesses. Embrace this community, respectfully and warmly

acknowledging brotherhood with saints and sinners, wisely acknowledging that you can no more know all about their lives than you can
know all about yourself." One remembers Goethe's advice that the
nature of true happiness consists in plumbing the depths of the knowable and quietly revering that which is unknowable.

At this point it is appropriate to introduce one of the peculiar factors in Dr. Petry's intuitive understanding of the shape of his own
learned ignorance. Never in attendance on any of his lectures or in
any encounter with him is one able to forget that Ray Petry never ignores the dimension of human sorrow, or the secret yearning (one of
his favorite words) of every human heart. More than once he has as-
sisted the young in breaking out of the chrysalis of self-centeredness
into the world of compassion. He delivers the tradition to each individual in a special way, because of the special needs of each individual.
Every individual has his own place with him. Dr. Petry is equally at
his ease, sitting at high table in the refectory of Mansfield College, or
discussing with a neighborhood child the virtues of running away
from home.

All that is here volunteered about Dr. Petry applies to him as a
churchman. Fiercely defensive of the tradition in the face of those who
spurn history and dissipate their inheritance, he is by no means conventional in his relation to the church. He guards well his own freedom which is as distinctive as that on the American frontier, as spontaneous as worship at Eastern rites. There are times when he attends
church for the explicit, though not exclusive, purpose of lifting his
voice in dissent. He does not settle for easy lines drawn between Christ
and culture any more than he tolerates barrier between market place
and university. In a real sense his study of history is the refinement and
practice of his awareness of others—not simply of his own generation,
but of whatever age, in whatever world. As he says obliquely in his
whole career, so he states explicitly in *Christian Eschatology* that the
temporal world which we know is "socially answerable to the eternal
order of life." The endeavor to fulfill the implied obligation informs
and explains his profession as historian, and his other activities, public
and private. The man is integrated, even though the dynamics of his
understanding and knowledge are not comfortably contained in their
existential prison.

Finally, what he is may perhaps best be exemplified in reference to
his relationship to his wife, the late Ruth Mertz. Affectionately de-

scribed in his published volumes as "collaborator," she was rare in her own right. The record of their marriage documents man's inability to be whole alone, and also reminds the questor that none need expect to escape loneliness. Ruth was so devoted and model a wife that to attempt to show how she deserved the distinction would probably stigmatize her in caricature. Nevertheless, she was an individual, perceptive and efficient, with a puckish sense of humor. Her integrity complemented his, and each was more distinctively individualistic in relation to the other. Ray Petry's theme has always been the application of the critical temper to the Christian tradition, the discovery of the true and ultimate community through all the uses of memory and mind. His relation with Ruth is an illuminating symbol both of the technique and the success of such a venture. Together they discovered the tradition—each enhancing the other's vision—because in the iconography of love they were already a part of the community which they sought to discover and enlarge. Everyone who passes along the tradition affects and is affected by it. Dr. Petry's career is a case in point.

He has taught us much more than history. Or rather, he has taught us that the tradition is constant in essence if protean in appearance, and that life exists in forms which we have not imagined.

The Divinity School
Duke University

Part I. Preaching in the great tradition

Preaching and pastoral care in John Tauler

B. MAURICE RITCHIE

In a useful study of John Tauler, James M. Clark[1] observes two striking aspects of the man, the eminently practical preacher and pastor, and the occasional speculative and mystic. Clark asks how one might bring these two seemingly divergent aspects of a single man together. His conclusion is that Tauler was at heart a mystic who was restrained in his public expression of his true feelings by the force of circumstances in which he worked. The tone of hesitation Clark detects surrounding the truly mystical passages of the sermons is to be explained by the unfortunate experience of Tauler's fellow Dominican, Meister Eckhart. But, moreover, "It was not Tauler's task to stimulate mysticism, but rather to restrain it, and to guide it into safe channels."[2]

Ignaz Weilner[3] recently observed that it is questionable whether Tauler was indeed "mystically gifted." There are references in the sermons which indicate that Tauler himself had not attained the highest levels of the mystical encounter with God, at least at the time from which the sermons stem. In Tauler one finds, according to Weilner, a true shepherd of souls who is not concerned with wonderful, yet extraordinary ways to God, but with the deepening of man's relationship to God charged to every willing soul.[4]

Tauler's personal mystical experience may indeed elude the industrious inquirer into the sermons, but the relationship of a mystical focus on the Christian's life to pastoral practice has not gone unnoticed in the history of scholarship. No less a figure than Johann Schneyer[5] has noted that, while the thought of the German mystics had parallels in Bernard, Albert the Great, Bonaventura and others, their preaching style reflected distinctive priorities of mystical thought. In contrast to the scholastic preaching style with its use of clever alle-

---

1. "John Tauler," *The Month*, XXV, no. 1 (Jan., 1961), 23–33, especially p. 33. See also Clark's *Great German Mystics: Eckhart, Tauler, and Suso* (Oxford: Basil Blackwell, 1949), pp. 36–54.
2. *The Month*, p. 33.
3. "Tauler und das Problem der Lebenswende," *Johannes Tauler, Ein deutscher Mystiker. Gedenkschrift zum 600. Todestag*, E. Filthaut, ed. (Essen: Hans Driewer Verlag, 1961), pp. 321–340. Hereafter cited as *Gedenkschrift* with the appropriate page(s). See also Weilner's *Johannes Taulers Bekehrungsweg: Die Erfahrungsgrundlagen seiner Mystik* (Regensburg: Verlag Friedrich Pustet, 1961).
4. *Gedenkschrift*, p. 331.
5. *Geschichte der katholischen Predigt* (Freiburg: Seelsorge Verlag, 1969), pp. 173–174.

gories in the interpretation of scripture and skilled resolutions of theological problems, the mystics sought to deal directly with the longing
of the human soul in its total relationship with God. These men moved
so close to the profoundest human experience of God in their preaching that they landed in misinterpretation and misunderstanding.

Adolf Korn's study[6] of Tauler's preaching and speaking activity
documents the psychological and spiritual proximity of preacher and
congregation. Korn's work confirms what the sermons themselves tell
us. John Tauler's preaching does not reflect a man caught in the *pro
forma* execution of a charge from a mendicant order, but a man in
service of the experience of God in the depths of the human soul. Not
ossified tradition, but tradition in its highest form, "living truth,"[7]
was the dynamic of this sermonic activity in the Dominican convents
in and around Strasbourg.

This consonance of thought and practice in the Rhenish mystics,
and particularly in Tauler, may not tell scholars anything regarding their innermost mystical experience, but it is not unimportant.
Schneyer and others have pointed to this with their observations on
the impact of mystical thought on preaching style in certain circles.
The question arises as to whether there was a distinctive sort of mystical pastoral care, a way of dealing with the cure of souls which went
against popular and prevalent practice. Preaching was and is an important part of the church's ministry in the cure of souls.[8] But what

6. *Tauler als Redner* (Muenster in Westfallen: Verlag der Aschendorffschen Verlags-
buchhandlung, 1928), pp. 63–98.

7. "And understand this as pure truth: Whatever man does not go this way [which you
have just heard], will never come to the living truth." *Die Predigten Taulers, aus der
Engelberger und der Freiburger Handschrift sowie aus Schmidts Abschriften der ehemali-
gen Strassburger Handschriften*, Ferdinand Vetter, ed. (n.p.: Weidmann, 1968), p. 153,
lines 35–36. This volume is a reprint of the original 1910 edition. With the exception
noted below, all references to Tauler's sermons will be to this edition. When possible,
citations will be given within the text proper by page and line: (153:35–36). All translations are based on Vetter's edition, unless otherwise noted, with assistance from the modern German translation by Georg Hofmann, *Johannes Tauler: Predigten* (Freiburg:
Herder Verlag, 1961) and the modern French edition, *Sermons de Tauler, Traduction sur
les plus anciens manuscrits allemands*, P. Hugueny, Thery, and A. L. Corin, eds. (Paris:
Editions de la Vie Spirituelle, 1927–35), 3 vols. For additional Tauler bibliography consult Georg Hofmann's study, "Literaturgeschichtliche Grundlagen zur Tauler-Forschung,"
pp. 436–479 of the *Gedenkschrift*. A lean and sober account of Tauler's life and work on
the basis of the scant sources which exist may be found in "Zur Biographie Johann
Taulers," by Heribert Christian Scheeben, pp. 19–36 of the *Gedenkschrift*.

8. For a treatment of preaching and the *cura animarum* see Ray C. Petry, *Preaching
in the Great Tradition. Neglected Chapters in the History of Preaching* (Philadelphia:
Westminster Press, 1950), especially ch. 1: "The Christian Heritage and Ministerial Responsibility," pp. 17–39. For a general treatment of the *cura animarum* from an historical

about the relation of the believer to the divine aids, the sacraments, and the church itself, particularly in its ordering of human life?

A reading of Tauler's sermons with an eye to these issues shows that there was a specific mystical focus on the cure of souls. It is true that much of what was taught was common Christian tradition, and indeed the best of the tradition. But the mystics were engaged in a real sense in refocusing the tradition, if not changing it, a point which has not been appreciated fully enough by those seeking to establish the soundness of mystical doctrine and its congruence with the church's teaching. Methodologically this brief study will proceed by inquiring cursorily into the mystical teaching which relates to the cure of souls and then searching for specific references in the sermons which may yield insight into actual practice in Tauler's setting.

One striking aspect of Tauler's teaching is the integrity of the human soul[9] which is called to the highest level of union with God. The call of God is an individualized affair.[10] One senses in at least one comment by Tauler a regard for order and arrangement between the individual soul and God which parallels the order of nature.[11] God tailors his grace to individualized need according to his own providence. It is incumbent upon the individual believer to search his own ground of soul to discover where it is, and for what, God has called him.[12] Some are not called to perfection, but they have no need to fear. God

---

perspective, see John T. McNeill, *A History of the Cure of Souls* (New York: Harper and Bros., 1951). The present study conceives of the cure of souls in McNeill's sense: "The cure of souls is, then, the sustaining and curative treatment of persons in those matters that reach beyond the requirements of the animal life" (p. vii).

9. By "integrity of the soul" is understood certain rights and privileges of the soul vis à vis the church and world which stem from the special covenant between God and the soul. Cf. Martin Greschat: "Der Bundesgedanke in der Theologie des spaeten Mittelalters," *Zeitschrift fuer Kirchengeschichte*, LXXXI, no. 1 (1970), 44–63, especially 50–52. It was profound respect for the soul and its communion with God which prompted Tauler to give so much attention in the sermons which survive to the concepts of vocation and order. The roles of the Pseudo-Dionysius and the *via negativa* are only suggested below. It will become apparent however that the Dionysian theme of the *deus absconditus* had specific repercussions for the way the shepherd of souls dealt with those in his charge.

10. "Each must have his manner, and as he is called, so must he come" (265:25–26).

11. "The ways of men to God are as diverse as men themselves: one man's life may be another's death, and the grace men receive is often arranged according to their make-up and nature. Therefore do not look to the ways of men, although you may take note of their virtues . . ." (433:28–32).

12. The phrase "ground of soul" is a translation of Tauler's word *grund*. The word is difficult to translate adequately into English, and "ground of soul" is perhaps as good as any, and at the same time rather literal. Says Tauler: We should ". . . turn to ourselves and await our call: how, where and in what way God has called us: one to inward contemplation, another to action, a third far beyond these both to a wonderful inward rest . . ." (400:9–12).

in his providence has provided a place for them also (337:15–20). But a call of God is issued to each man, and each must discover his own way to God.[13]

The ways to God are as diverse and individual as the calls themselves.[14] The way always leads over faithful exercise of the virtues and practices of Christendom.[15] But there is no single way which is inherently better than another,[16] and there is no way to God which is immune to perversion by a creaturely possessed ground of the soul (203:25–204:10). Every way can become foul; no way is guaranteed to lead directly to mystical union. The individualized way is again given to a man in a manner consistent with God's providence and the believer's nature. Even the smallest and most insignificant exercise, when faithfully performed, can become a way straight into the divine abyss.[17]

Ideally the divine call is sounded over creation and holy history, although it is only claimed in the ground of the soul. Everything is accordingly a potential way[18] to God when it is related to as God has ordered it.[19] The tragedy is that man's voluntary bondage to creatures prevents the right relation to God's creation. Man's relation to nature and history is properly worked out only from within a state of possession by God, not possession by creatures.[20] Thus man in his earthly

13. "Let each search with his inward eyes [to discover] what his own way is, and in which way of these three, of which you have heard, God wants him" (243:4–6).

14. In addition to 433:28–32, see also 243:4–22.

15. "I do not mean that one should dispense with good exercises. One should always practice pious works. But he should not build [his spiritual life] on them, nor rely on them" (6:24–26).

16. Tauler does however find the Eucharist the shortest and best way in some sermons. He would certainly adhere strongly to the validity of the sacramental way, and seems to prefer it in some sermons, but it is not immune to corruption by a creaturely possessed ground of soul. On the corruptibility of ways, see 203:26–204:10, and on the sacrament generally, Vetter, sermons numbered 60c, 60f, 32, and 33. References in the text proper to entire sermons in the Vetter edition will be made according to the number of the sermon there: (Vetter #60c, 60f, etc.), not by page and line. On the sacraments in Tauler see: P. Adolf Hoffman, "Sakramentale Heilswege bei Tauler," pp. 247–267 in the *Gedenkschrift*.

17. "And you should know this: the least, most pitiful work, done in true obedience—that very work, because of obedience, is more worthy, better, and more profitable than all the great works which any man does" (326:30–327:1).

18. "Do you think God wanted to give his kingdom to wretched creatures and that he poured out his precious blood and gave his dear life for that? . . . God gave everything to be a way to him and he alone should be the goal of this way, and nothing else, neither this nor that [thing]" (221:23–28).

19. In this context one is to understand Tauler's frequent references to order in the sermons, e.g. 417:10ff.; 384:10f.; 365:28ff.; and elsewhere.

20. See particularly 191:6–28, on human deafness to the Divine.

pilgrimage is inclined to substitute a penultimate for an ultimate goal, and to make his abiding place time rather than eternity.

In this setting the holy faith, the sacraments, and the word of God are the wonderful divine aids given by God for the attainment of the ultimate goal: union with the Father himself. Tauler is insistent on viewing the church and the sacraments as servants of the soul in its journey to God. The monastic vocation and the operating rules of monastic orders exist to serve the attainment of inwardness or inward prayer, understood by Tauler as union.[21] The sacraments are also subjected to this interpretation. Tauler sees the Eucharist particularly suited to this service of inwardness. It is the best way. The church, as Christ's mystical body, with its marvelous diversity of vocations and ministries also serves this inward prayer,[22] this divine eliciting of the human soul to its ultimate destiny, simultaneous rest and work in God.

Where this scheme becomes problematical for the cure of souls is at the level of incipient union. Tauler holds to the threefold way of union: the sensible, the intellective, and the spiritual. The mass of humanity is to be located on the first two levels, either pulled down to a kind of animal existence on the first level, or living a mixed life on the second, but short of perfection or union. The second, or intellective level, is that of forms and images. Perfection as union is the pressing through and beyond image and form to oneness, direct union with God without means. On this uppermost, or deepest, level the soul abides in eternity.[23]

Tauler does not speak so much of this final level as scholars would like. Whatever the explanation for that may be, Tauler addresses himself more to the man on the way to union, to the human suffering of the divine in a kind of twilight zone between time and eternity. This is where the rigorous exercise of the faithful soul has brought it. The active purgation of the soul which had been exercised by the believer

21. "Now in order that the counsels of God might be followed properly and well, holy church, by inspiration of the Holy Spirit, instituted religious communities and orders, that in them one might follow God's counsel. And these have many rules, all of which pertain to this [same purpose]" (242:22–25).

22. "Every form and activity of holy church aims at the inner man where there should be consecration and true renewal without ceasing. And all these outer exercises call, entice and admonish us to a true preparation that God may have a perfect reception in us" (377:4–8).

23. "Those who come to this [divine union] act outside time in eternity, out of createdness into uncreatedness . . ." (29:18–20).

and God together gives way to the passive suffering of God.[24] Here the last breaths of self-love must be stilled and man born into the purity which is fit for union with God. In this state, anticipatory to actual union, the soul in its passivity is totally in the hands of God.[25]

Caught between two ends, certainty and uncertainty, knowing and unknowing, time and eternity, the soul experiences great pain and pressure.[26] In this condition everything which has brought it to this point, e.g., the precious images, the holy thoughts, and everything God ever gave it, appears now to be coarse (171:23). Although the old ways no longer satisfy it in this state, the new has not yet fully come. The pressure is insufferable and painful; the world becomes too narrow (51:31ff.).

The danger to the soul in this condition is that it will not suffer through, that it will prematurely release the divine pressure by some act of its own will. It is in this context of the deflection from the ultimate goal that Tauler discusses the role of the divine aids.

> In this state three things will hinder you, three things of which you must be deprived: the body of our Lord, the word of God, and your own exercises. For all aids are, on this level, a hindrance for you. Be certain, dear child, that if you could bear through this suffering without breaking out of it, that would be much more useful and better for you than all activity. [315:2–6]

Because of the intensity of the pressure, however, and especially the deprivation of the ordinary Christian aids, many break out and chase after this teacher and that, or search out a confessor who will release the pressure (172:5–19). Tauler regards this as the loss of an opportunity which may not come again for years, so rare an attainment and gift is this suffering of God (168:12). This exalted interpretation of the divine suffering led him to assert that whoever learns and lays hold of suffering needs no other exercise (163:13), that there is more growth in this suffering than the world accomplishes in all outward exercises (172:27; 313:14).

24. "When a man has come into this house [his own ground of soul] and sought God there, then the house is turned upside down; God seeks him and turns up his house again and again, as one would who was searching for something there. He flings one thing here, another there, until he finds what he is looking for" (144:14–17).
25. The sacramental sermons reflect this divine activity and human passivity well. See footnote 16 above, and especially Vetter #6oc.
26. A beautiful statement of this and what follows is in Vetter #6of, especially pp. 314–315.

Tauler's great regard for this birth of God in the ground of the soul gave him the utmost caution toward persons caught up in it. Because they can so easily be distracted, one must deal with them very carefully. They must be left alone to suffer through to union, and not be deflected from their destination, union with God. Positively, the entire community should help those who are on the narrow way (219: 5–8). Negatively, one should give them room to move with the divine will. "Dear children, no one should lead these astray by drawing them out somewhere into multiplicity, but let God deal with them" (168: 11–13). Holy church and the pope do not interfere with them (352:17) because God has set them free (258:17).

These noble souls have gone beyond the visible way of comfort and assurance which leads through the church, its aids and helps. They have entered onto the unknown and dark way which issues into the divine abyss. They are in the hands of God and they must endure the pressure until God releases them and not before. They are beyond the helpful reach of creature; creaturely activity on this level is a deflection.

> Here there is only renunciation, a transformation, a hidden divine darkness concerning which St. Dionysius has extensively written. Here poor human nature is led another way into an assault not only inward, but outward as well, destitute of every support and consolation. One withdraws the sacrament on the basis of the ordinance of God. Before the soul attained this stage I would have admitted him daily to the Lord's Supper, but now by no means. He must go another way which is beyond himself, where the spirit rests in the Spirit of God in a hidden stillness in the divine essence.[27]

A careless reading of such passages as this could easily lead one to see in Tauler a certain antisacramental strain. Yet it is clear that what he is dealing with is a human experience of God which has grown through religious exercise, including all the church has to offer, and beyond it. The several passages where Tauler tries to work out the contemplative and active life clearly demonstrate that he is trying to show the integration of the two, not eliminate the one or the other.[28] Thus the soul in union returns to the daily round to make its still

27. 411: 25–33. See also 161: 8–29.
28. Ray C. Petry speaks to this in: "Social Responsibility and the Late Medieval Mystics," *Church History*, XXI, no. 1 (March, 1952), 9–10.

greater contribution to the communal life of Christendom, but a contribution which is a continuation and extension of the contemplative experience.[29] The experience Tauler speaks of above is one he might well have said is so far superior to the outer ecclesiastical exercises as running is superior to walking (337:31–32). He is witnessing to an experience so deep within the Body of Christ, the Church, that the soul has forgotten its way there, although the way was certainly through the visible body.

Thus there is a development of the soul which can lead it beyond the ordinary means of the soul's cure, if even only temporarily. The confessional, the Eucharist, the church's ordered life in the form of the conventual rules, these salutary services and ministries may at times distract and disperse a collected mind. In love for the birth of God in the soul they must be suspended momentarily. Tauler is clear that there is no inadequacy in the divine aids themselves.[30] The threat to the soul in suffering does not lie in the nature of the aids, but in the soul itself which must be subjected to this height of self-denial to be fitted for union with God. The fullness of the divine darkness can be embraced only when one is stripped of those divine lights given man in this life. The soul is already entering into eternity in these last gasps of mortal self. If the divine abyss is to dwell in the human abyss, the latter must be empty of every creature, but also of every prop. It must bear the suffering of the indwelling of the divine abyss alone. Once the soul has suffered through, it will receive the full fruits of those aids. But in the meantime Tauler cautions repeatedly against not suffering through, and running to Aachen, Rome, or the cloister as an escape, or worrying confessor and teachers with repeated visits, all in order to avoid the fullness of the encounter with God (213:26–29).[31]

Tauler did not fail to see the implications of this for the dispensing

29. "Our Lord sat in the ship and taught the people. God abides in these men and rules and directs the world and all creatures in these people" (175:1–2). The idea also occurs several times more in the sermons, e.g. 153:23 and 340:32.

30. Cf. Petry, "Social Responsibility," p. 10.

31. Of course Tauler is also exercising a critique of the religious life in his attention to these matters. For in his continual insistence on the divine aids as subordinate to the ultimate goal of union, he underscores their role as means and not as ends in themselves. No divine aid is good in itself; they all imbibe their goodness from the end they serve. The suffering which results from a right use of the church's religious exercises is hierarchically higher, or deeper, on the way to God, than the exercise itself. To abort suffering for the sake of another exercise would be to deny the ordained divine fruit of the exercise in order to sink back to the level of images and forms.

of the divine aids. To know when to refuse a soul's admission to the Eucharist took great perceptivity, but no more than that demanded of a soul in suffering to know whether to seek out a confessor or partake of the Body of Christ. These exceptional souls challenged the cure the church sought to exercise. The question was whether the church would give the Spirit the room it needed to operate in these men. Would the church operationally recognize the limitation the activity of God himself was placing on its own cure? Again the question was not the integrity of the divine aids themselves, their indispensability for the Christian life. Rather the issue thrust upon the church by these exceptional persons was whether the church would serve the work of God in men, or pervert its divine mission by insisting on mastering God's activity.[32] Whether he intended it or not, Tauler in fact exercised his own critique of the church by addressing these issues in his preaching.

At several points in the sermons Tauler reveals a special sensitivity for persons in the agony of the birth of the divine within. He knows their temptations and their needs and places his office and person as well as his teaching in their service. In a sermon already cited (Vetter #60f), Tauler seeks to work out the issue of the frequency of the Sacrament of the Altar. Having commended its use in the first stages, he cautions against it in the final stage of union. The temptation is to break out of the death of self by running to preaching and the Eucharist. He pleads: "Be still, and true being will be born in you" (315:7–8). But human reason fights against this stillness and seeks instead some appropriate object for its activity. "What are you doing?" asks reason. "You should be doing something else. You are wasting your time. You should meditate and pray" (315:10–13). But this is not the only assault the soul must withstand. There is in addition the temptation of activity. "Then comes the enemy [Satan]. 'Why are you sitting here? You should undertake some spiritual exercise. Get up. You are losing time. Do this good work, or that.' "[33] The final encounter is with the misunderstanding of other men. "Then come the gruff sorts and say:

32. See Petry, "Social Responsibility," p. 10. "Nevertheless, this [interior cultivation of the holy mysteries] is no repudiation of hierarchical function and external sacraments—only a call to the fuller realization of what the sacraments themselves involve beyond the sheer externality of cult."

33. "And so it [man's nature] would gladly possess something and know something and will something. The going gets rough for human nature before these three 'somethings' die in it" (383:5–7).

'Why are you sitting here and not listening to God's word?' " (315:15–16). This threefold assailing of the tempter moves the soul to become its own assailant and say to itself: "You should use the help of the Lord's table" (315:17–18). This imaginative projection of Tauler in the midst of a sermon shows his own intimate acquaintance with the difficulties he sought to address. On the basis of this human dilemma he goes on to say that this sort of soul would not receive the sacrament from him, unless of course he could determine that God had brought that person to him. Too often it is human weakness or custom seeking a premature release from the divine suffering which sends such persons. "Ah, nature would rather go [on a pilgrimage] to Rome than suffer through [this pressure], but this suffering would be better for you than all the exercises you might do, for suffering is better than doing" (315:23–31).

At least two episodes in the sermons reflect Tauler's seriousness and independence regarding his pastoral practice. On one occasion he found it necessary to defend himself against a false accusation that he would hear no one's confession who did not promise to do as he wanted (202:30–32). Tauler denies ever having said this. He demands, he says, only what stands written regarding the confessional. The incident reveals a practice which evidently went against the notions of at least some of Tauler's congregation. The experience, however, does not indicate any specifically mystical teaching. The complaint may have stemmed from an interpretation of the church's teaching on the confessional which was considerably stricter than the popular or prevalent one.

The second reference does appear to reflect Tauler's use of church teaching in a way both offensive to some persons and reflective of mystical teaching. The context in this case is a discussion of the importance of stillness, waiting, and suffering. Those who possess detachment, renunciation, and humility, says Tauler, could remain an entire day in the midst of activity to no ill effect. "But if you are too weak," adds Tauler, "then go your own way."

Children, where I find this genuine ground [of the soul], I advise what God instructs me to advise. Let people swear at me and scorn me as much as they will. On this matter our sisters have a good practice. Whenever someone wants to turn inward, they are glad and give her as much latitude as she wants. That is far and away beyond your rules. That is a precious and holy thing, established by the Holy Spirit. [371 : 1–6]

No passage in the sermons reflects so vividly Tauler's profound regard for the integrity of the individual soul before God and his own willingness to support it in its journey toward union.[34] The point of contention, and thrust of the passage, is the freedom of the individual soul to move in response to the divine will, to go its own way as God instructs directly in the soul or through a good confessor. Since the good confessor and true mystic placed his person and office in the service of special ways to God, the reference to the swearing and scorn of others is not to be taken lightly. Tauler's independence of ministry evidently rubbed some the wrong way. Some either could not, or would not, understand what he was about with these special friends of God. Yet Tauler did find sympathy from the administration of the religious house where he was preaching and he compliments them on their own willingness to set the rules of the house in the service of inwardness, as Tauler interpreted their divine intent from the beginning. As seriously as Tauler took the church and her regulated life, he could not be referring here to a suspension of canon law. Rather he sees a flexibility with the monastic rule which is a recovery of the divine order of things whereby all things are subordinated to the service of the inwardness of man. Monastic rules are thus the servants of the divine will and activity with men, not the master.

This same pastoral posture is evidenced in another sermon, indeed one of Tauler's more mystical ones. His text is First Peter 3:8: "Beloved, be of one mind in prayer" (Vetter #39). The issue which emerges in the course of the sermon is the relation of outer activity and inward prayer. How is one to reconcile conventual obligations on prayer and inner union which is the epitome of prayer for Tauler? Tauler tries to explain how it is one can leave off outward prayer and yet fulfill the requirement of the convent for prayers. Significantly enough, the sermon progresses to a consideration of the relation of the inner and outer natures of man, and how it is one can be joined with God while active in the world, or be gathered in mind while diversely engaged with the powers one possesses. Not surprisingly, this issues in a reflection on the diversity and unity of the mystical Body of Christ,

34. It is not inconsequential here that Tauler is expositing a text of Saint Paul, Ephesians 3:14f.: "I bow my knee before the Father of our Lord Jesus Christ . . . ."

the Church. When Tauler finally comes to discuss the threefold nature of the mystical life, the relationship of inner and outer again impinges on his thinking, but this time in terms of the relation of the soul on the way to union to the convent itself. Since it is God who is assisting these persons in their death to self and growing similitude with the divine, it

> should be forbidden all men to take charge of these dear ones or to hinder them or to distract them with coarse outer works and ways. It is no concern of the prior where a brother goes from the chancel after the liturgy, unless it is a matter of a frivolous man. That man's way and work must be watched. [160:27–32]

Thus Tauler not only draws attention to the particular position of certain souls and their need for special consideration, he also interjects himself between the conventual leadership and the brothers (or sisters) on behalf of the latter. He therefore recalls in this specific situation the rights of the religious and the limitations of the offices of those in their charge. In so doing he does not seek to go beyond church teaching but simply to make clear distinctions which will preserve the integrity of the constituent parts. The very context of the sermon itself refuses any interpretation which would suggest modern individualistic notions. Because there is one body, there is integrity for each calling and function. "All in one, and one in all" (159:1).

The depth of Tauler's feeling on the diversity of ways and callings emerges very plainly in a sermon which has been almost universally cited in the literature on him. Explaining First Corinthians 12:6ff., he cautions that all members of the Body of Christ cannot be eyes and pursue the contemplative life all the time. Some must work, but Tauler does not intend that this should exclude the contemplative aspect of the religious life. Thus he tries to demonstrate briefly how the two can exist side by side, the contemplative and the active. But this appreciation of the diversity of gifts and works exceeds the understanding of some.

> Then come the presumptuous persons, and this is their way: everything must be thus and so. And they want to direct everyone according to their own notions and their own understanding and in their own manner. And these same persons have glistened forty

years with the religious life and do not know to this day what it is all about.[35]

After these exceedingly sharp words Tauler discusses his own confessional practices with persons in the grips of the birth of God in the soul. He admits that he is occasionally at a loss as to how to deal with them. There are times, he says, when there is no instruction from the Lord, and in these instances he simply refers the souls to their own private counsel. "Dear children, search out the Lord yourselves, and he will surely answer you" (180:13–14). In contrast, those whom Tauler addresses want to show each his place and judge him according to their own nature and way of thinking. These "worms" come out to devour the good plants that ought to grow in God's garden. "These persons say: 'This is not our custom. This is a new way and born of a new spirit,' and do not consider that the hidden ways of God are unknown to them" (180:17–19).

This episode shows the struggle which Tauler's teaching and confessional practice encountered in at least some of the convents where he was active. While it is true that he operated as teacher and confessor within the limits of the traditional teaching of the church, it is also true that he dared in both teaching and pastoral practice to go against prevalent pious practice. The latitude which he granted the soul in its communion with God in his teaching, he granted as well in pastoral practice. Specifically what other aspects of Tauler's instruction and practice hit sensitive nerves is difficult to tell. On one occasion he did grant those in his charge permission to dispense with their verbal prayers if they were a hindrance to true, inward prayer.[36] Tauler promised to assume responsibility for their action. Or maybe his congregation failed to grasp his distinction between the value of religious exercises and the danger of building on them. At any rate, there was occasion-

35. 180:6–10. Line 6, *nasenwise lute* has been translated "presumptuous." It has the connotation of "keen-nosed." See Jacob and Wilhelm Grimm, *Deutsche Woerterbuch* (Leipzig: Verlag von S. Herzel, 1889), VII, col. 417. Cf. also Curt Kirmsse, *Die Terminologie des Mystikers Johannes Tauler* (Leipzig: Inaugural Dissertation, 1930), p. 92. Kirmsse is an indispensable reference for Tauler's terminology.

36. As in Vetter #39, especially 38:14–18. "And if any exercise or outer prayer or work hinders you, drop it—at my responsibility—except those which are set for specific times; besides, all verbal prayer is like chaff and straw compared to the finest wheat. As our Lord said, 'True worshippers pray in spirit and in truth.'" Naturally the boldness of such an utterance would have to be measured against its setting, the precise nature of which is lost.

ally tension between the friends of God and their surroundings. This is documented by several passages where Tauler warns persons on the narrow way that they can anticipate suffering from the world. Commenting on a text from Saint Augustine concerning humility, Tauler says:

> Know that a man must be annihilated in his own mind and in the eyes of all men: He must be stripped of all substance and all that he is, and it all must be gambled away in his own sight, as was the case with our Lord. That means: you must be mocked and scorned to such a degree, your life misunderstood and deemed folly to such an extent, that those around you cover you with shame, and say to your face that they consider your way of life erroneous or heretical and hate it.[37]

It is tempting to dismiss such a passage as a mystical romanticizing of suffering. But as important as suffering was in the mystical theology of John Tauler, it never became anywhere an end in itself. Tauler was not skilled as a preacher in only one direction. The imagery of the dry cisterns (Vetter #6ob) of the spiritually barren religious hearts is matched in power by the injunction to enthusiastic pruners (ascetics) to hold their knives until they know what to cut out of their lives (Vetter #7). Repeatedly Tauler restrained the passions of self-appointed martyrs even as he underscored, before the religiously complacent, the necessity for suffering.

If Tauler is not romanticizing the cost of Christian discipleship, then he must be addressing himself to a specific historical reality. Just what this reality was is hinted at in a small number of additional references in the sermons.

In a sermon on renewal the passage above may be understood more specifically.

> Before it was heathen and Jews who martyred holy men. Now those will martyr you who appear holy, who excite a lot of attention, and perform more pious works than you. This criticism will cut you to the bone, for these men will say you are mistaken and that they have

37. Georg Hofmann, . . . *Predigten*, p. 463. The original text of this sermon, contained in the appendix of Dick Helander, *Tauler als Prediger. Studien* (Lund: Dissertation, 1923) was unavailable at the time of writing. Helander's research is the basis of sermons numbered 60, 70 and 71 in the Hofmann translation. References to this source are cited as H and the appropriate page number. Thus here: H463.

seen a lot, heard the great preachers, and know what is right. Ah, and you will not know what to do or where to turn! [265:15–21]

In a parallel passage Tauler is even more pointed. There it is the neighbor who makes the accusation. "You turn to God and they say you are confused, spiritually sick, a crank, and deluded" (Hofmann 548). These passages suggest that the scorn Tauler experienced for some of his own practices was experienced as well by those close to him. The emphasis appears again to be on the special way of these persons, a way of piety and the religious life which did not suit the mold which was fostered either by the monastic community at large, its leadership, or substantive elements within it.[38]

The conflict of those on the narrow way is also reflected in another group of passages, those dealing with the interference of some persons in the lives of others. The citation above to presumptuous persons who would not leave others alone, but would arrange their lives according to their own way, was no isolated incident. For Tauler, more was at stake than a simple matter of privacy for those in the convent. The issue was the integrity of the vocation of each and his own special way to God. This is shown clearly in a passage set in the context of a discussion of the biblical authority and the force of the commandment that one is not to judge others. He sought rather to explain the tragic implications of an unwarranted interference in the lives of others.

What do you know about your neighbor's ground [of soul]? What do you know of God's will for him or of the way by which God has called and invited him? And you want to direct his works according to your own notion, murder God's will for that man and arrange his life with your false judgment? [112:31–35]

It is similar sorts who, seeking to heal a neighbor's scratch, strike him two or three wounds in the process (260:34–261:3) and thus bring judgment on themselves.

It must be emphasized that Tauler nowhere denies the responsibility of those in charge of conventual life to exercise the authority given them by the church and the Holy Spirit. On the contrary, in one passage he discusses how one in authority might discharge his responsibility to supervise others without falling into judgment (113:4ff.).

38. As in 265:23–26. "Thus these would appoint each person according to their own notions and push everyone towards one goal, and that cannot be. Each must have his way, and as he is called he must come."

The import of these passages surrounding the divine call indicates that Tauler's frequent discussions of the hiddenness of God and his ways with men were for him no mere convention. He genuinely believed there was no certain way to God available to men which did not involve the total investment of an individual believer in the discovery of God's will for him. The statements in the sermons which reflect the tailoring of the divine activity to individual need and nature were no mere scholastic theology for John Tauler. He believed them with all his being and adhered accordingly to a deep respect for the integrity of the human soul as it confronted the divine. At certain points in men's relation to God he was willing to acknowledge not only the desirability but the necessity of those souls' self-direction in deepest accord with the operation of God's will within them. In so doing he underscored the limitations of his own office and person, and gave these exceptional souls the support of both his person and office as they worked out their special ways to God in response to God's call.

It was Tauler's willingness to observe the diversity of callings and to give men freedom to work out their divine vocation which brought tension between his own ministry and specific situations where he was active, as well as conflict between individual nuns and their communities. He sought to implement the central implications of his mystical theology by granting souls in his care a latitude of movement which was not always the custom of the houses where he worked.

Tauler's was not a new way in the long tradition of the church. He was always very much aware of what church teaching and practice permitted. But in the specific convents where he preached it doubtlessly struck some as new. It was the recovery of the venerable tradition, but with a pointed mystical focus, which most characterized Tauler's pastoral activity. It is perhaps in this context, as much as any other, that contemporary students should read the letter of Heinrich of Noerdlingen to Margaretha Ebner:

> Pray God for our dear Father Tauler. . . . He is generally in much suffering because he teaches the truth and lives it as fully as any teacher I know.[39]

---

39. Philipp Strauch, *Margaretha Ebner und Heinrich von Noerdlingen. Ein Beitrag zur Geschichte der deutschen Mystik* (Amsterdam: Verlag P. Schippers N.V., 1966), 263, ll. 83–86. This is a reprint of the 1881 edition.

Clarity and dilemma—the *Forty Sermons* of John Wyclif

WILLIAM MALLARD

What sort of man and reformer was the adamant biblical theologian, John Wyclif? A convincing portrait has begun to emerge, even though scholarship has not yet provided us with a definitive account. The concern of this article is to offer one small fragment in the developing mosaic, based upon a particular segment of the reformer's works—the so-called *Forty Sermons* of Wyclif, which have long been noted for their seeming orthodoxy and for omitting many of his characteristically violent denunciations. The aim here is to use this special little preaching collection in order to glimpse Wyclif outside the lecture hall at the height of his powers, even as he was swiftly evolving toward the isolated, irascible reformer that he finally became. Happily, the *Forty Sermons* seem able to give us a quick sketch—Wyclif, a primarily moralistic preacher, addressing some of his widest and most varied audiences.[1]

I

A natural question to ask is why all of Wyclif's sermons should not be used for this undertaking. Why just these forty? Certainly the collection of all his sermons does constitute evidence for the thought and proclamation of Wyclif. Nevertheless these forty tend to be separable from the rest (1) by their distinct character and tone, and (2) by our ability to assign reasonably reliable dates to the majority of them. The other sermons in volumes I–III and the rest of volume IV unfortunately do not serve the historian's purposes as well. For one thing, the aging Wyclif put them through a more thorough and final edition before he died. Apparently some time between his forced departure from

---

1. The collection referred to is the *Sermones Quadraginta* of the old Bohemian catalogues, published in *Wyclif's Latin Works* in the 4 vols. of *Sermones*, ed. J. Loserth in the Wyclif Society edition (London: Truebner and Company, 1887–90), IV, 197–492, nos. 23–62. Loserth's comments on the group may be noted, ibid., I (Intro.), xxi, xxvii–xxx, and IV (Intro.), iii–xii. For fuller documentation on the history of the collection, cf. my article, "Dating the *Sermones Quadraginta* of John Wyclif," *Medievalia et Humanistica*, Fasc. XVII (1966), pp. 86–105, hereafter referred to as, e.g., Dsq, p. 86. The collection of forty will be referred to by initials, number of the sermon in the Society edition, and pages, e.g., SQ *31*, 264–265.

Oxford and his last stroke in late 1384, Wyclif did the editorial work on the general corpus of his "rude sermons for the people."[2] Except for this special forty, the sermons must have been considerably recast and rewritten, and at the same time put in almost perfect liturgical order. The introduction of new, late material is indicated, as for example, the many instances of Wyclif's attack on the friars, a polemic that occurs monotonously again and again.[3] Significantly, Wyclif's break with the mendicants was no seething quarrel until at least 1380. The form of the sermons as we have them therefore postdates that year; yet Wyclif could not conceivably have written and delivered over three volumes of such sermons in the last four years of his life, three years of which he spent in exile at Lutterworth in failing health. Furthermore, he sees those declining months of forced "leisure" as devoted to "collecting" the sermons, not producing a whole new set. Clearly, then, Wyclif took sermons accumulated over a number of years and edited them, writing new and timely material into many of the homilies. They may have therefore served his own ideological cause all the better; but he effectively spoiled an enticing project for the historian: the attempt to correlate the sermons as he originally gave them with his unfolding development as theologian and activist.

How, then, did the *Forty Sermons* escape this procedure? The group as we now have it betrays efforts at editorial work, but undertaken only with considerable haste and with uncertain results—which turns out to be a happy fault as regards historical data, since the subject matter was little revised and many internal clues to former serial arrangements remained unexpurgated. The present intermediate stage of editing must represent either a hurried assembling for limited circulation before he left Oxford, or a task cut short by illness and death at Lutterworth, or more likely something of both. As a result, the *Forty Sermons* point to John Wyclif as preacher prior to the late, acrimonious years, while they constitute material that also is more plain and less scholastic, more broadly practical and less subtle, more popular and less intricate. Why, then, did Wyclif as his own editor leave these until last (or until too late, from his point of view)? Could he have felt that the more heavily scholastic sermons were more important and carried more intellectual ammunition for his cause? Possibly so. Wyclif

2. "... videtur quod in illo ocio quo a scolasticis ociamur et in particulari edificacioni ecclesie in fine dierum nostrorum sollicitamur, sint sermones rudes ad populum colligendi ...," *Sermones*, I, Praefatio.

3. Ibid., I, 104, 153, 226; IV, 9, 39, 108–112, are among countless examples.

was a schoolman to the end and must have felt that his professional hope and strength lay in university acceptance; thus the reader is continually impressed with how academically heavy-handed he is in most of these so-called "rude sermons for the people." He may have considered the more elaborate exegesis as more important for posterity and for his message.

On the other hand, the time-span most likely for presentation of the forty may offer an additional clue. I have elsewhere attempted to propose a list of dates for the *Forty Sermons*, based on their references to saints' days and to one another in certain series.[4] Although not strictly proven, most of these dates will be used here as trustworthy; such dating obviously opens the way for orienting the collection to the events in Wyclif's career. Now the range of years seemingly correct for most of the forty is from January, 1375, to September, 1379. Here, then, are sermons (surely not all of his during that four-year period) of a plainer and more practical sort, stretching from early in his public, political involvement right up to the "beginning of the end." For the fall of 1379 disclosed his "heresy" concerning transubstantiation, through his treatise *On The Eucharist*. The watershed that led to his public rejection lay distinctly in that autumn. At the same time, while the *Forty Sermons* reveal almost none of his violence of the last years, they clearly expound many of the mature, doctoral views appropriate to his *On Civil Dominion* (1376) and the years immediately following. Surely the more established and experienced a theologian, the more free he was to apply his doctrinal themes widely and to address broader, popular issues. Would it be unreasonable that the forty are a collection of just such sermons? They would represent the "plainer" sermons of application during the last years when Wyclif preached on a regular basis. In other words, instead of being "early," as traditionally proposed—because lacking in "heresy" and extreme denunciation[5]— they may precisely have been "late," relative to the body of his sermons as a whole. Their "late" intent of popular application may have seemed more valid to the exiled Wyclif than the cloistered, scholastic nature of so many other sermons he had on hand. He might naturally

4. Cf. Dsq, pp. 86–105. On p. 105 note a complete table of proposed dates.

5. "Constat omnibus quod iste Wycleff quadraginta sermones istos scribens fuit alius a se ipso hic quam alibi, ut apparet legenti, quia demptis paucissimis pene in omnibus hiis scriptis sequitur ecclesiam in fide et ritibus et modo loquendi katholico," Codex pa. Vindobonensis 3928, a marginal note that Loserth reckons of a fifteenth-century Bohemian scribe; cf. *Sermones*, IV, v, and Dsq, p. 86.

turn first to the larger body of material to alter its scholastic heaviness by applying the concerns of his last four years. Whatever full improvements he desired for the forty never finally got attended to. In their unrevised form they were neither as scholastically impressive nor as useless to the current cause as the larger corpus. Some such logic may lie behind our possession of the *Forty Sermons* today, with their greater original integrity and the light they shed on a few specific years in Wyclif's career.[6]

In summary, the *Forty Sermons* do offer distinctive insight into Wyclif's pulpit fare at an advanced stage of his career, running a fairly "late" parallel to certain more complex, scholastic sermons. Being less revised than countless of their sister pieces, they hold out hope of our knowing Wyclif as preacher, prior to his final rebellious posture. If their preservation was due at all to their direct practical nature, then that quality in itself increases their inherent interest. Under considerable stress and caught up in the antagonism between spiritual and temporal orders in England, what themes did Wyclif emphasize in his widespread personal effort to exhort the laity and the lesser clergy?

II

If the *Forty Sermons* promise something special by their character and place in things, an initial reading of them may result in some disappointment. As medieval sermons go, they are quite conventional rehearsals of the austere Christian life, doggedly obligated to a single pattern of biblical interpretation, and drawing upon *exempla* and exhortations that were highly standard. Wyclif was not especially original in what he did, but only in the astonishing persistence and intellectual thoroughness with which he did it. And that, of course, locates the historical interest of the man. His theological "contribution" was an Augustinianism so internally consistent and immobile that it lim-

6. What has been said admittedly does not clarify the relation between the forty and the other sermons. I have undertaken a comparison of each of the forty with its parallel sermon outside the forty, based on a common biblical reading. Dependency of one on the other is suggested when Wyclif "repeats himself" with one version much more studied and full and the other a brief, dependent recollection of the first. On that basis, *Sermones* I, *11, 12, 17, 18, 22, 24*, look as if they may have been sources for SQ *27, 28, 32, 33, 36, 42*, respectively. And SQ *46, 47, 49, 53, 60, 62*, appear as sources for I, *34, 35, 42, 50, 57, 58*, respectively. The ten other parallels with sermons in vol. I suggest to me no dependency of any kind. Of nine parallels with vol. III and one with vol. II, only two suggest dependency: III, *23* on SQ *35*, and SQ *54* on III, *53*. If reliable, the comparisons suggest the SQ as *not* earlier than all the other sermons, while some SQ were earlier and even partial sources for others.

ited and reduced its own model in the great doctor of Hippo. Yet Wyclif is interesting because his pursuit of such a theology occurred when
and where it did, undertaken by a man of his prominence, and with
results far transcending his own life. So it is in particular with the sermons. Their inherent importance would be much reduced but for
who preached them and the destiny that he faced. As it is, the single-
ness of purpose that pointed the message of the sermons, plus their elements of correlation with surrounding events, provide considerable
interest. Wyclif viewed his historical moment as one in which the
forces of God and the Devil were polarized to extreme clarity and decisiveness. Only the longer, ironic view of history knows the matter as
far more complex and tragically distressing.

With some variations, the recurring themes and stresses of the *Forty
Sermons* are clear enough. Briefly, the whole series is an exhortation
to "be strong!" Two modes of life are offered to men—the blessed and
the corrupt—and the strong, wise man will fight unflinchingly in the
earthly "stadium" till he wins his heavenly reward.[7] Consistently, one
finds Wyclif a Christian thinker absolutely confident of the truth he
knows, though dismayed that human weakness lays fearful odds against
its acceptance. Foolish boys will kill each other for a handful of cherries; that single *exemplum* epitomizes Wyclif's absolute self-assurance
regarding sin and error, as well as his scornful horror at man's choice
of self-destruction.[8] If in so saying Wyclif appears arrogantly to de-
value the good of "cherries" in a full and significant life, one can only
remember how blatant was the lust for money in late medieval England. The raw appetites Wyclif knew around him evidently drove him
to his prudish derogation of natural good, and inspired the self-right-
eousness that so favored invisible and abstract things.

Thus the interpretive framework of the entire *Forty Sermons* is
Wyclif's stout, hierarchical view of spirit over flesh, abstract mentality
over physical concreteness—one aspect of the created life in disciplined
sway over the other. Such was Wyclif's celebrated theory of "dominion." His views on the topic had been developed in several important
treatises during his early doctoral years, 1373–1376;[9] not only so, his

---

7. E.g., SQ *55*, 429: "Ideo oportet militem Christi primo pugnare in stadio. Nam hoc
seculum est spectaculum Deo et angelis intuentibus pugnam et desidiam Christianorum
in exercitu diaboli."

8. SQ *44*, 362: "Unde simile videtur pugnare pro dominio vel questu temporalium et
pueros vulnerare se letaliter pro colleccione ventilatorum lapidum ceresorum . . . ."

9. His *De Divino Dominio* evidently followed hard upon his taking the doctorate in

approach to dominion had laid the basis for his engagement in politics from about 1374, climaxing from 1376 to 1378. If the *Forty Sermons* indeed represented an austere "popularizing" mostly concentrated during these same latter years, clearly the motif of dominion might heavily inform them. And so it does. Simply stated, the theory is a strong resurgence of early medieval neoplatonist realism on Wyclif's part: the order of the universe is a principle of rectitude[10] in which our reason participates; that principle finally and inexorably governs all of nature, just as one's own rational spirit is meant to govern his body. This same principle of rectitude is simply another term for the ideal Law of God, through which the Deity keeps universal dominion and by which he determines, indeed predetermines, all things. The man who is eternally elect to be in harmony with God's Law therefore himself shares in that divine dominion, or has rightful governance over whatever the divine order entrusts to him—his own selfhood, his family, his property, his church and nation, and ultimately all things. The approach is simple, stark, and exhaustive of all the possibilities. Wyclif may have had a nineteenth-century reputation for some early modern "democratic sense," but his every shred of interest in "the people" assumes this austere hierarchical outlook: the elect are destined to oversee the reprobate, and every office of dominion on earth ought ideally to reflect that election and authority.[11]

Wyclif's theological method is no less strict than the outlook itself. As the final reference for his position, he asserts a remarkable, precise coincidence between rational and revealed truth. Authority derives from the Bible; but authority derives no less from philosophical reason of the neoplatonizing, realist school. To grasp biblical thought is to be of the elect; but to grasp biblical thought is also to be rational, which coincidentally is no less a mark of election. Thus philosophizing

1372. Continuing its theme, the *De Mandatis Divinis* appeared probably in 1373 or 1374. There followed *De Statu Innocentie* (1375?) and the major work, *De Civili Dominio* in 1376–77. Each of these is available in the Wyclif Society edition for the years 1890 (ed. R. L. Poole), 1922 (both *DMD* and *DSI*—ed. J. Loserth, F. D. Matthew) and 1885–1904 (ed. Poole and Loserth), respectively. I am indebted for comments on these treatises, and especially for his analysis of the second one, to John F. McCristal, O.F.M., "A Study of John Wyclif's Treatise *De Mandatis Divinis*," an unpublished thesis, MS B. Litt. d. 667, the Bodleian Library, Oxford University, the Hilary term, 1958.

10. I.e., *jus*. Cf. infra, p. 27, n. 19.

11. E.g., SQ *58*, 459, where lords must correct sinful subordinates, but subordinates must also correct sinful lords, or decline to serve them. Cf. SQ *56*, 442, the strict rule of husbands over wives. For the dominion theory as such, cf. SQ *32*, 281: the more men love riches, "de tanto plus elongantur ab earum vera possessione . . . ." Also, SQ *55*, 432. Cf. *DCD*, I, ch. 1, p. 1; ch. 7, p. 47; and passim.

correctly means penetrating God's truth. Also, reading the Bible correctly means exactly the same. The two inquiries merge in what Wyclif called "the logic of Holy Scripture," while in the *Forty Sermons* all the elements clearly meet together: right philosophy, right exegesis, the biblical text itself, and the truth of daily living. Wyclif does not explicate his scholastic method as such in the sermons, but the power of "scriptural logic" is nevertheless plain enough. His recurring emphasis, indeed his despair of mankind, is how irrational and lacking in self-interest sin is, and how reasonable and clear and even "easy" is the opposite way of faith. Why are men not both rational and faithful? Wyclif the theologian becomes so thoroughly self-consistent in his realism that philosophy and the Bible seem to him as if a single daylight, while those who disagree appear to stumble in darkness.[12]

Thus reason and faith both declare that an ethical spirit of rectitude makes of a man a kind of "lord of all things," despite his having no such apparent position in social affairs.[13] Regardless of how one of Christ's followers may be abused, his place in God's order remains untouched, and he sees with incontestable reason the certainty of his vindication. No matter how poor a man may be, such faith and insight are open to him. On the other hand, the man is a fool who grasps for temporal security through abuse of God and neighbor, for he sacrifices all claim on both the present and the future. Only the man who is under electing grace holds genuine authority over things, although circumstances may not for the moment acknowledge him. Does Wyclif therefore suggest that the just man rise up and assume the dominion

12. E.g., "Cum enim omnis fidelis debet emere dictum regnum pro merito, notanda est facilis, placabilis et utilis condicio huius mercandie. Est enim facilis, cum precium sit bona voluntas qua nichil est facilius vel plus in hominis potestate [in the sense that a material price would be out of some men's reach] . . . . Magna ergo cecitas mercacioni sumptuose, laboriose et infructuose insistere ista dimissa condicionis opposite. Ego non video quin *Deus huius seculi cecavit mentes* hominum infidelitate et odio divino . . . ," SQ *61*, 476, 477–478 (italics his). He insists that only sin deteriorates the rational creature (SQ *60*, 471), whereas natural law favors heavenly reward (SQ *57*, 446–447, "Ergo de lege nature debet christianus inimico debita dimittere . . ."), and natural reason even/ necessitates the confessional (SQ *33*, 286). Only the most foolish will depart clear reward for clear damnation (SQ *26*, 224, "O supina stulticia!"). For all this clear rationality, Wyclif never hesitates to insist that the powerful recourse of all Christians is to Holy Scripture (". . . scriptura sacra turris fortissima . . ."), for every creature might be more easily destroyed than that one iota of Scripture should fail or pass away (SQ *25*, 220). On Wyclif's "logic of Scripture" as the coinciding of the intelligible being of all things with the meaning of the scriptural text, see, e.g., *DMD*, ch. 7, p. 61; cf. *DDD*, I, 11, pp. 81, 89. Cf. McCristal, op. cit., pp. 172, 174–175.

13. SQ *26*, 222: ". . . paciencia convertatur in perfectum dominium, quia in regnacionem perpetuam super totum universum . . . ."

that is rightly his?—a highly important question for the times in which he lived. The almost monotonous emphasis of Wyclif throughout the *Forty Sermons* is indeed quite the opposite. With only minor qualification, Wyclif again and again exhorts his hearers to adopt an attitude of "patient suffering." The initial logic of the position is straightforward enough: if a man knows that he is in the right and will find ultimate vindication, certainly in heaven, then to take the risk of seeking present redress (other than passive resistance) is just not in his own best interest. He may fall into greed for the property he seeks, or into hatred for his opponent, or even into murder; then an infinite paradise is lost in exchange for paltry satisfactions and passions—never the outcome for one who maintains patient suffering via the New Testament counsels.[14] Does Wyclif therefore advise against all ordinary recourse to the law or to just sanctions for righting wrongs? His intense feeling does approach such radical exclusion. Nevertheless, he is willing to admit (though without enthusiasm) that just acts of redress are possible granted the right conditions. For example, he allows for the just war (following St. Augustine), but his definition is hedged in very tightly indeed. Not only must the cause be just, while the enemy's is unjust, but the intention must be one of "loving correction"; the justified warriors must not love the temporal possessions of the enemy, but rather love the enemy's true prosperity.[15] Wyclif admits the difficulty (!) of such warfare, "since for each one maintaining the rule of love, a hundred fail." Therefore, the true Christian "will suffer seizure of his goods with joy" before he will take the risk of erring in so ambiguous a situation.[16] Instrumenting justice on earth is not excluded, but the conditions for it are set so high that Wyclif hardly disguises his preference for suffering passivity, a heavenly behavior realized on earth.

Indeed, this Gospel discipline has still another level of theoretical support. For universal justice so fully prevails, as Wyclif sees it, that *in*justice scarcely has any reality at all, other than appearance only.

14. The passages are legion, but note, e.g., ". . . omnes homines et specialiter predicatores verbi Dei disponerent se ad pacienciam pro defensione iusticie." SQ *32*, 278. Again, love of the enemy is bound to bring a more copious reward than we can gain by blasphemous revenge ("Quis ergo non racionabiliter diligeret inimicos?"). SQ *42*, 346. Whatever our misfortunes, they will work "ad augmentum nostri premii si paciencer sufferimus." SQ *56*, 442. Christ himself taught us "tam verbo quam opere vincere paciendo . . . ," SQ *37*, 312. Cf. SQ *23*, 204; *26*, 222; *40*, 331; *44*, 363; *46*, 374.

15. "Si enim plus amo temporalia inimici quam eius prosperitatem, pecco contra regulas caritatis que docent diligere inimicos . . . ," SQ *24*, 210.

16. Ibid., p. 211.

Even the most severe violations of just relationship, seen *sub specie aeternitatis*, disclose their very incorporation into the everlasting and just order of God, not by being altered but simply by being seen in true perspective. Thus the man who lustfully tyrannizes may seem victorious, but really he is condemned already. The man who, to the contrary, is abused and wasted, and yet bears up with steadfast love toward God, knows his very pain as part of the ultimate justice that will richly reward him. Deprived or exiled, he knows that all this injustice is right, because it is part of *his* righteousness in the eye of his ultimate and just Vindicator. Reality is fixed; change can only mean letting false appearances give way to true ones. So Wyclif tells us that "it is impossible for a man to suffer except justly," for if he suffers without complaint, then it is merit for him; and if he does complain, then he deserves to suffer for sinning against his own potential good.[17] All suffering is actually just, and all creatures serve God willy-nilly, regardless of what they do.[18] The God of absolute order knows that every disruption is either an agony meritoriously borne and rewarded, or a sinful collapse that will find its ordered place in hell. Consequently, because he is the just determinor of all occasions, God is pleased with every instance of suffering by man. However bleak and terrifying such a view, Wyclif found it consoling for the Christian, a solid base for the steel-like posture of patient suffering.[19]

It may seem surprising, in the light of eternal justice and patient suffering, that another major theme in the *Forty Sermons* is that of "fraternal correction." If things already are what they must be, little would seem gained by attempting to alter either people or circumstances. Yet in a deeper sense Wyclif finds it much in keeping to exhort

17. SQ *26*, 223.

18. ". . . debemus scire quod nulla sit pena nisi iusta et a Deo inflicta . . . Ergo debemus omnem penam in nobis inflictam velle esse . . . ergo quilibet debet amare omnem punicionem." SQ *56*, 441. Cf. ". . . omnis passio hominis sive iusti sive iniusti est iusta et per consequens placens Deo." SQ *25*, 213. Cf. also SQ *36*, 305.

19. For a source of these motifs in Wyclif's theological treatises, cf. *DMD*, ch. 1-2, pp. 1-15, a fundamental exposition of *jus* or "right." *Jus* is perpetual will and consequently a term applied only to God; it signifies uncreated truth and is therefore exemplar for every created justice, assigning to each thing what is proper to it (ibid., pp. 2-3). Thus *jus* is the ground of *justitia*, the principle of *dominium*; true *dominium* results in *premium*, heavenly reward, the final disclosure of one's harmony with primal *jus*. If a man never pays a debt, nonpayment must be just—since whatever is is God's will, and the divine will is forever just and irresistible (ibid., p. 5). Therefore, suffer seeming injustice patiently (ibid., p. 8). Recompense wanting here will be paid in eternity via the penalties of the damned, from which the blessed will derive loving, everlasting joy ("Cum enim beati habent quicquid boni voluerint, patet quod habent de dampnatorum penis caritativam leticiam sempiternam . . . ," ibid., p. 11). Cf. McCristal, op. cit., pp. 15-21.

the correction of one's erring brother. Material human history is absurdly turned away from God's one true Order. At the level of that history, men are assuredly unequal in power and wealth; but such outward inequality has no bearing on their inner possibility for love and good will; at the center of his life, *any* man is possibly a free man. And that mysterious election to spiritual freedom will prove itself if the man can be summoned from apparent blindness into daylight, from corrupt behavior to a life under the Commandments. Wyclif himself not only preaches for moral results; he also insists that his hearers correct their fellowmen. Interestingly, his virtual prohibition of retributive acts against others (bear all injuries patiently) parallels this substitute approach, brotherly correction. He not only permits such reproof, he requires it of a true Christian, and especially a priest.[20] Any follower of Christ has the obligation not only to keep Christ's Law in full seriousness for himself, but also to awaken others to how wrong they are, to what infinite treasure waits upon their own simple power of choice. When so few are devoted to the narrow way, the Christian is all the more compelled to speak up and to call in question those around him. The ones who harden themselves forever against the summons betray their eternal destiny to a just hell-fire.[21]

Brotherly correction is thus simply another mode of declaring the gospel. Consequently, Wyclif hedges it about with the conditions appropriate to a charitable concern for the other. Biblically, he appeals to the procedure enjoined in Matthew 18:15–17, of going to the brother first privately, then with two or three, and finally in the presence of the entire congregation.[22] Again, he lays down the proper attitudes to employ:[23] first, a discretion willing to see doubtful matters "in better part" and to chastise sharply or gently as the case requires; secondly, a motivation of "sincere love for the person corrected and for Holy Mother Church," not vindictive zeal or love of money. Wyclif thus insists that all such chastisement must meet an austere criterion

20. ". . . sacerdotes propter excellenciam dignitatis renuunt correpcionem fraternam accedentes ad luciferinam superbiam." SQ *47*, 382. Cf. ibid., pp. 384–385 for the recommended character of reproof. Cf. also CQ 25, 218; *50*, 399; *55*, 431 (keeping silent when the cause is hard pressed); *57*, 447.

21. Of course Wyclif admits that we are finally ignorant as to who will be saved; therefore it behooves us to love our neighbor ". . . quem quantumcunque peccaverit, ignoramus utrum habebimus in celo patronum. . ." (!) SQ *50*, 399.

22. Loc. cit., a clear biblical rebuke to the current ecclesiastical practice of settling such matters through fines or simoniac payment.

23. SQ *47*, 385.

of willing the other man's good, the hope that he will see the truth and change his life. He rests his cause finally upon love. Yet just as the atmosphere of court procedure pervades his stated methods and attitudes, so his approach to love stands in a severe context of law. Indeed, if one of these, love or law, may be said to predominate, then clearly Wyclif finds law to be the prime reality, of which love is a kind of function. Love appears as the power of harmonious inclusion within the eternal, just order, even when it is love of neighbor. Love means being at one with omnicompetent, rational Will. Little wonder that a spirit of rational order dominates Wyclif's view of Christian *agape*. Indeed, the topic recalls Wyclif's synthesizing view of faith and reason, that whatever the New Testament commands coincides with right philosophy. So he tells us that natural reason moves us to love our enemies, since we not only thereby irritate our enemies, but also profit ourselves.[24] The reader ends with the sense that brotherly love and chastising has brought this survey back to where it began: to a matter of intense personal strength in the service of hierarchical truth, of spirit over flesh, of right over wrong—such that even compassion must have an edge of "correction," and love express itself as an adjustment to law. Against the framework of his combined biblical and philosophical clarity, Wyclif inevitably saw the order of love in the most strict, uncompromising light.

III

Wyclif's inflexible outlook on faith and morals is much more understandable in light of the absurd corruption and public loss of confidence during his day. If Wyclif offered a stiff antidote for the nation's sins, the public distress around him was much to blame. England was mired down in the intermittent Hundred Years' War with France, an empty and sordid affair. The king was dottering and incompetent. The papacy had long been in its Babylonish captivity, and Wyclif lived to see it break apart in the Great Schism. Across Europe, the dread onset of plague had so reduced population and production that what goods were available invited increasing graft and intrigue. And the English, as did many peoples, suffered for lack of money and yet had to watch a great deal of it vanish into most questionable hands. It

24. "Sic enim oportet nos crucialiter diligere Deum supra nos, sicut et inferiora homine in natura et a dextris ac sinistris tam amicos quam inimicos. Et movet ad hoc racio naturalis, cum plus sic quam exasperando inimicos proficimus nobis ipsis." SQ *40*, 332.

is all too easy to read Wyclif's heavy and methodical sermons and forget the moods of crisis, the frustration, the panic that informed their
setting. Who could be sure, while wasteful campaigns continued across
the channel, when the nation might be invaded by an alien, armed
force? August of 1370 disclosed a French fleet off one coastline, while
July of 1372 saw preparations for a possible French invasion through
South Wales; at the same time, the northern border with Scotland
remained tense. Nevertheless, Edward III could order an embroidered
vest for £350 and amass heavy unpaid bills for wine. Equally grotesque
absurdities loomed in papal financing. Gregory XI imprisoned so many
Waldensians in southern France that he was forced in 1376 to issue
an indulgence whose income would sustain the prisons. The pope's
use of mercenary armies was unceasing, including one under an English leader, John Thornbury, against the visconti of Milan. In 1375
Wyclif had to endure the appointment of the mercenary's son, a young
priest in distant Italy, to a prebend in Lincoln, in partial payment for
his father's war-like prowess; Wyclif himself had been promised an
appointment to Lincoln that was never forthcoming.[25] More distressing during Wyclif's last years was the outrage of having to watch from
his Lutterworth exile the crusade of Bishop Spencer. The bishop was
another English mercenary fighter with Italian experience, whose reward had been consecration to the See of Norwich. Nevertheless, his
personal aptitudes remained strictly military, such that the Peasants'
Revolt (1381) found him with sword and armor leading in the slaugh-
ter, including the beheading and quartering of one peasant rebel. His
"crusade" to Flanders, sponsored by Urban VI against those loyal to
his rival, Clement, saw a great outpouring of private possessions and
funds for Urban's plenary indulgence. The pious affectations, the
wealth, the vain indulgences, the sordid destruction and killing, produced only an agony of waste. Meanwhile, Wyclif saw his own stature
and personal credentials reduced to those of an alien.[26]

The Wyclif of the *Forty Sermons* was a man heavily reacting to such
a state of affairs, even though the Peasants' Revolt and Spencer's cru-

25. H. B. Workman, *John Wyclif* (Oxford: the Clarendon Press, 1926), I, 204–206. Cf.
DCD, I, 387–388; III, 334. Also, J. H. Dahmus, *The Prosecution of John Wyclif* (New
Haven: Yale University Press, 1952), p. 5.

26. For an overview of the above conditions, see Workman, op. cit., e.g., I, 206, 214,
226, 293–300; II, 64–70. Cf. K. B. McFarlane, *John Wycliffe and the Beginnings of English Nonconformity* (London: English Universities Press, Ltd., 1952), ch. 2.

sade were still pending. We have already reviewed the major themes of the sermons, with their clear counterattack on corruption and hypocrisy. Let us ask further how the sermons were instrumented. To what kind of audiences were they directed, and with the hope of what achievement? Wyclif obviously had no leverage of power in the higher councils of the church. What hope did he have of altering conditions, especially the state of Christianity? Significantly, the sermons appear again and again to address themselves to secular priests. Others were undoubtedly included among his hearers, for the sermons are not that specialized; yet an emphatic concern often develops for the labors of the priest, particularly his preaching. He notes, for example, that preaching requires "industrious work by the preacher," and again, that persecution must be borne, "since patience is of the highest necessity for a preacher."[27] At one point of intense exhortation, he declares, ". . . if all of us, certainly of us priests, would stand together with the help of the church triumphant, how could the enemies of the church fail to be defeated?"[28] Indeed, there are moments when Wyclif almost recognizes secular priests as a kind of group, from whom he is hoping for high things. In one sermon series in particular, he addresses his hearers as "your fraternity," and at least two of these five homilies are pointedly directed to the work of priests, one to preaching and the other to the confessional.[29] "Your fraternity" would seem likely to refer to some association of secular priests, as that of the city of London.[30] Again, his hopeful sense of cameraderie arises when he admits that the ones preaching "this religion" are accused of blasphemy and heresy; "nevertheless, with miracles plain to see, they confess the truth of our order."[31] With Christ's "religion" and "our order" used in wry, contrasting criticism to the many monastic "religious," Wyclif seems to hope that preaching by ordinary secular priests will offer a renaissance of true Christianity. Perhaps he most clearly betrays his strategy in one statement of keen desire: "O if in every parish church

27. SQ *30*, 257; *32*, 276. Cf. also a major sermon on preaching, SQ *31*, in which the word of God is dispensed by the priest of the Lord, "misso ad gignendum et nutriendum populum verbo vite" (p. 264).

28. SQ *47*, 386.

29. SQ *31*, 35. Note "Ex quibus elicio michi tria *fraternitati vestre* per ordinem declaranda." SQ *31*, 263 (italics ours).

30. A suggestion by Principal A. B. Emden of St. Edmund's Hall, Oxford, to whom I am grateful. Cf. Dsq, p. 92, n. 13.

31. SQ *59*, 462.

one priest would be found, refined and discreet, teaching the faith of Christ to his subjects both in deed and in word, how splendid and peaceful would the kingdom be, even if her other ecclesiastical prelates did not join in." [32] The plea aptly epitomizes Wyclif's goal as a secular divine who has no power with the hierarchy, but has the ear of many ordinary priests. Such an effort would be natural for a doctor of theology highly reputed as a platform speaker, [33] so that here may reside a kernel of truth in the exaggerated claims for Wyclif's "order of Poor Priests." [34] Apparently, he initiated no such movement in a distinct and formal way; he simply yearned for each parish priest to be an agent of his gospel and sought by preaching and lecturing to bring it about. How such an influence relates to the later unlicensed preaching by Lollards is quite another question.

If Wyclif thus intended to arouse ordinary parish priests, his goal of influencing the national society also included much more. Indeed, it is a commonplace of his biography that he engaged in political affairs, notably in struggles between church and state. A milestone of such involvement was a summons for Wyclif to appear before the King's Privy Council—then dominated by the king's son, John of Gaunt—on September 22, 1376. The sequence of events is known only in outline: the summons was issued; Wyclif was then found preaching in London during the autumn; he was arraigned before the bishops at St. Paul's the following February and was physically protected by Gaunt at that encounter. [35] Precisely what links together these disparate facts has been a matter of much opinion. An alliance of some sort between Gaunt and Wyclif appears almost certain. If so, what was the resultant aim and content of the London preaching during the autumn? Workman proposes that Gaunt "made Wyclif's scheme of disendowment . . . peculiarly his own," implying that the London sermons were styled to that end; [36] McFarlane goes further in speaking of Wy-

32. SQ *43*, 359. Cf. *DCD*, II, 14.   33. McFarlane, op. cit., p. 88.

34. Workman, op. cit., I, xxxviii, boldly inserts into Wyclif's chronology: "? 1377 Wyclif begins sending out his Poor Priests . . . ." And so he is memorialized in a bas-relief sculpture at the Lutterworth church. On the lack of evidence for such, cf. McFarlane, op. cit., p. 101.

35. Cf. Workman, op. cit., I, 275–288; McFarlane, op. cit., 69–76; Dahmus, op. cit., ch. 2. Cf. the major source in *Chronicon Angliae*, ed. E. M. Thompson in the Rolls Series, no. 64 (London: Longman et al., 1874), pp. 115–121.

36. Op. cit., I, 278. Workman seems to contradict the direction of his statements (p. 275) that the duke did *not* adopt the principles of Wyclif's program. This latter view would seem more nearly correct.

clif as Gaunt's "clerical hireling" dispatched "to stir public opinion against his patron's victim," i.e., William Wykeham, bishop of Winchester, a political rival.[37] On the other hand, Dahmus suggests the detachment of Gaunt from the London preaching altogether, citing the duke's own policies of supporting clerical endowment and of using the clergy in government; why then would he employ Wyclif to preach exactly the opposite?[38]

Both sides of this question seem exaggerated beyond the most natural implications of the evidence: Wyclif need not have been Gaunt's mouthpiece; he was too stubbornly independent for that. Yet Gaunt need not be unrelated to the autumn preaching just because he differed on the disendowment theory. Indeed, Gaunt's situation that autumn, 1376, fits nicely into a clear usefulness of Wyclif to him, since his major concern was a struggle to keep certain powerful ecclesiastics out of the king's government. He was busy, in fact, reversing the deeds of the Good Parliament done the past spring. Now the Good Parliament had itself attacked clerical abuses; but its overwhelming impact had been to impeach members of the king's council and replace them with others, including Wykeham and William Courtenay, bishop of London. The days before 1371 were thus recalled, when the government around the aging king had been composed of Wykeham and other bishops. Gaunt's interest was to keep these powerful prelates out of the council without seeming to violate too blatantly the popular moral zeal of the Good Parliament. He needed a zealous, moralistic preacher, related by reputation more to the king than to the bishops, who could be his "answer" to the Good Parliament. Wyclif was not only ideally suited, but also his normal homiletical fare—the worldliness of the church—fit naturally into the duke's specific campaign against Wykeham and Courtenay. Gaunt had no need to risk proposing what Wyclif should say, nor was it of any relevance that he agree with Wyclif's theories. He had only to tell Wyclif that the king was disturbed at the increasing worldly power of the prelates (and indeed Gaunt was much disturbed!), and invite him to speak his mind in the London churches. In such preaching, one would thus not expect to find Wyclif strictly concentrating on disendowment, least of all on Wykeham himself, as an assigned topic. He would seem very much his own man, building a general atmosphere of church reform that was

37. Op. cit., p. 70.   38. Op. cit., pp. 14–19.

dissociated from the bishops' leadership. He would fit quite well into Gaunt's purposes, yet see himself as furthering only his own conscientious message.

If the dating of the *Forty Sermons* is reliable, it is interesting to find that those apparently falling within the autumn of 1376 are just the sort that could have been appropriate to the above situation.[39] Significantly, Wyclif nowhere in this series blatantly advocates disendowment of the church by the state. Rather the major themes of the whole *Forty Sermons* are found here: spirit over flesh, the two ways, the logical choice, patient suffering and fraternal correction. What distinguishes this particular cluster is that these issues are drawn with an almost apocalyptic urgency, bracing intensely for impending harshness, and exhorting to steadfastness. And though moral decay across the society is attacked, the greater number of these barbs is leveled at the church. Emphatic with this group is the sense that Wyclif is looking for a critical "show-down" on the grand issues. Citing at one point Antichrist's flagellation of the earth through warfare, he notes that from this "persecution" will arise a people called to faith, adding significantly, "among many of whom the grace of final perseverance will be wanting."[40] Yet a man must live as if "that trumpet always seems to resound in his ears" (quoting St. Jerome).[41] Satan wishes to postpone Judgment Day; so those are satanic who wish to delay Christ's religion "by inducing worldly desires";[42] while those are truly praying, "Thy kingdom come," who labor for the church's perfection. Clearly, he wishes to blend the standard medieval urgency on Doom's Day with the imperatives inherent in the state of affairs around him. A part of the church is lying spiritually sick, feverish "in a field of fatness," wicked in its pride, satiety, and idleness.[43] At one point he attacks the foolish legacies given the church to pray for the dead (a very sensitive thrust at a vast source of income), and suggests that the dead be prayed for, not according to money, but according to the kind of life they lived on earth![44] Nowhere else in the *Forty Sermons* does he

---

39. Dsq, p. 105 (series *59–55–56–57–62–60*, for October 19, 26, November 2, 9, 16, 23) and pp. 98–99. To these should perhaps be added a major part of 23 (November 30; cf. Dsq, p. 99–101), and in that case add 26 (December 7; cf. Dsq, p. 89). Interestingly, within this group we find three concrete references to London or a London site (SQ *59*, 460; 23, 205 "Westmonasterium"; 26, 229), as against only one other time in the forty (cf. SQ *28*, 239).

40. SQ *55*, 428. 41. SQ *23*, 205–206.
42. SQ *56*, 440. 43. SQ *56*, 435.
44. SQ *55*, 432: "Ex quo patet stulticia . . . dicencium quod executores sui rediment

concentrate so many injunctions to speak out for the cause, to beware of keeping silence, to correct one's brother in love. "The ones keeping silent seem treacherously to consent to the enemy."[45] On the other hand, the truly just will suffer many things, but they will suffer patiently without retaliation. For "whatever merits we achieve will have to be through voluntary punishment," or freely consenting to "sheer patience in tribulations."[46] Whatever crises lie ahead in the struggle, Christ's (and Wyclif's) true hearers will be loving in every criticism of others, and humbly patient through every blow against themselves. Wyclif does suggest that the state cannot permit flagrant abuses of wealth, lest the social fabric be destroyed, and he also alludes to his principle of dominion only through grace and rectitude.[47] But he nowhere directly exhorts the government to strip the church of her possessions—a significant omission for this London series, since in principle he had defended such dispossession in *On Civil Dominion*.[48]

Besides the sermon group for autumn, 1376, two other clusters show evidence of the same apocalyptic urgency or sense of critical encounter, and both of these bear a specifiable relation to the autumn preaching. In two sermons for January 25 and February 1, 1377, Wyclif emphasizes that he and his hearers are living in the "eleventh hour" of history and that the preachers must not be idle, since "our time is short in comparison to the fathers before us."[49] These two sermons properly continue the spirit of public exposure and concern from the autumn, a period of time climaxed in Wyclif's arraignment before the bishops at St. Paul's. Gaunt and Courtenay on that February 19, 1377, confronted each other directly, with Wyclif's interrogation as the setting.

The other sermon cluster having an air of impending *eschaton* about it is one dated in the late fall of 1377.[50] Now we know that in May of that year Gregory XI took the step of issuing bulls against Wy-

---

animas eorum defunctorum pecunia." Cf. SQ *56*, 435: The prayer of the church is for the "capaces mortuos secundum dignitatem qua dignificarunt se in via . . . ."

45. SQ *59*, 465.   46. SQ *26*, 222. Cf. SQ *56*, 442; *60*, 474; *23*, 204.

47. Cf. SQ *62*, 483; *26*, 222.

48. I, ch. 37, pp. 265–272. Note that his defense in principle abjures all expertise as to whether present circumstances warrant such action; that is a decision for statesmen only (p. 269). Contrast the implication of J. Loserth that London heard him at this time advocating disendowment, ibid., IV, x (Intro.), based on the brief summary by Thomas Walsingham, *Historia Anglicana*, ed. H. T. Riley in the Rolls Series, no. 28 (London: Longman et al., 1863), I, pt. 1, 324–325.

49. SQ *29*, 251. Cf. ibid., 246–247; SQ *30*, 258; *32*, 275; Dsq, p. 91.

50. SQ *61*–24–25 with hypothetical dates of November 22, 29, December 6; to this may be added SQ *58* for October 25, though this is less certain. Cf. Dsq, pp. 88–90, 103.

clif and his theory of dominion, though it required until December
for these to be published in England. Nevertheless, by the time of this
sermon group Wyclif had become aware of the papal threat;[51] thus it
fits well that a sense of crisis was upon him. How much better, he declares, to be a martyr for Christ than a martyr for one's own stomach!
—especially since Christ's innocent ones will sit in judgment with him
on that Last Day.[52] Therefore be vigilant, since the Devil fights more
sharply approaching the final hour of Doom's Day, as well as the hour
of one's individual death.[53] Then for the first time in the *Forty Sermons* Wyclif levels a direct attack on the pope: The Bishop of Rome,
whose deeds are the direct opposite of Christian law and doctrine, "is
the crafty Antichrist, and likewise are all who consent to him in these
matters."[54] A sharp line now clearly separates Wyclif from the highest
church officialdom, outside mere academic debate. Not only so, Wyclif
uses the same occasion to put drastic limits on seizure *by anyone* of
another's goods. Clearly he has in mind the pope and his mercenary
armies, but he also includes "laity instructed by a cleric."[55] Seizure of
another's wealth must be out of love for the rich man, and not love for
his riches.[56] If love and good will do not motivate the act, then dispossession is sinful and self-destructive. The portrait is beginning to
emerge of Wyclif increasingly his own man, uncompromising with
either clergy or laity. Secular rulers may dispossess others only by an
act of love clearly too idealistic for this world. Also the cleric who
counsels the secular action must be sure that it is not for his own pride
or mundane honor.[57] In brief: Wyclif speaks not as a politician plot-
ting victory with the state, but as an ascetic preparing to suffer with
Christ.

By such demanding intensity Wyclif has now moved to polarize his
biblicism against the organized church *and* the strategies of government. A silent implication is that Wyclif is speaking in his own right

51. Dahmus, op. cit., p. 55; McFarlane, op. cit., pp. 80–81. Cf. Workman, op. cit., I,
293–300, 304–305.

52. SQ *61*, passim 479–481.　　　　　53. SQ *24*, 206.

54. SQ *25*, 218. That no such reference occurs in any previous sermon is not provable,
but the correlation with the date here is interesting. A tract opposing the bulls and
ascribed to Wyclif may likely be dated this same autumn, 1377; it is also a rather public
document and also refers to the pope as "Antichrist." See Thomas Netter, *Fasciculi Zi-
zaniorum*, ed. W. W. Shirley in the Rolls Series no. 5 (London: Longman et al., 1858), p.
490. Cf. Workman, op. cit., I, 304–305.

55. SQ *25*, 218: Correcting another by seizing his temporalities ". . . non pertinet clero
sed laicis a clero instructis."

56. Ibid., pp. 218–219.　　　　　57. Loc. cit.

as a true vicar of Christ, a kind of papal voice of an oddly transformed sort, but nonetheless absolute in his vision and his commitment to passive suffering. Increasingly critical of actions by both church and state, the Wyclif of late 1377 certainly anticipates the Wyclif who will become disillusioned with the newly elected Urban VI (1378), will go his own way into Eucharistic heresy (1379), will attack the friars (1380), and will finally depart Oxford rather than curb any of his pronouncements (1381). Even his early alignment with the king and with John of Gaunt gets short shrift, for he discloses a final unwillingness to hope in anything except New Testament perfection as he conceives it.

Especially as church and state found certain inevitable compromises,[58] the isolation of Wyclif fell into increasingly stark relief. The tragic dilemma of Wyclif was that the more clarity and certainty he evolved, the more he substituted his own suffering and self-despite for a living encounter with affairs. Perhaps his outstanding ability was itself his undoing, since at a time of late medieval scholastic doldrums he really lacked the competition at Oxford that could have shocked his dogmatic certainty. Nor was it simply his unwavering stand "for the truth" that renders his self-initiated exile suspect. As the *Forty Sermons* makes more than clear, a key to Wyclif was his logical and emotional determination to "suffer patiently" without retaliation, with nothing but love and "brotherly correction" for his mounting hosts of opponents. Unhappily, not one of his intellectual categories could enable him to grasp a concept of "passive aggression"; yet he was apparently consumed with it. His enormous hostility toward those rejecting his perfect coincidence of philosophy and faith he chose to turn back in on himself, in the name of New Testament charity. Thus he became the model of his own patient suffering, ideally fixed in an immense antagonism. With no protecting sense of irony whatever, his view of Christian good will drove him out of general affairs, out of Oxford, and in a few brief years, out of life itself, under enormous self-imposed demands. Inevitably, such a tragic result claims the man who attains a sense of total truth, only to have it outraged again and again. Death becomes the last complaint of an ultimate faith-reason synthesis against the imperfect.

The *Forty Sermons* suggests to us a certain greatness in Wyclif's capacity to challenge the entire prevailing mood of his day, theological and institutional. His preoccupation with the Bible promised greater

58. Cf. Workman, op. cit., I, 314.

things to come, in form if not in substance. Yet he was unfortunate enough to catch the disease that he so courageously battled. The rejection of life itself in favor of an illicit security was the besetting evil of the age, faltering as it was. It hardly discredits a man that in bending all his powers to recall his age to sanity, he assumed too much, and ended by constructing his own illicit comfort, a system of truth so coherently uniform that it left the world behind instead of engaging it.

Part II. Christianity and the arts

Durandus and the interpretation of Christian worship

JAMES F. WHITE

The events of recent years have demonstrated anew the importance of interpreting Christian worship for the benefit of both clergy and laity. If it is true, as some have argued, that liturgy is the theology of the laity, then it becomes even more necessary that care be given to instruction of the laity in the meaning of worship. And certainly the clergy stand equally in need of careful education in their understanding of worship.

Since Vatican II the Roman Catholic church has been engaged in a vigorous program of educating the laity to take "that full, conscious, and active participation in liturgical celebrations which is demanded by the very nature of the liturgy."[1] This is nothing new; it has been a goal of the Liturgical Movement since the beginning of the twentieth century. But the changes in the liturgical books effected by the Consilium for the Implementation of the Constitution on the Sacred Liturgy and those changes in the regulation of worship approved by the various national conferences of bishops have added fresh urgency to the reeducation of both clergy and laity in the meaning of worship.

Protestants have been hardly less affected. The advent of new forms of worship have exposed the great confusion of both clergy and laity as to the whole purpose of worship. Much experimentation has floundered in meaninglessness, largely due to a failure to understand the pastoral, theological, and historical foundations of Christian worship. And hence a massive program in education of both clergy and laity as to the meaning of Christian worship seems essential in our own time.

Despite the apparent novelty of such situations, the underlying demand for catechesis in Christian worship has been with the church since the start. Paul faced the problem of glossolalia and the incomprehension of others (I Cor. 14:2ff.) with a clear preference for "five intelligible words" *in ekklesia*. Justin Martyr, a century later, found it necessary to interpret Christian worship for the non-Christian.[2]

---

1. "Constitution on the Sacred Liturgy," Walter M. Abbott, S.J., ed., *The Documents of Vatican II* (New York: Guild Press, America Press, and Association Press, 1966), p. 144.
2. "First Apology," chs. 65–67.

Ever since, Christian writers have produced a tremendous literature of interpretation of worship, most of it for Christian consumption.

It is doubtful that anyone has ever done this with greater success than William Durandus in his *Rationale divinorum officiorum* written shortly after 1286. We shall trace the background of this work and its influence on Christian worship over many centuries. Though highly criticized at present for its "fanciful explanation"[3] of worship, that does not diminish this volume's importance in shaping Christian understanding of worship for over six centuries. And the *Rationale* remains today a basic source of data on medieval worship, particularly in southern France and Italy during the late thirteenth century. Josef Jungmann, in his great work, *The Mass of the Roman Rite*, refers to Durandus no less than 124 times.[4] The usefulness of Durandus has changed; it has not disappeared.

As we have suggested, Durandus stands within a long sequence of interpreters of Christian worship beginning with the early apologists. The Carolingian renaissance had seen a flowering of this form of writing, part of it directed to preparing priests for yearly examinations on the liturgy, a requirement instituted in 742 for parochial clergy.[5]

Our chief interest at this point is the move toward allegorical interpretation of worship, especially of the mass, that comes to the fore in the West from this time on. Though Alcuin himself may have been the first to apply such a treatment to the mass, it was his student, Amalarius of Metz who brought this method to full development. Amalarius' masterpiece, *Liber officialis*, was completed by 823 and expanded in 831. It set the stage for medieval expositions of the mass. Amalarius (about 775 to about 850) was at one time bishop of Trier, though there has been controversy about this identity.[6] His allegorical interpretations did not go unopposed but were condemned by the synod of Quiercy in 838. Nevertheless, though interpretations continued to be written which gave little scope to allegory, it increasingly came to be the vogue for such writing.

Amalarius' *Liber officialis* set the style for a numerous progeny. His first book deals mainly with the season of lent and the related process

3. Louis Bouyer, *Liturgical Piety* (Notre Dame: University of Notre Dame Press, 1955), p. 278.

4. (New York: Benziger Brothers, Inc., 1951–55), 2 vols.

5. Ibid., I, 85–86.

6. Cf. his life by Johannes M. Hanssens, S.J., in *Amalarii episcopi opera liturgica omnia* (Vatican City: Biblioteca Apostolica Vaticana, 1948), *Studi e testi*, CXXXVIII, 58–82.

of Christian initiation. Book II takes up the rites of ordination and the appropriate vestments. Most interesting of all is Book III, which deals with the mass, while Book IV gives an exposition of the divine office and seasons of the year. Typical of Amalarius is his imaginative interpretation of his materials. He frequently produces both Old and New Testament references, though he often seems oblivious of the original function of a worship practice itself. The stole is connected with the yoke of Christ *"leve ac suave"* and it represents humility to him who wears it.[7] The kiss of peace brings no comment as to its original sense of reconciliation (Mt. 5:24, *Didache* 14). Instead it has become a moment of anxiety because of carnality and is limited to clergy with *"nullam titillationem libidinosae suggestionis."*[8] For moderns, the kiss of peace has been an important recovery of symbolic action. Coming at the point where it was in the Roman mass, no obvious reference to the offertory remained. But Amalarius' imagination does not fail him at most points and his accounts of a great variety of aspects of worship are fascinating, even though not the functional analyses our age favors. Though he was open to the attack of his contemporaries that these interpretations represented innovations, Amalarius had opened the door to allegorical explanations in many a subsequent *expositio missae*. For the most part, Amalarius' allegorical interpretations had stressed Christological references and the mass itself becomes an itinerary through the life of Christ. The final benediction of the mass, for example, is depicted as a recalling of Christ's blessing of his disciples before his ascension.[9]

Through this door entered many subsequent commentators on worship and the mass in particular. There were some, to be sure, such as the twelfth century Parisian, John Beleth, who wrote simply and plainly. Beleth saw the final benediction simply as a recalling of men to their heavenly Father where in giving thanks we always live happily.[10] But other forces were stimulating interest in allegory. Among the greatest of these was the popularity of the theology of Pseudo-Dionysius. From the year 835, Dionysius the Areopagite, St. Denis, third-century bishop of Paris and martyr, and Pseudo-Dionysius (probably a fifth-century Syrian) had been considered as a single individual. The writings of Pseudo-Dionysius were thus enhanced by apostolic

---

7. *Studi e testi*, CXXXIX, 242–243. 8. Ibid., CXXXIX, 364.
9. Ibid., CXXXIX, 368.
10. Joannes Belethus, "Rationale divinorum officiorum," *Patrologiae latina*, CCII, 56.

and heroic associations. In some of the writing of Pseudo-Dionysius, especially *The Celestial Hierarchies,* there is an emphasis on the ascent to the divine through the material. A similar neoplatonic strain is present in Augustine ("I saw thy invisibility [*invisibilia tua*] understood by means of the things that are made").[11] Pseudo-Dionysius had elaborated, making "earthly lights a figure of the immaterial enlightenment" and thus "similitudes can be fashioned from material things to symbolize that which is intelligible and intellectual."[12] Dr. Petry has noted:

> Dionysius leaves the implication that the ecclesiastical orders are to respond, not only in symbolic fashion, but also in life impulses, to the heavenly orders. It is this significant influence which becomes so pervasive in all medieval thought.[13]

Much of medieval iconography found inspiration in such a philosophical foundation. In his rebuilding of the Abbey Church of Saint Denis, Abbot Suger speaks rapturously of the beauty of the church as "transferring that which is material to that which is immaterial (*de materialibus ad immaterialia*), and his being "transported from this inferior to that higher world in an anagogical manner."[14] Suger and others were building and decorating churches which were, in effect, books of allegory. Suger describes in *De administratione* XXXIV the iconography based on typology he helped develop for new stained glass windows of the Abbey Church. We realize now the role of sacred geometry in the construction of medieval cathedrals and other churches so that their measurements reflect number ratios of symbolic significance.[15] Allegory was being built, glazed, carved, and painted long before the thirteenth century.

Less obvious, but more important, was the gradual liturgical fixation as practices continued without obvious meaning. As we have seen, Amalarius seems ignorant of the signification of the kiss of peace as an act of reconciliation. Yet such the practices remained and, following

11. "Confessions," VII, 17 in *Confessions and Enchiridion* tr. and ed. Albert C. Outler (Philadelphia: Westminster Press, 1955), pp. 151–152.

12. *The Mystical Theology and the Celestial Hierarchies* (Fintry, Brook, Surrey: Shrine of Wisdom, 1949), pp. 30, 34.

13. *Christian Eschatology and Social Thought* (New York: Abingdon, 1956), p. 178.

14. "De administratione" XXXIII in Erwin Panofsky, *Abbot Suger* (Princeton: Princeton University Press, 1946), pp. 62–65.

15. Cf. Otto von Simson, *The Gothic Cathedral* (New York: Pantheon, 1956) and George Lesser, *Gothic Cathedrals and Sacred Geometry,* 2 vols. (London: Alec Tirenti, 1957).

Amalarius, became encrusted in allegorical interpretations. Most of these explanations focus on the life of Christ beginning with the anticipation in Old Testament types and going through to the ascension. As historical and geographical reasons for practices became increasingly forgotten, allegorical interpretations took their place, a practice certainly not confined to the Middle Ages (e.g., Cyprian's reasons for the mixture of water and wine or Protestant explanations of Genevan tabs). The alternative, abandonment of practices now vacant of meaning, seems rarely to have been considered.

A fully-developed exposition of Christian worship occurs in the *De divinis officiis per anni circulum* of Rupert of Deutz (d. 1135).[16] Here the scheme is the course of the church year but the theme is familiar, the remembering of Jesus Christ through hours, days, vestments, and each item of the mass. Even more important was the interpretation of the mass, composed shortly before his election, by Pope Innocent III. The six books of his *De sacro altaris mysterio* are replete with Christological references. The alb, for example, represents the longest distance from the skins of animals that Adam put on after his sin, the newness of life which Christ gives us at baptism, Christ's clothing at the transfiguration, and the earthly vestments of a sinless Christ.[17] Or the moment of silence after the offertory recalls one to the instance in the passion of the Lord (John 11:54) in which Jesus and his disciples went into hiding at Ephraim.[18] The silence after the Lord's Prayer recalls the sabbath during which the Lord rested in the tomb.[19] Of special interest to moderns is Innocent's list of the four liturgical colors which he distinguishes according to the properties of the different days of the calendar.[20] This is the earliest such list we have. Except for the use of black for advent and lent, the scheme is basically that in general use today in the West.

The climax of the interpretation of Christian worship through the use of allegory came at the end of the thirteenth century. It is surprising that the climax of allegorical interpretation should come at such a time since the thirteenth century represents the greatest achievements of scholastic theology. The philosophical foundations of allegorical writings were heavily platonic. The fascination with symbols was "nothing more, really, than the logical consequence of carrying

---

16. *Patrologiae latina*, CLXX, 10–332.
17. Ibid., CCXVII, 787–788.   18. Ibid., CCXVII, 831.
19. Ibid., CCXVII, 906.   20. Ibid., CCXVII, 799–802.

through Plato's theory of knowledge, with its sharp separation of the world of sense and the world of ideas."[21] But the new philosophical approach, with its Aristotelian emphasis on the world of sense as the basis of knowledge, stood in direct opposition to allegorical interpretation of worship or of anything else. Albertus Magnus ridiculed many a popular allegorical interpretation of the mass in his *De sacrificio missae*.

Scholasticism did not triumph in this instance. Indeed, allegorical interpretations were actually strengthened as an indirect result of scholasticism. Jungmann points out that scholasticism contributed a more systematic and theological approach to the writing of an *expositio missae*.[22] And it is quite possible that the popularity of Durandus' work is due in part to the carefully-ordered sequence and concern for the relationship of the parts to the whole that distinguish his *Rationale* from previous works. One senses a different spirit in Durandus' careful attention to the sequence of each part of the mass and his discussion of ways of dividing the structure of the mass.

William Durandus was born in southern France about 1230.[23] As a young man he went to study in Italy and eventually became a professor at Bologna, then Modena. About 1262 he became a part of the Roman curia, rising to important functions in the administration of the papal patrimony. In 1285 he was elected bishop of Mende in southern France though he is not known to have visited his diocese until 1291. In 1295 he was recalled to Italy to pacify some of the papal possessions and died in Rome the following year.

Despite the press of his administrative duties, Durandus managed to continue his scholarly interests. His was a most distinguished name among canonists for his *Repertorium iuris canonici* (date uncertain), two editions of *Speculum iudiciale* (before 1276 and after 1286), and *Constitutiones synodales* (after 1292). Of more liturgical interest is his *Pontificale*, written as bishop, sometime between 1292 and 1295. Though his pontifical incorporates items peculiar to his cathedral church, it gradually became a rival to the pontifical of the Roman curia. When the pontifical was first printed in 1485, it was felt most bishops were using copies of the text edited by Durandus.[24] There are

21. Jungmann, I, 113.   22. Ibid., I, 114.
23. Michel Andrieu, *Le Pontifical Romain au Moyen-Age: Le Pontifical de Guillaume Durand* (Vatican City: Biblioteca Apostolica Vaticana, 1940), *Studi e testi*, LXXXVIII, 3–5.
24. Ibid., LXXXVIII, 20.

curious parallels between Durandus' edition of the pontifical becoming a rival to the Roman prototype and Alcuin's earlier influence on the Roman missal.

Our present interest in Durandus, however, centers in his work, *Rationale divinorum officiorum*,[25] written sometime after his election as bishop but probably before he went to Mende in 1291. Few books, if any, have enjoyed the long-lasting popularity that this one had as an interpretation of Christian worship.

The *Rationale* is remarkable for its thoroughness in giving a comprehensive explanation of Christian worship. Durandus begins the Proeme by telling us that all things of which "ecclesiastical offices and furnishing are formed, are full of divine signs and mysteries and overflow with heavenly sweetness" (Proeme 1). This is not always easy to grasp since often what things in church and the offices signify "is not seen." "For the figures have withdrawn and today is a time of truth. And we ought not Judaize" (Proeme 6). He goes on to say that "in divine scriptures there are the historical, allegorical, tropological, and anagogical senses" (Proeme 9). "In this work," Durandus tells us, "many of these same diverse senses are used and transitions are made from one to another" (Proeme 12). This can be justified as long as all are used "in praise of God." Durandus also mentions the variety of uses in different churches, intending only to treat the most common. Throughout the work are scattered such remarks as "in certain places they sing the creed" (IV, xxv, 14) or other references showing the variety of local practices before printing brought standardization. His intention was to set forth those things in which "for the daily use of the clergy understanding is necessary" just as he had previously done for magistrates in the *Speculum iudiciale* (Proeme 16).

Durandus' *Rationale* is divided into eight books. The first deals with churches, ecclesiastical places and furnishings, and consecrations and sacraments. In Book II he treats the ministers of the church and their offices. Book III is on priestly and other vestments. Book IV, dealing with the mass, and Book VI, discussing Sundays and feasts of Our Lord, are the longest by far. Book V treats the other divine offices. In Book VII, the feasts of the saints are described and VIII investigates time and the calendar. As can be seen, it is a comprehensive survey of Christian worship as practiced in the medieval West. In short, it represents a complete textbook or *Enchiridion* (as it is sometimes subtitled)

25. I am using an edition published in Lyons in 1592 by Jean Baptiste Buysson.

of Christian worship. Durandus bemoaned that priests and bishops in his day had meager understanding of those things they used daily "what they signify and why they were instituted." He applied the words of Isaiah (24:2): "And so will the people be as [is] the priest" (Proeme 3). The *Rationale*, then, is a massive effort (more than nine hundred pages in octavo) at continuing education of the clergy.

Durandus made it quite clear that he was content to lean on his predecessors. This is especially the case in Book IV on the mass. Durandus began this book by saying that he intended to follow, with some additions and subtractions, the four-part division of Innocent III (IV, i, 2). This is true of many details also. Innocent stated that the *confiteor* was not private confession *"non (ut quidam minus provide faciunt) in specie"*[26] and Durandus repeated: *"non (ut quidam minus provide faciunt in specie)"* (IV, vii, 2), or in similar words both writers urged that the final collect ought always be for the living rather than the dead[27] (IV, xv, 16).

The *Rationale*, then, is important not just for its original sections but as a compilation of medieval understanding of the mass and other forms of worship. One could make a rather loose comparison between it and Peter Lombard's *Sentences* as works pulling together the bits of liturgical or theological information available at the time.

But, for us, the *Rationale* also serves another purpose—as a witness to practices extant in the late thirteenth century in southern Europe. There are some surprising survivals. For example, the dismissal of the catechumens which we usually assume had disappeared much earlier in the West, is mentioned (VI, lvi, 11) though Durandus disapproved of the practice, in some places, of their dismissal before the gospel lection. Or we learn that the gospel is read, the symbol of faith (creed) is professed, and *then* "preaching is made to the people as exposition of the words of the gospel and symbol" (IV, xxvi, 1). This is the sequence Anglicans and Methodists have followed for four hundred years but now seem to be about to give up to follow the modern Roman Catholic sequence of gospel, sermon, and creed. Sometimes details in the *Rationale* are amplified in Durandus' *Pontificale*, such as the putting on of the maniple during mass (IV, vii, 4).[28]

The medieval love of symbolism appears in the practice (*nonnullis*

26. *Patrologiae latina*, CCXVII, 806.
27. Ibid., CCXVII, 815.   28. *Studi e testi*, LXXXVIII, 634.

in locis), eliminated at the time of Pius V, of making the sign of the cross on the altar "with three fingers extended" as a sign that "all are acting in the faith of the Trinity" (IV, xxxix, 7). In many instances, a single symbolic reference does not exhaust Durandus' ingenuity. For the triple sign of the cross after the *Te igitur* Durandus finds five different symbolic explanations: the death on the cross, the triune God, in figure of the triple union in receiving the Saviour, the memory of three crucifixions (the Pharisees' decision to crucify him, the clamor of the crowd, and the actual crucifixion), and three crosses in the times of the tribes before the giving of the law (Abel in the lamb, Melchizedek in bread and wine, and Abraham in his son—all of which prefigured the sacrifice of Christ) (IV, xxxvi, 8). Numerical symbolism was always tempting, if not irresistible, to Durandus, but the explanations are usually a bit more restrained than this one. This example shows Durandus' constant lifting of the most mundane of matters to a heavenly level and also his delight in Old Testament types. Other actions are described whimsically: the altar is incensed "that all evil demons may be repulsed from it," they apparently being allergic to the "fumes of incense" (IV, x, 5).

We have cited a few examples to give an indication of the wealth of Durandus' imagination in giving meaning to all objects, acts, words, and times used in worship. His method of explanation may seem to us to create more obscurity than enlightenment though it just might be that postliterate man could profit from probing the forms and understanding of worship that seemed most natural to preliterate man. Durandus' symbols are largely visual and graphic. They appeal to the imagination that could conceive of worship as more than the diet of words it tended to become after Gutenberg. Maybe Durandus is ahead of us as well as behind us!

Certainly Durandus' *Rationale* had an appeal in the Gutenberg era too. Indeed it formed an important part in the early history of the printed book. Not only was it one of the very first books to be printed but it was one of the most frequently printed works of the fifteenth century. Only the Bible, a missal, a psalter, and a Latin grammar of Donatus are known to have been printed prior to the *Rationale* and but small fragments of the first printing of Donatus remain. Next to the Bible and the two service books, the *Rationale* is the oldest complete printed book to survive. The first printed edition of the *Ratio-*

nale divinorum officiorum appeared on October 6, 1459 from the Mainz firm of Fust and Schoeffer, successors to Gutenberg. The second edition was a product of the press of Günther Zainer of Augsburg and appeared on January 22, 1470.

Even more remarkable than the fact of being the fifth printed book is the number of early editions of the *Rationale*. Before 1501 at least forty-four editions (GW) had appeared as compared with only nineteen (GW) of Augustine's great work, *The City of God*, or sixteen (GW) of Caesar's *Commentary on the Gallic War*. At least thirteen more editions of the *Rationale* appeared during the sixteenth century. Durandus' *Speculum iudiciale* appeared in at least fifteen editions during the fifteenth century. The obscurity of Durandus in modern times hides from us his popularity on the eve of reformation. It is interesting to speculate on the reasons for such popularity. We can assume that there were so many editions of the *Rationale* because of demand for the work since publishers were probably as sensitive to sales opportunities then as now. But why was such a book on the fifteenth century best-seller list for so long? It may not be surprising that it outsold other interpretations of worship but to rival major theological and classical works is a bit surprising for liturgists in any age. Apparently there was a deeply felt need on the part of literate people, living in the half-century before the Reformation, for an explanation of Christian worship. Perhaps the Reformation too hastily and too impatiently answered this need by discarding much that seemed incomprehensible rather than taking the slow and patient course of explication. Martin Bucer is perhaps typical when he accuses the "Romish Antichrists" of continually turning "sacred ceremonies for the worship of God into various wicked shows, so that today those signs among the great majority of people serve more for the maintenance and increase of superstition and show than of piety and religion."[29] For people who are ignorant of the meaning of ceremonies, such acts certainly are not of much value, but perhaps liturgical interpretation would have been more useful in the long run than subtraction and iconoclasm.

The popularity of Durandus' *Rationale* apparently declined sharply during the seventeenth century. No less than fifty-nine printed edi-

29. "Censura" in *Christian Initiation: The Reformation Period*, ed. J. D. C. Fisher (London: S.P.C.K., 1970), pp. 99–100.

tions had appeared by 1614 yet none was published thereafter for 229 years. Its reappearance came about in an unusual way. Two Anglican priests, John Mason Neale and Benjamin Webb, published an English translation of the portions of the *Rationale* dealing with church architecture. It was a major effort in their campaign to recover medieval forms of worship and architecture in the Church of England. The volume was published in 1843 and again in 1906 under the title, *The Symbolism of Churches and Church Ornaments.*[30] A 127-page introductory essay by Neale and Webb leaves no doubt as to the purpose of the translation. It is propaganda for the revival of medieval architecture based on "correct" symbolism, i.e., that with the authority of medieval precedent. Undoubtedly, many Victorian church building committees succumbed to the "authority" of Durandus and included a piscina in their churches, not because they had felt a real need for a piscina but because Durandus had said it represented the mercy of Christ through whom we are washed from the filth of sin at baptism and penance (I, i, 39). Building committees like to be told how to do things right and Neale and Webb saw to it that Durandus was used to inculcate true medieval guidelines. At about the same time the entire *Rationale* was translated into French,[31] a gothic revival and new interest in medieval music being current in France, too.

The only other translation into English was that done by another Anglican priest, T. H. Passmore, at the end of the nineteenth century.[32] His purpose, too, was propaganda, this time to encourage the use of traditional vestments. Ritualism had been promoting their use ever since Neale helped reintroduce them in the Church of England in 1850. To this end, Passmore translated Book III of the *Rationale*, that dealing with vestments. How many bishops were persuaded that they ought to wear a tunic because it signified "perseverance" (III, x, 1) or how many priests adopted a maniple "on the left arm, noting that they ought to be restrained regarding earthly things but unbound with respect to heavenly" (III, vi, 2) is unknown. It may have convinced a few.

Durandus' *Rationale* would persuade few men today to adopt practices because of their symbolic references. But it remains a valuable

---

30. Leeds: T. W. Green, 1843; London: Gibbings & Company, 1906.
31. C. Barthelemy, trans. (Paris: 1848–54), 5 vols.
32. *The Sacred Vestments* (London: Sampson Low, Marston & Co., 1899).

source for the study of the forms of worship contemporary with the author. It is a carefully-organized catalog of medieval customs in worship. Today Durandus' explanations may fascinate us less than those things he tries to interpret. The *Rationale divinorum officiorum* has been used for explanation, propaganda, and source material in different centuries. In each function, it has been of foremost importance.

The eschatological function of the iconography in the Dresden Manuscript of the *Sachsenspiegel*

GERALD H. SHINN

On first opening the Amira edition of the Dresden MS.,[1] one is struck by the profusion of the illuminations. If the document were a Book of Hours, a Breviary, a Psalter, or a Missal, the illuminations would be readily understandable. In the Middle Ages such theological works were expected to be illuminated. Why, however, illuminate a "secular" civil and feudal code of law?

F. J. Mone in *Deutsche Denkmäler* (1820), Büsching in his *Wöchentliche Nachrichten IV* (1819) and more recently H. C. Hirsch in his translation of the "Lehnrecht" of the *Ssp.*, have maintained that *D* was illuminated for those persons who could not read the written text.

> The illuminations of the feudal law were taken from Sachsenspiegel manuscripts. The purpose of the illuminations was to clarify the laws of the Sachsenspiegel for its "readers", especially those who could not read.[2]

We are led to believe by these scholars that the illuminations of the *Ssp.* were to perform the same function for legal science that the images in the churches did for theology. Malcolm Letts exhibits a comparable approach in his article on the *Ssp.* and its "illustrators."

> The artist has followed the text very closely, although here and there he has missed a point. As a result practically the whole work can be read, title by title and paragraph by paragraph, in the illustrations.[3]

Such a naive interpretation of medieval pedagogy is appealing, and, at first blush, quite plausible. Pope Gregory the Great's letter to

---

1. The Dresden MS. (hereinafter abbreviated *D*) of the *Sachsenspiegel* (hereinafter abbreviated *Ssp.*) was almost totally destroyed by water damage during the fire bombing of the city of Dresden in World War II. Karl von Amira's first volume, in two parts, of 1902 contains the text and photographic facsimiles of *D*'s illuminations (six plates are in color) and is, consequently, the sole source for the study of the complete MS.

2. Eike von Repgow, *Der Sachsenspiegel Lehnrecht*, tr. H. C. Hirsch (Halle, 1939), p. 232.

3. Malcolm Letts, "The Sachsenspiegel and Its Illustrators," *Law Quarterly Review*, XLIX (1933), 557.

Bishop Serenus of Marseilles is often fondly recalled in support.[4] With specific investigation of the text and illuminations of *D* there are several questions which might be raised against such an interpretation. If *D* were produced for those persons who could not read writing, then we should, first of all, expect each article and paragraph to be illuminated. Secondly, we should anticipate that the illuminations be self-explanatory. In regard to the first question we find that all articles and paragraphs are *not* illuminated; for example: articles 50, 53, 55 and 70 in Book II; 14, 24, 28, 30 and 43 in Book III. We would assume, consequently, that the "illiterate" readers would and could know nothing about the building of boundary fences, tree limbs overhanging a neighbor's property, majority rule in a village, protection of goods won in a court decision, rights of the plaintiff to take the defendant into custody until the time of trial, reversal of court decisions, persons declared dispossessed of legal rights, the fact that a judge shall adjudicate all people in the same manner regardless of wealth or political position, and goods, taken unjustly by force, being returned intact. Not only whole articles but also a great many paragraphs were left unilluminated: *Ssp.* II; 20, 2; II; 21, 2 and 4; II; 51, 2 and 3; II; 58, 1; II; 59, 4; II; 61, 4 and 5; II; 64, 4 and 5; III; 1, 2; III; 5, 4.[5] The person unable to read the text of *D* would clearly have a rather incomplete picture of the civil law in Saxony.

Secondly, even the articles and paragraphs which are illuminated stand incomplete, for the illuminations are not self-explanatory. For instance, *Ssp.* III; 2, says clergy and Jews who carry weapons are to be treated as laymen and, therefore, are open to armed retaliation. This statute is based upon the King's Peace which states that clergy and Jews are not to carry weapons. Yet, Amira plate 72, illumination 5, pictures only a monk and a Jew, astride horses, wearing swords. The crime is shown, true. The fact that it is a crime for Jews and clergy to carry weapons and the punishment for such action can only be known by a reading of the text.

Amira plate 84, illumination 2, depicts scenes from the crucifixion of Christ, Hell and the creation of Adam. But what do they have to do

4. "Pictures are placed in our churches in order that people who cannot read may learn from gazing upon the walls what they cannot get from books." Letter quoted with references in Eleanor Shipley Duckett, *Alcuin, Friend of Charlemagne* (New York, 1951), p. 50. For an attack upon the modern patronization of medieval art see G. G. Coulton, *Medieval Faith and Symbolism* (New York, 1958), pp. 246–249.

5. See Amira, I, 1, 21, for a more complete list of unilluminated paragraphs.

with the civil law of Saxony? Only the text explains the relationship *(Ssp.* II; 42). Because God had created man in His own image and Christ has died to save all men, even descending into Hell, it is not right for anyone to own or have slaves.

Amira plate 69, illumination 5, pictures the ascension, creation of man, crucifixion, resurrection and judgment day. Again, what do they mean? The text elucidates *(Ssp.* II; 66). There are four days in the week which are "peace days" *(nefas)* when court cannot be held—Thursday, Friday, Saturday and Sunday. Why? Because on Thursday Christ ascended into Heaven, on Friday man was created by God and on that same day man martyred God. On Saturday God not only rested from creating but also reposed in the grave. On Sunday He rose from the dead, and on Sunday He shall come to judge us.

Illuminations 2 and 3, Amira plate 8, refer to *Ssp.* I; 3, 1. They show Adam, Noah in his ark, Abraham, Moses, David and the birth of God. And what is the meaning portrayed? Without the text the illuminations would remain unfathomable enigmas. Adam, Noah, Abraham, Moses, David and the birth of God symbolize the six ages of the history of mankind. The seventh age is yet to come, Eike says, and we do not know the date.[6]

Not only, therefore, would a person who could not read writing

6. The two major sources for Eike's historical divisions of the ages of mankind are St. Augustine, bishop of Hippo (354–430), and Isidore, bishop of Seville (c. 560–636). Augustine says: "After that, I have proceeded from the first man down to the flood in one book, which is the fifteenth of this work; and from that again down to Abraham our work has followed both (cities) in chronological order. From the patriarch Abraham down to the time of the Israelite kings, at which we close our sixteenth book, and thence down to the advent of Christ Himself in the flesh, to which period the seventeenth book reaches, the city of God appears from my way of writing to have run its course alone; whereas it did not run its course alone in this age, for both cities, in their course amid mankind, certainly experienced chequered times together just as from the beginning." Taken from St. Augustine, *The City of God,* tr. Marcus Dods, G. Wilson, and J. J. Smith ("The Modern Library" [New York, 1950]), Book XVIII, chap. I, p. 609. Latin text in *OC,* XXIV, 407 (*PL,* XLI, col. 559). Isidore writes in Book V, chap. 38:5 on "Generations and Ages." "Age (aetas) is used properly in two ways: for it is either the age of man, as infancy, prime, old age; or the age of the world, whose first age is from Adam to Noe; the second, from Noe to Abraham; the third, from Abraham to David; the fourth, from David to the migration of Judah to Babylon; the fifth, from then to the coming of the Saviour in the flesh; the sixth, which is now in progress and which will continue until the world is ended." From Ernest Brehaut, "An Encyclopedist of the Dark Ages," *Studies in History, Economics and Public Law,* XLVIII (1912), 179. Latin text in Isidori Hispalensis Episcopi, *Etymologiarum sive Originum,* ed. W. M. Lindsay (Oxford, 1911), I, Book V, chap. 38:5. Augustine's and Isidore's influence may be seen in another Medieval historian, namely Rudolf von Ems (d.c. 1254), a contemporary of Eike's. See Rudolph von Ems, *Weltchronik,* lines 60–146. Text given in Gustav Ehrismann, "Rudolf von Ems Weltchronik," *Texte des Mittlelalters,* XX (1915), 2–3.

have an incomplete knowledge of the Saxon laws because certain sections are unilluminated, but he would and could not understand the meaning of the text even with the illuminations.

If the illuminations in *D* were not intended for the illiterate, what purpose and function could they possibly have? In 1816 a much more mature suggestion concerning the function of the illuminations of the *D* MS. was offered by Johann Wolfgang von Goethe. In his letter to Johann Gustav Büsching, professor of German studies at Breslau (d. May 4, 1829) and son of the famous geographer Anton Friedrich Büsching, concerning a pictured copy of the Oldenburg MS. of the *Ssp.*, Goethe stated:

> In any case, it seems significant to me that what had already occurred with sacred books and illuminations should be accomplished also for legal, political and civil literature. We shall eventually come to the realization that not only the uneducated but the thoroughly educated, natural man will want to see with his own eyes what comes to him through the ear. . . .[7]

In the Middle Ages reading was usually oral.[8] It is not enough, however, for a person to read aloud or listen to writing, he must also be able to see vividly the conceptual images of the meaning in his mind in order to appropriate them. The illuminations in *D* provide a moving picture of legal principles in living color in order for the reader and hearer to appropriate their intent and it is only by appropriation that one begins to comprehend. Reading, therefore, was not a mere matter of the ability to read words or writing, one had to comprehend the ideas which the words and writing reflected. Ancillary illuminations, consequently, helped tremendously to focus the mind and present sharp, clear images to the understanding.[9]

7. Ludwig Geiger, *Goethe-Jahrbuch* (Frankfurt a.M., 1880), I, 254–255.

8. See E. Wattenbach, *Das Schriftwesen im Mittelalter* (Graz, 1958), p. 385, who states that the function of the illuminations of the *Ssp.* is to facilitate the understanding.

9. "Die Glasmalerei. Sie war für das romanische Kirchengebäude ein Schmuck, für das gotische ist sie eine Notwendigkeit. Dabei ist sie für sich nichts. Sie ist nicht nur mit ihrem materiellen Dasein sondern mit ihrem tiefsten Wesen an die architektur gebunden. . . ." From Georg Dehio, *Geschichte der Deutschen Kunst* (Berlin and Leipzig, 1930), II, 82. Gothic art, then, necessitates pictured representation by its very nature. Zaroslava Drobna in *Gothic Drawing*, tr. Jean Layton (Prague, n.d.), p. 16, reflects a similar approach to the meaning of Gothic art in Bohemia: "Hence it would be incorrect and inconsistent to consider mediaeval drawing as an autonomous artistic form of expression. Even in the case of single independent examples of such drawings, their function is clear: it is always clear that it was a working auxiliary function." Dr. Ray C. Petry gives a more thorough treatment of the relationship between art, writing and symbolism in chap. 9 of *The History of Christianity* (Englewood Cliffs, N.J., 1962) I, 382ff.

There is yet a higher purpose and function of the illuminations in the *D* MS. At the outset, a clarification is in order concerning the technical meaning of an illumination in the Middle Ages. The pictures in the *D* MS. are illuminations. That is, the artist made use of gold and silver metals for color.[10] Gold and silver are Gothic colors whose function it was to place the reader or listener in direct contact with God who in the *D* MS. is the author of the law. In fact He is law. "God is Himself law, therefore law is beloved by Him."[11] Illuminations, as a result, perform an eschatological function. They help place the earthly in touch with the heavenly.[12]

That gold denotes light and is a characteristic symbol of the Gothic *Zeitgeist* and *Weltanschauung* can be illustrated from a few primary sources. The literary historical background for these sources appears to be St. Augustine and the mystical writings of Pseudo-Dionysius the Areopagite (c. 500) translated into Latin by John Scotus (c. 850).[13] Medieval light symbolism, which was also allied to contemporary mysticism, drew deep draughts from these two wellsprings. Almost all sources indicate an intrinsic eschatology.[14]

St. Augustine couples the neoplatonic theory of light with the

10. John W. Bradley, *Illuminated Manuscripts* (London, 1920), pp. 2–5.

11. Karl August Eckhardt, "Sachsenspiegel Land-und Lehnrecht," *Monumenta Germaniae Historica, Fontes Iuris Germanici Antiqui,* n.s. (1933), I, 13. Hereafter referred to as *MGH.*

12. Gold stands for that light in which Divinity dwells. It is the color of revelation of the Holy Spirit (I Tim. 6:16). Silver stands for purity (Ps. 12:7). The godly Word is likened unto silver and also the tongue of the just is called silver. See Klementine Lipffert, *Symbol-Fibel* (Kassel, 1957), pp. 83–85. This point, moreover, is not mere academic reflection about the life and times of the medieval folk. Kings, monks, popes, university professors, students, knights and their ladies, serfs, farmers and their wives normally thought of gold in connection with, and in relation to, divinity. How can this be known? By the fact that these people were the raw material from which saints were made, and even more important, they were the people who made the saints! It was the medieval folk themselves who had the saints wear the golden cloaks, the golden nimbi, the golden chains and golden crowns in order that the divinity exemplified in their saintly lives might be made manifest in their golden icons. For example, the twelve-year-old girl of Agen martyred by the proconsul Dacian in 303 A.D. became St. Foy (6th of October). Her golden figure in Conques still dazzles onlookers today as it did the eleventh century traveler Bernard of Anger who termed it a "golden majesty." For a general treatment see E. Mâle, *L'Art religieux du XIIIème siècle en France* (Paris, 1924), pp. 200–202. For the detailed study of the origins and iconography of St. Foy see Louis Reau, *Iconographie de l'art chrétien* (Paris, 1958), III, pt. i, 513–516.

13. For further information see the article by W. J. Sparrow, "The Influence of Dionysius in Religious History," in *Dionysius the Aeropogite on the Divine Names and the Mystical Theology,* tr. C. E. Rolt (New York, 1951), pp. 202–219. See also Edgar de Bruyne, *Études d'esthétique médiévale* (Brussels, 1946), III, 16–18.

14. Cf. Ray C. Petry, *Christian Eschatology and Social Thought* (New York, 1956), pp. 177–180.

Christian doctrine of the creation.[15] The uncreated light is God Himself who creates light.

And he spoke, saying, "Light be formed!", and light was made. But the light which is born of God is different from the light which God made. The light born of God is the wisdom of God. True created light is everywhere mutable, whether incorporeal or corporeal.[16]

His light enlightens all men.

Therefore it is said, "You are the light of the world" (Matt. 5:14). But light, not true light. Why? Because *He* is the true light which enlightens all men (John 1:1).[17]

The uncreated light and the created light are, however, to be distinguished.

The light which is God is different from the light which God made. The creator light is incomparably better, for it lacks nothing.[18]

Still, the created light is the means by which objects are revealed to us.

Fittingly, moreover, this light (the creator) allows the suitable light (the created) to make things manifest.[19]

Pseudo-Dionysius begins his *Celestial Hierarchies* with the image of the Father of lights whose light proceeds from Him and converts men to a resemblance of His unity and simplicity.[20]

15. See Clemens Baeumker, *Witelo, Ein Philosoph und Naturforscher des XIII Jahrhunderts* ("Beiträge zur Geschichte der Philosophie des Mittelalters" [Münster, 1908]), III, 372–377. Hereafter referred to as *BGPM*. Also de Bruyne, III, 17.

16. St. Augustine, *de Genesi ad litteram, inperfectus liber*, ed. Joseph Zycha ("Corpus Scriptorum Ecclesiasticorum Latinorum," [Prague, 1894]), chap. 5:20, XXVII, pt. 1, 472. Hereafter referred to as *CSEL*. Latin text also in *Patrologiae cursus completus, Series Latina*, ed. J. P. Migne (Paris, 1887), XXXIV, col. 228. Hereafter referred to as *PL*. See also *De Trinitate*, Book VIII, chap. 2:3 where Augustine quotes I John 1:5—"Hoc enim scriptum est: 'Quoniam Deus lux est,'" in St. Augustine, *Oeuvres complètes*, ed. and tr. Peronne, Vincent, et al., Latin text and notes according to the Benedictine edition (Paris, 1871), XXVII, 344. Hereafter referred to as *OC*. See also *PL*, XLII, col. 949.

17. St. Augustine, *Sermo IV, De Jacob et Esau, OC*, chap. 5:6, XV, 619 (*PL*, XXXVIII, col. 56).

18. St. Augustine, *Contra Adversarium Legis et Prophetarum*, Book I, chap. 7, *OC*, XXVI, 466 (*PL*, XLII, col. 609).

19. St. Augustine, *de Genesi ad litteram, inperfectus liber*, chap. 5:24, *CSEL*, XXVIII, pt. 1, 474 (*PL*, XXXIV, col. 229).

20. From Denys L'Aréopagite, *La Hiérarchie Céleste*, Roques, Heil and Gandillac (Paris, 1958), p. 70. We find a very similar note in Plato's *Republic*, Book VI, Divisions 18

Robert Grosseteste, bishop of Lincoln (1175–1235), wrote a treatise on light which reflects the Pseudo-Dionysian philosophy of illumination.

And the form and perfection of all bodies is light (lux): but the light of the higher bodies is more spiritual and simple, while the light of the lower bodies is more bodily plurified. Nor are all bodies of the same form or species, though they have originated from a simple or plurified light; just as all numbers are not of the same form or species though nevertheless they are produced by the greater or lesser plurification from unity.[21]

Thomas Aquinas (1225–1274) treats light metaphorically instead of anagogically in both his *Summa Theologica* and his *Summa Contra Gentiles*. This is very likely a result of his Aristotelian orientation. The bond between divinity and light, nevertheless, is not broken; it is only reinterpreted.[22]

Hence it is necessary that some supernatural disposition should be added to the intellect in order that it may be raised up to such a great and sublime height. Now since the natural power of the created intellect does not avail to enable it to see the essence of God . . . it is necessary that the power of understanding should be added by divine grace. Now this increase of the intellectual powers is called the illumination of the intellect, as we also call the intelligible ob-

---

and 19 (pp. 99ff. in vol. 2 of the *Loeb Classical Library*, tr. Paul Shorey [Cambridge, Mass., 1942]) where light is discussed as the third element necessary for vision. Plato speaks of the "sun," i.e., one of the divinities in heaven, as the author and cause of light: "Whose light makes our vision see best and visible things to be seen." In Plotinus' *Enneads*, we find essentially the same idea of "fire" and "light" as the "Forming-Idea" which stretches from the primary to the ultimate (Book IV, 3 :10 in Plotinus, *The Enneads*, tr. Stephen MacKenna [London, 1930]), p. 269. See also IV, 5:3 and VI, 4:7. For a treatment of light denoting a divine presence in central Asia see M. Eliade, *Traité d'histoire des religions* (Paris, 1949), pp. 68ff., and especially the chapter on "Le Soleil et les cultes solaires." The Divine Light and Shekinah Glory play an essential role in the Bible, for example Gen. 1:3–4, Ex. 34:17, Ezek. 1:27, Hab. 3:4, Is. 60:19–20, Dan. 2:23 and John 1:5–7. See also chap. 4, para. 6 in Pseudo-Dionysius' *The Divine Names* where he speaks of God as "He who enlightens all intelligence," "He is the source of all lights," and "He is Lord of all light," in *Oeuvres complètes du Pseudo-Denys L'Aréopagite*, tr. Maurice de Gandillac (Paris, 1943), pp. 99–100. For further information on Pseudo-Dionysius' use of light see Walther Völker, *Kontemplation und Ekstase bei pseudo-Dionysius Areopagita* (Wiesbaden, 1958), pp. 210–211.

21. Robert Grosseteste, *On Light, or the Incoming of Forms*, tr. Charles Glenn Wallis (Annapolis, 1939), pp. 7–8. Latin text by Ludwig Baur, *Die Philosophischen Werke des Robert Grosseteste, Bischofs von Lincoln, BGPM*, IX, 56–57.

22. Wolfgang Schöne, *Über das Licht in der Malerei* (Berlin, 1954), pp. 79–81.

ject itself by the name of light or illumination. And this is the light spoken of in the Apocalypse (21:23). "The glory of God hath enlightened it," viz., the society of the blessed who see God. By this light the blessed are made deiform—that is, like to God, according to the saying: "When He shall appear we shall be like to Him, and [Vulgate: because] we shall see Him as He is" (I John 3:2).[23]

Hugo of St. Victor (1096–1141), a native of Saxony, in his *De Sacramentis* commenting on the Genesis text says:

> Therefore, He Himself who was to do truth, did not wish to work in darkness; but He came to light and made light, that He might make Himself manifest through light. For He did not make light that He Himself might see by light, but that He might make His works manifest by light, because they were done in God.[24]

Book One, Part One, Chapter 13:

> For if He saw His other works in the light, that they were good, in what light did He see the light, that it was good, and did He divide the light from darkness and call light day and darkness night? For nothing can be seen without light. But not even darkness is seen without light.[25]

Suger, abbot of St. Denis (c. 1081–1151), reports in *De Administratione*, Division XXVII, the words on the gilded doors:

> Whoever thou art, if thou seekest to extol the
> glory of these doors (portarum),
>   Marvel not at the gold (aurum) and the expense
> but at the craftsmanship of the work.

23. St. Thomas Aquinas, *The Summa Theologica*, tr. the Fathers of the English Dominican Province (London, 1920), pp. 130–131. Latin text in St. Thomas Aquinas, *Summa Theologiae* (Ottawa, 1941), pt. 1, Q. 12, art. 5, pp. 65b–66a. See also St. Thomas Aquinas, *Summa Contra Gentiles*, tr. the English Dominican Fathers (London, 1928), pp. 126–128. Latin text in St. Thomas Aquinas, *Opera Omnia*, Book III, chap. LIII, pp. 126–128, ed. Vernon Bourke (New York, 1948), V, 199.

24. Hugo of Saint Victor, *On the Sacraments of the Christian Faith*, tr. Roy J. Deferrari from an unpublished Latin text edited by Charles Henry Buttimer (Cambridge, Mass., 1951), p. 14. Latin text available in *PL*, CLXXVI, col. 193. Also in Hugonis De S. Victore, *Opera Omnia*, ed. studio et industria canonicorum regularium, regalis Abbatiae Sancti Victoris Parisiensis (Rothomagi, 1648), III, 491.

25. Hugo, tr. Deferrari, p. 19. *PL*, CLXXVI, col. 197. *Opera Omnia*, III, 493. See also Paul Wolff and Hans Rosenberg, *Die Viktoriner Mystischen Schriften* (Wien, 1936), pp. 49–50, and Martin Grabmann, *Die Geschichte der Scholastischen Methode* (Freiburg, 1911), II, 250ff.

Bright is the noble work; but, being nobly bright, the
work should brighten the minds, so that they may travel,
through the true lights (lumina vera),
To the True Light (verum lumen) where Christ is the
true door (janua vera).[26]

Dante Alighieri (1265–1321) utilizes the same sort of light symbolism that is exemplified in the above in his *Divine Comedy*, Paradiso,
Canto 1, lines 1–3:

Shine through the world we see all-mover's glory,
all penetrating, but more bright reglowing
in world-frame's higher than in lower story.[27]

Again in Canto VII, lines 139–141:

The life of brute and plant, howe'er gradating,
is drawn from compounds thereunto potential by sacred
moving lights here radiating.[28]

The symbolic, conjugal relationship between gold and light is distinctly seen in the iconographic nimbus.[29] The medieval artists universally adopted the nimbus to symbolize holiness and divinity. It is
not surprising, therefore, to find the nimbus almost always painted
with gold, the color of light and fire.[30] Such is the case in William

26. Abbot Suger, *On the Abbey Church of St. Denis and Its Art Treasures*, ed. and tr.
Erwin Panofsky (Princeton, N.J., 1946), pp. 47–49. Work includes Latin text of *De
Administratione*.
27. Dante Alighieri, *Dante Theologian, The Divine Comedy*, tr. Patrick Cummins (St.
Louis and London, 1953), p. 254. Italian text in Dante Alighieri, *The Divine Comedy*, tr.
John D. Sinclair (London, 1946), III, 18–19. For a discussion of the *Lumen Gloriae* in
Dante see Etienne Gilson, *Dante und die Philosophie* (Freiburg, 1953), pp. 53–58.
28. Dante, tr. Cummins, p. 278. Dante, tr. Sinclair, III, 108–109.
29. The relationship between gold, light, and nimbus presupposes a knowledge of the
influence of literature upon art in the Middle Ages. Emile Mâle has shown that art and
literature are not separate enterprises in the Middle Ages. Art depends upon literature
for its symbolism and vitality. See for instance Mâle's treatment of the *Commentary on
the Book of Revelation* by Beatus of Liebana in *L'Art religieux du XIIIème siècle en
France* (Paris, 1924), pp. 6ff., and the *Meditations on the Life of Christ* attributed to Bonaventure in *L'Art religieux de la fin du moyen-âge en France* (Paris, 1931), pp. 27ff.
30. A few representative examples will have to suffice. Giotto (1267?–1337) has St.
Francis wear the golden nimbus as he gives his cloak to a poor man in a fresco of the
Upper Church of San Francesco, Assisi. Plate can be seen in Jacques Dupont and Cesare
Gnudi, *Gothic Painting*, tr. Stuart Gilbert ("The Great Centuries of Painting" directed
by Albert Skira [Switzerland, n.d.]), p. 59. Hereinafter referred to as *GP*. Giotto paints
St. Anne and the angel with a golden nimbus in the Scrovegni Chapel in Padua. The
woman (a maid?) outside the door with the spindle in her hand, however, goes bare-
headed, *GP*, p. 61. Simone Martini (1284?–1344) has the angel and virgin with the golden

Durandus, the author of *The Symbolism of Churches and Church Ornaments* (c. 1286). "So also all Saints are pourtrayed as crowned, as if they said: Ye children of Jerusalem, behold the Martyrs with the golden crowns wherewith the Lord hath crowned them."[31] Similarly in Cennino Cennini's manual for budding artists (c. 1398) we are told how to "turn glories, engrave the gold, and indent the outline of the figures."

> When you have burnished and finished your panel, you must first take the compasses and describe the circles for the glories or crowns. Engrave them, add fringes, indent them with small stamping tools so that they glitter like grains of millet. . . .[32]

Gold, consequently, was a representative color for the light of divinity in the Medieval Age and characteristically displayed its *Zeitgeist*. *D*'s illuminations reflect the inherent light symbolism of their medieval milieu which "lighted up the text" and placed the reader and listener in galvanic contact with the Creator, Lawgiver and Redeemer. Words and pictures are not reality, but rather, reflections of reality. The illuminations perform the identical function of handwriting which is to mirror reality for those who can read. The iconography and calligraphy of the *Ssp.* direct man beyond his temporal world to the real eternal world.

In the concept of Eike von Repgow and the illuminator of the *D* MS., the reading of the written and illuminated word of the Saxon law led to a participation and appropriation of the Being behind and within existence, that is, God Himself. The text and illuminations of the *D* MS. have a functional unity. Both text and illuminations of *D*

nimbus in the Annunciation, *GP*, pp. 86–87. Duccio (?–1319) in his Madonna of the Franciscans has the angels, Mary and Christ with the golden nimbus. The Franciscans themselves do without, *GP*, p. 72. In the *Sacred Chronology*, folio 27, MS. 9174 in the Belgium Royal Library, the birth of Christ forms the center of a circular genealogy. Mary, Joseph, Christ, the angels and the Magi have the golden nimbus, whereas the shepherds are conspicuous by the absence of a nimbus. The outer circle is composed of Christ's forefathers who are wearing the golden nimbus and who are pointing to the birth of Christ. Angels with golden nimbi are peeking out between their shoulders, *Miniatures Médiévales*, pp. 58–59. For a discussion of the meaning of the nimbus in Trecento painting and its relationship with the problems of tridimensionalism see Wolfgang Braunfels, "Nimbus und Goldgrund," *Das Münster*, 3 Jahr, Heft 11/12 (1959), pp. 321ff.

31. William Durandus, *The Symbolism of Churches and Church Ornaments*, tr. J. M. Neale and B. Webb (Leeds, 1843), p. 66. Latin text in Gulielmus Durantis, *Rationale divinorum officiorum*, ed. Boneti de Locatellis (Venice, 1491), Book I, p. 5a, col. 1.

32. Cennino Cennini, *The Book of Art*, tr. Christiana J. Herringham (New York, 1939), p. 115. See Cennino D'Andres Cennini, *Il Libro Dell' Arte*, tr. Daniel V. Thompson, Jr. (New Haven, 1933), p. 85.

attempt to place the reader in the presence of the divine. Because God is the law and reveals Himself as law in the text and illuminations of *D*, the inference can be made that to know the law is to know God, and to love the law is to love God. The epistemological presupposition of the *D* MS. of the *Ssp.* is that those who can read the text and illuminations of *D* can know God.

The ontology present in the *D* MS. of the *Ssp.* is consonant with its epistemology. For Eike and the illuminator of *D* the presentation of this world, the temporal order, is a representation of the eternal order. The temporal microcosm reflects the eternal macrocosm. Eternal realities are reflected when *D* pictures a peasant plowing a field or a king taking the oath of coronation. The details of everyday life, however insignificant they may appear, mirror the eternal.

The ontology of Eike von Repgow and the illuminator of *D* is most vividly seen in their concept of history. History, the record of God's saving acts among men, reflects His law. Wherever law is, there too is the divine.

The basic ontological principle for the codification of the Saxon law was the revelation of God as law in the history of mankind.

> God, who is the beginning and end of all things, made heaven and earth. He created man on earth and placed him in paradise. Man broke the obedience of God and brought us all to grief. Therefore, we have all gone astray like shepherdless sheep until the time the Lord freed us with his martyrdom. Now that we have repented, God has again revealed to us His will and law through the teachings of wise and spiritual men, and also by means of the Christian kings Constantine and Karl. Consequently, His law is now followed in Saxony.[33]

There are three major sources in the code: Roman law, canon law and Biblical law. If Saxon law did not reflect these same sources in its jurisprudence, then it would not reveal God and, consequently, not really be law. In the *Ssp.* God is the unity in the multiplicity of law.[34] All the

33. MGH, Fontes Iuris Germanici, n.s., 1, 13–14.
34. Gierke's summation of the intrinsic principle of the Divine Unity in the law of the Middle Ages is cogent. "The fundamental principle of the entire world is the principle of unity. God, the simple, pre-existent, omnipotent and unifying Being in the multifarious complexity of the world, is the source and goal of all particular beings. The divine intelligence, moreover, permeates all manifestations of multiplicity with eternal law (lex aeterna). The divine will manifests itself in a world which, although composed of the many, strives unerringly towards the One" (Gierke, III, 515).

Saxon laws in the *Ssp.* are related to and find their reference point in the divine. God is the foundation of Saxon jurisprudence in the text and illuminations of the *D* MS. Whatever the situation of the everyday life in the thirteenth and fourteenth centuries, marriage, inheritance, relation of church and state, counterfeiting, heresy, witchcraft, rape, the author of the text of the *Ssp.* and the artist of the *D* illuminations felt the laws governing these situations were related to and directly dependent upon God. The purpose of the illuminations in the *D* MS. of the *Ssp.* is eschatological. They are designed to implement the human response of obedience to the divine initiative in order that the *unus corpus Christianorum* be created on earth as it is in heaven.

Part III. Reform, dissent, heresy

Images of Catharism and the historian's task

GEORGE H. SHRIVER

Only four decades ago one of the present leading medievalists in this country was not allowed to write a dissertation in the area of Catharism. In turning down the request, the director made reference to the paucity of sources for undertaking such a study.[1] In view of the variety of materials currently available, one finds it nearly unbelievable that such a delimited area of research has been given so much attention in the interim, in the manuscript finds,[2] translation work,[3] and multifold secondary interpretations which have touched on a variety of subjects including sex,[4] song,[5] and diet. Whenever a topic in the field of history edges out biblical studies, contemporary theology, and the latest witless fad in religion in *Time* magazine (the entire religion section, no less),[6] perhaps it can be said that that topic has become lively enough to engage even the grass-roots level of historical interest. Sparkling brilliance has been added to Cathar scholarship through the studies of such scholars as Runciman,[7] Söderberg,[8] Borst,[9] Dondaine,[10] Man-

1. Lynn White, Jr. shared this interesting piece of information with his seminar in the summer of 1969 at the Southeastern Institute of Medieval and Renaissance Studies, Chapel Hill, N.C. He was the young graduate student forbidden to write on the Catharists at Harvard.

2. For excellent bibliographies of manuscripts and other works see the following: Daniel Walther, "A Survey of Recent Research on the Albigensian Cathari," *Church History*, XXXIV (June, 1965), 146ff.; Walter L. Wakefield and Austin P. Evans, *Heresies of the High Middle Ages* (New York, 1969), pp. 820–846; and Herbert Grundmann, "Bibliographie des études récentes (après 1900) sur les hérésies médiévales," in *Hérésies et Sociétés*, ed. Jacques le Goff (Paris, 1968), pp. 407–467. These extensive bibliographies offer detailed assistance in relation to any single part of the Catharist story.

3. For brief translations see Ray C. Petry, *A History of Christianity* (Englewood Cliffs, 1962), pp. 342–358. In *Ecritures Cathares* (Paris, 1968), René Nelli makes available in French translation the *entire* corpus of Cathar texts with an introduction and fine notations. Wakefield and Evans, in their amazing translation project, *Heresies of the High Middle Ages*, make available over seventy different primary source documents with introductions, notes, and bibliographies.

4. See John T. Noonan, *Contraception* (Cambridge, 1965), p. 179ff. Among other intriguing observations, Noonan suggests that the Roman Catholic idea of procreation as an absolute value in intercourse developed in the twelfth century as a definite reaction to Catharism. He states: "In relating intercourse to procreation the reaction to the Cathars left its deepest mark on the doctrine of contraception" (p. 199).

5. Among others, cf. Denis de Rougemont, *Love in the Western World* (New York, 1956), passim, for a discussion of Catharism and the troubadours and their songs.

6. *Time*, April 28, 1961, p. 54.

7. *The Medieval Manichee* (Cambridge, 1947).

8. *La religion des Cathares* (Uppsala, 1949).

9. *Die Katharer* (Stuttgart, 1953).

10. See Walther, passim, for Dondaine's contributions.

selli,[11] Roché,[12] Nelli,[13] Russell,[14] Wakefield,[15] le Goff,[16] Thouzellier,[17] Griffe,[18] and Roquebert.[19] And yet, as is obvious, there are still unanswered or partially answered questions and the necessity for continuing scholarship which will engage even more facets of Catharism.

In a sense the past does not really exist—all that exists is the debris left by long-since vanished ages. The historian, who involves himself in searching through this debris, is driven by at least two motives: to concern himself with that highest of human functions, understanding, and to engage himself, sometimes unknowingly, in that function of "knowing thyself." He lays humanity on the couch and learns from history, though not in a predictive sense. The study of history teaches him the wide range of possibilities in history. Lynn White has addressed himself to the historian's task and in this context has said: "The past does not exist. What we call the past is our present thinking about what went on before us. Today the past is changing with incredible rapidity because our ways of thinking are in flux and expansion."[20] Elsewhere on the same subject, he has stated:

> History is worth knowing, historians believe, because the past happened, and our race is possessed by a spiritual necessity to try to understand all that was or is. As for the future and molding of it, most historians have an equal conviction about the study of history. From the kaleidoscopic and iridescent record of mankind, we can learn chiefly this: the possible range of human thought, emotion, organization, and action is almost infinite. In facing today's problems, we must therefore liberate ourselves from presuppositions as

11. Ibid., pp. 164–165.

12. *L'Eglise Romaine et les Cathares Albigeois* (Arques, 1957).

13. Among many other works, one of his most recent is *La vie quotidienne des Cathares* (1969).

14. *Dissent and Reform in the Early Middle Ages* (Los Angeles, 1965).

15. *Heresies of the High Middle Ages.* Also see his "Notes on Some Antiheretical Writings," *Franciscan Studies*, V (1967), 285ff. and "The Family of Niort in the Albigensian Crusade and before the Inquisition," *Names*, XVIII, nos. 2, 4 (1970), 97ff., 286ff.

16. *Hérésies et Sociétés* (Paris, 1968). This most helpful volume covering a wide gamut of topics resulted from a colloquy held in 1962 which engaged the leading European historians of heresy—Puech, Manteuffel, Thouzellier, Manselli, Morghen, Borst, Obolensky, Grundmann, Leff and others. Happily enough, the panel discussions which followed the papers are also recorded in this work.

17. Among others, see her *Hérésie et Hérétiques* (Rome, 1969) and *Catharisme et Valdéisme en Languedoc* (Paris, 1969). In process by her are also critical editions of *The Book of Two Principles* and the Cathar Latin *Ritual*.

18. *Les débuts de l'aventure cathare en Languedoc* (Paris, 1969).

19. *L'Epopée cathare, 1198–1212: l' envasion* (Toulouse, 1970).

20. "The Changing Past" in *Frontiers of Knowledge* (New York, 1956), p. 72.

to what may or may not be possible. Knowledge of history frees us to be contemporary.[21]

There you have the tension worth a lifetime of commitment to the task: "The past does not exist" and yet "the past happened." Grappling with various facets of the Cathar story, one is well aware that much of life escaped the documents, that there must be a place for intuitive perception at times. It is also obvious that the discovery of subhistory and the history of the "losers" in history (and the Cathars were certainly losers) involves the employment of the new canons of our culture—the canon of the globe, the canon of the symbol, the canon of the unconscious, and the canon of a spectrum of values replacing a hierarchy of values.[22] For these and other reasons it is an important part of the historian's task to look once again and freshly at Catharism. The counter-culture typology offers one valuable contemporary construct through which the Cathars might be observed, especially in relation to causes, expressions, goals, successes, failure, and relevance for present and future. This, of necessity, involves a wholistic approach—an approach which is extremely important for looking at Catharism, and, unfortunately, one which has not always been followed in the past both in popular and grass-roots efforts[23] and in ostensibly scholarly works.[24] Studies in Catharism illustrate *par excellence* the extreme intricacy of the task of the historian as he uses the new canons of our culture to research the past which happened. The word "subculture" was defined in 1947 by Milton Gordon as a

> sub-division of a national culture, composed of a combination of factorable social situations such as class status, ethnic background, regional and rural or urban residence, and religious affiliation, but forming in their combination a functioning unity which has an integrated impact on the participating individual.[25]

It is obvious that there is a necessity for subdivisions and the inclusion of subtypes. J. Milton Yinger proposed to call one of these "contraculture." He refined further by saying that a contraculture is in existence

21. *Machina Ex Deo* (Cambridge, 1968), pp. 9–10.
22. Ibid., p. 11ff.
23. For a ludicrous (though taken seriously by certain grass-roots folk) example see J. M. Carroll, *The Trail of Blood* (Lexington, 1931), passim.
24. Cf. Jacques Madaule, *The Albigensian Crusade* (New York, 1967).
25. Milton M. Gordan, "The Concept of the Sub-Culture and its Application," *Social Forces*, XXVI (Oct., 1947), 40.

wherever the normative system of a group contains, as a primary element, a theme of conflict with the values of the total society, where personality variables are directly involved in the development and maintenance of the group's values, and wherever its norms can be understood only by reference to the relationships of the group to a surrounding dominant culture.[26]

In the contraculture or counter culture, there is a sharp conflict of values with the dominant culture. More recently, in the wake of youth movements, Theodore Roszak has defined counter culture as "a culture so radically disaffiliated from the mainstream assumptions of our society that it scarcely looks to many as a culture at all, but takes on the alarming appearance of a barbaric intrusion."[27] These definitions certainly overlap in the direction of the church historian's use of "sect," "schism," and "heresy." Sometimes the emotional freight which these terms have carried has really obscured the real nature of a movement which has emerged in conflict with the dominant culture. Calvin Redekop has rightly suggested that "a more constructive and fruitful way to view religious differentiation is to see it as the emergence and operation of the contraculture process. Seen from this perspective, attention is drawn away from the normative and pejorative dimensions and is focused on the dynamics of the origin of the contraculture and the nature of its persistence."[28]

Religion can well be observed as a main source of subculture and counter culture. This has certainly been the case with the Christian religion, with the record continuing. Religious counter cultures themselves become dominant cultures and the wheel turns again, as internal schism and division results in another counter culture which says it affirms the essence of the culture or protests the very nature of reality held by the dominant culture.

Was then Catharism a "counter culture," given these various descriptions? "Yes" and "no" answers must be given. The "yes" answers will deal more with religious questions in the main. In fact, Catharism may legitimately be referred to as a "counter church," another world religion alongside Christianity and in serious competition with it.

26. J. Milton Yinger, "Contraculture and Subculture," *American Sociological Review*, XXV (Oct., 1960), 629. Also see the excellent article by Calvin Redekop, "Church History and the Contrasystem: A Case Study," *Church History*, XL (March, 1971), 57ff.

27. *The Making of a Counter Culture* (New York, 1968), p. 42.

28. Op. cit., p. 58.

The "no" observations will be more involved with political and so-ciological considerations as well as with problems of origin and evolu-tion. Indeed, the Midi of France was a subculture, but it can hardly be said that this subculture became so alienated from the dominant culture that it became a counter culture unless we refer only to the religious side of counter culture. But, then, a constellation of view-points perhaps throws more light on this thorny question than any one simplistic either/or fragmented approach.

Since Runciman's *The Medieval Manichee* the origins of Catharism have been given increasing attention. Eastern filiations and relation-ships, especially with the Bogomils,[29] have certainly been proved be-yond the shadow of any doubt.[30] And, yet, the most prodding recent studies have been scintillating in their description of the role played by reform movements in the Western church in the eleventh and twelfth centuries. Jeffrey Russell, following Raffaello Morghen, has made a strong case for seeing "Catharists" before the 1140's as reform-ists in the church with puritanistic interests. These interests derived from the New Testament and the very tradition of the Christian church (thus, first fruits of a counter culture which says it is affirming the essence of the culture) but led them on to an exaggeration of dual-ism in Christianity.[31] Gordon Leff correctly notes: "There is much force in these arguments, though the inadequacy of the sources robs them of decisiveness."[32] Of course the same notation could be made about Eastern filiation *prior* to the 1140's. The argument stressing the indigenous nature of the reform movement is very convincing from the sources and perhaps is also illustrative of the process of intuitive perception as well. This argument offers that important point-of-contact for more thoroughgoing dualism coming over the trade routes and through the ports of southern France. It is no happenstance that "tisserand" later became a synonym for heresy.[33] But an engaging question, indeed, is why after the 1140's did a subculture become a religious counter culture or counter church in a rather delimited strip

29. See Dmitri Obolensky, *The Bogomils* (Cambridge, 1948), passim, as well as *The Medieval Manichee*. Also see Söderberg, op. cit., p. 36 and A. Dondaine, *Le Liber de duobus principiis* (Rome, 1939), p. 16.
30. In addition to Runciman, see Thouzellier, *Hérésie et Hérétiques*, pp. 1–17, 223–263.
31. *Dissent and Reform*, p. 188ff. Also see Russell's excellent essay, "Interpretations of the Origins of Medieval Heresy," *Mediaeval Studies*, XXV (1963), 26ff.
32. *Heresy in the Later Middle Ages* (New York, 1967), II, 446, fn. 1.
33. Cf. Austin P. Evans, "Social Aspects of Medieval Heresy," in *Persecution and Liberty* (New York, 1931), pp. 93–116.

of Western geography stretching across northern Italy and southern France? By no means is there a simple answer to this question. The forces behind the successes of Catharism in the period after 1140 are indeed plural and doubtless intertwined. Were the deepest dynamics of this success economic, social, and political or were they religious and intellectual? Perhaps putting it this way lends too much encouragement to the development of a pyramid of forces in one's answer rather than the intertwined community of forces more illustrative of a wholistic approach.

Some scholars would have the entire Catharist movement as simply one part of that larger and longer story of the evolution of national unity in France.[34] With this position the whole episode then becomes the drama of the Capetians of the North versus Languedocian independence in the South with the suggestion that the counts of Toulouse would have set up their own state if the Capetians had not successfully intervened. This highly tenuous "if" of history is rather intriguing, for if this had happened another "if" is a possibility—would Catharism have been adopted as a state religion in this small part of the West and have offered lively and more abiding competition to Roman Catholicism? This "if" of history is intriguing, but far too simplistic. However, the reminder of the political forces at work at this time helps interpret the dynamics of heresy by underscoring the fact that far more was at stake than the religious alone.

What of the social and economic factors leading to the rise and early successes of Catharism? To change A. H. M. Jones's well-known essay title somewhat, were medieval heresies disguised social movements?[35] Jones is certainly correct: heresies have resulted from far more complicated factors than simply "personality flaws of the leaders of such movements,"[36] though some ancient and medieval churchmen seemed to think otherwise. Why did Catharism have such an appeal to the "little people" of southern France as well as to the aristocracy? Do simple answers afford more truth at this point than complicated meanderings? From the side of the aristocracy was there at least (not to say at most) an exploitation of heresy for other ends?[37] To pose such questions is to suggest positive answers. To the simple folk, Catharist lead-

34. For example, see Madaule, op. cit., passim.
35. See *Were Ancient Heresies Disguised Social Movements?* (Philadelphia, 1966).
36. Ibid., p. v.
37. See Russell, "Interpretations of the Origins," p. 33.

ers spoke an indigenous language of severe doctrine. To people already used to an austere life from day to day, such doctrine would have been very attractive. The "losers" in the history-that-happens were offered the opportunity of being "winners" in the history-that-matters. There was already very little, if anything, to be given up by these "little people" and so very much to be gained from the kind of eschatological program projected by the "good men," the "pure ones." For simple people simple answers were given for the crises of evil and suffering to be faced anew every morning.

Another intriguing part of the social setting of southern France at this time was the troubadours. Were the troubadours bards of heresy? Did their concept of courtly love derive in part from Cathar dualism? At present perhaps the least we can say is with de Rougemont, "Courtly lyrical poetry was *at least inspired* by the mysticism of the Cathars,"[38] or with Nelli, "the poems of many troubadours . . . were certainly influenced by the Cathars. . . ."[39] This segment of cultural relationships remains open to more intense scholarly investigation,[40] certainly, but it is important to note that in a counter-culture setting, even musical expressions bear the effects of that counter culture.

But, indeed, Catharism made claims to being the true church and evidently with intense commitment. The religious dimension is certainly not the *only* dimension to be treated as images of Catharism are sketched, but it is the most important one and one which sensitively touches on motive, commitment, and the very springs of life itself. Nelli is right when he says:

> Doubtless before 1209 Catharism was partially related to the feudal system in its anticlerical interest; and, after the Crusade, for other completely different and more general reasons, it was related to the merchant bourgeoisie, which in itself provided the guarantee of a new economic order founded on the first private capitalism. But I am also convinced that men who were able to live as ascetics and to go courageously to death at the stake must also have been as free from social and economic conditioning as they were from hunger, thirst, and fear of death. . . . They were courageously involved in authentic human existence.[41]

38. Op. cit., p. 100. 39. *Ecritures Cathares*, p. 9.
40. See A. J. Denomy, "An Inquiry into the Origins of Courtly Love," *Mediaeval Studies*, VI (1944), 175ff.
41. *Ecritures Cathares*, p. 10.

One might quibble with some of the tensions in this statement, but the point is well made that the Cathars were religiously motivated as well as having been conditioned by social and political influences.

It would of course be impossible in such an essay as this to survey even rapidly the religion of Catharism[42] or to examine the numerous and relevant testimonies by Cathars themselves[43] or by Catholic sources.[44] Let it be noted that Catharism was itself fractured and not so homogeneous as some works seem to imply. The sectarian spirit in the Middle Ages often took its toll from its own kind and the new "one true church" was itself broken in pieces.[45] The spirit indeed spoke but somewhat discordantly. The most important parts of the religious image of Catharism will be surveyed here while only fleeting attention will be given to evolutionary details and differences.

It is an over-simplification to make corruption in the church the sole or root cause of heresy and the growth of a counter church, but whenever the church displays in its leadership and style of life a way which is in little conformity with the apostolic ideal, the soil is fertile for primitivist and restorationist seeds among both clergy and laity.[46] Catharism then first appears in the context of sensitive Christian spirituality; it is inscribed in a larger renewal movement involving the evangelical Christian spirit. Initial or primordial renewal is quite different, however, from later sectarianism and counter church. But it is rather clear that dissatisfied Christian believers interested in renewal formed the nucleus of early Catharism. Due to a constellation of circumstances, Catharism evolved into a counter church, especially in southern France and northern Italy, and was certainly in the farthest frontiers of Christianity, or, as is more likely and the viewpoint sug-

42. Perhaps Söderberg's *La religion des Cathares* and Borst's *Die Katharer* remain as the most complete accounts of the Cathar religion.

43. Nelli brings together under one cover in his *Ecritures Cathares* the complete corpus of Cathar writings in modern French translation with excellent notations. A Catharist New Testament is also made available by L. Cledat, *Le Nouveau Testament traduit au XIIIe siècle en langue provençale, suivi d'un rituel cathare* (Lyon, 1887).

44. Wakefield and Evans's volume now makes available in English translation dozens of Catholic sources related to Catharism. For the most complete inquisitor's manual on Catharism, see G. Mollat's edition of Bernard Gui's *Manuel de L'Inquisiteur* (Paris, 1926). Long sections of this manual are also to be found in Wakefield and Evans.

45. See le Goff, op. cit., pp. 119, 213, and passim. For the most dramatic illustration of schism among the Cathars themselves, see the Cathar work *The Book of Two Principles*, translated in Wakefield and Evans as Document 59, p. 511ff.

46. See Georges de Lagarde, *La naissance de l'esprit laique* (Paris, 1956), I, 82ff., and Morghen's essay, "Problèmes sur L'origine de L'hérésie en Moyen-Age" in le Goff, op. cit., p. 121ff. The primitivist flavor is also to be found in both the Provençal and Latin Cathar *Rituals* (see Wakefield and Evans, pp. 468, 483).

gested here, beyond the very borders of Christianity with what it considered to be legitimate claims as another world religion.[47] Could it be, however, that Catharist leadership in its dualism and double morality brought an acceptable style of life as *model* before the rank and file *credenti* which had been terribly lacking in Catholic circles? In religious circles there seems to be a universal need for these "models," the "pure ones," the true Cathari who exude security and vicarious purity for the vast majority of believers and followers on the grass-roots level. With these Cathari models around, eternal security for every man was a strong possibility by means of the *Consolamentum*, the liturgical celebration of spiritual baptism just before death.[48]

Catharism was ahistorical in its major impulse and thrust, yet a striking part of its image is restorationism or primitivism. Perhaps this is always an inbuilt tension in sectarianism. In its objections to Roman Catholicism it spiritualized the sacraments and committed itself to a correlative or supplementary principle in objective authority by means of the ministrations of the *perfecti*. And, finally, Catharism was extremely esoteric, making firm claims to a unique grasp of ultimate reality to the exclusion of any other claimant. When Catharists said they were the true church, they meant it![49] In the most recently identified Catharist documents, the following is said of the church:

> We propose to recount some testimony from Holy Scripture in order to give knowledge and understanding of the Church of God. This Church is not made of stones or wood or of anything made by hand. . . . But this Holy Church is the assembly of the faithful and of holy men in which Jesus Christ is and will be until the end of the world. . . . And this holy and unblemished Church is the chamber of the Holy Spirit. . . . This Church suffers persecutions and tribulations and martyrdom in the name of Christ. . . . This Church per-

47. Lynn White, for one, shares this opinion with me, though with more confidence in far Eastern filiation than I am willing to admit at this time. For instance he sees the tenet of reincarnation as "presumably" received from India (see *Machina Ex Deo*, p. 92).

48. See Wakefield and Evans, p. 468ff. for the complete liturgy as well as Nelli, *Ecritures Cathares*, p. 207ff.

49. See Wakefield and Evans, p. 308ff., for Moneta of Cremona's *Summa* against Cathars. Catholic polemics against Catharism probably reached a peak in this work. Moneta is rather exercised to point out in Catholic reaction just which church is the true church. For instance he practically shouts: "What is the essence of the Church (quid sit ecclesia)? In resolving that question, I say that the Church is the congregation of the faithful. Moreover, no matter what its enemies may pretend, the Church is the one which is called Roman" (p. 323).

forms a holy spiritual baptism, which is the imposition of hands through which is given the Holy Spirit . . . . Hence, no man is saved who is not baptized with this baptism, just as all those who were outside the ark were drowned in the flood. . . .[50]

Exclusivistic ecclesiology to say the least! But this ecclesiology never lent itself to any kind of unity—hierarchical or otherwise. The sectarian spiritualistic interpretation of the church forever becomes a victim of its own ecclesiology and splintered pieces are part of the unhappy result.[51]

Permeating Catharism was an extreme preoccupation with one of those basically insoluble problems which it nevertheless insisted it solved—the problem of evil. The religious image of Catharism is bound up with the strands of this multi-fibered problem. Gnostics, Marcionites, and Manicheans also struggled with the same nemesis and reached conclusions similar to those of Catharism. An intriguing project in itself, though too space-consuming for this essay, is tracing the element of dualism found in so many of the sect groups existing earlier than the Catharists.[52] Catholic faith also wrestled with the same question, as have all major world religions, but with different conclusions and rationale than the Catharists. One seriously wonders whether the Catharists' dualism was more an attitude of life than a reasoned-out philosophy in a strict sense. Did their preoccupation result from a fundamental psychological aversion to matter?[53] Was the root of their interest in the problem of evil despair itself? If the answer to this question is positive, as is likely, then from the normative Christian standpoint the Catharists were of all men most evil—for "we always act in an evil manner when we cease to believe in the world, when we cease to believe in what we are doing, and . . . when we cease to believe in what God wants us to see and do in order for the world to be 'good'."[54] The kind of dualism, whether mitigated or radical, to which the Catharists were committed in their solution of the problem of evil, resulted in faulty doctrines of creation, man, Christ, redemption, and eschatology. With such key doctrines as these negated, diluted, and distorted, it is not too rash to conclude that Catharism

50. Wakefield and Evans, p. 596ff. The document is entitled "A Vindication of the Church of God."
    51. Ibid., passim, but especially p. 515ff. and the entire *Book of Two Principles*.
    52. See Runciman, op. cit., passim and Nelli, *Ecritures Cathares*, p. 12ff.
    53. Nelli, *Ecritures Cathares*, "Introduction," passim.
    54. Georges Crespy, *From Science to Theology* (Nashville, 1968), p. 112.

proper (the finally evolved product) was outside the Christian circle and should be referred to as another world religion in the medieval period (that is, a religion making practical claims as such through missionizing and evangelizing as well as theoretical claims at having final truth). With them creation was the result of evil forces rather than good intentions; man was split into pieces with some pieces not even worth saving; Christ was less than God, more than man, and a non-participant in the history-that-happens; redemption consisted in the restoration of "soul pieces" out of the materialistic fix into which they had unfortunately come; and eschatology was the final and complete removal of being from actual nothingness. In brief, judged by normative Christian ethics and theology, the Catharists did some of the right things for most of the wrong reasons.

Isolated circumstances, whether in medieval or modern times, have often given rise to subsocieties and subcultures which have evolved into counter cultures. Lack of open channels of rapid communication can result in sectionalism. Across the mountain there may always be another mind at work, not always plugged into the same ideas and conclusions as the dominant culture. When a challenged institution finally becomes aware of this, how must it react most effectively? At the least, any reaction is hazardous and perhaps only in retrospect can most appropriate decisions and judgments be made, for one may easily and beautifully rationalize contemporary or at-the-moment reaction as most appropriate for the total situation.

There are "pluses" and "minuses" on the Catholic side in its reaction pattern to the Catharist counter church. The "search and destroy" missions are well rehearsed and well known stories. Unfortunately, the casual student of medieval history who knows anything about Catharism, knows more about and judges harshly the Inquisition and Crusade.[55] Often this is the only reaction of the Catholic church of which he is aware. Indeed, here was, as Paul Tillich might put it, a demonic persecution of the demonic, partially as a result of the anxiety in the church concerning the presence of the demonic.[56] But take the medieval mind, the past treatment of heresy and heretics, the nation-

55. For extensive annotated bibliographical notations on the Inquisition and Crusade, see Walther, op. cit., p. 163ff. and Wakefield and Evans, passim. There are also sympathetically written novels available such as Hannah Closs's *High Are the Mountains* (New York, 1959) and *Deep Are the Valleys* (New York, 1963), as well as Zoé Oldenbourg's, *Destiny of Fire* (New York, 1961), and *Cities of the Plain* (New York, 1963).

56. *History of Christian Thought* (New York, 1968), p. 149.

alism, the concept of truth in the church. Then mix these with a hefty amount of anxiety and several other ingredients and the Inquisition becomes highly predictive and not so startling. And yet, given the very rise of Christianity itself as a heresy, this reaction must be called the most grievous of "minuses" whether appearing in medieval or modern garb. One keeps hoping that the Christian institution will rise toward its ideal rather than being pulled down by institutional self-interests.

So often the institutional rhetoric of opposition, false association, and insinuation of immorality is used against those who may indeed be outside the circle and yet doing some of the right things (in this case, including others, projecting hope, allowing personal contact with leadership, calling forth lay participation, raising the level of ministerial ethics).[57] The use of rhetoric to associate heresy with all forms of immorality (thus, to discredit the cause and the leadership) was especially widespread. Guibert of Nogent described "Manichaeans" near Soissons in such discrediting terms. Of their religious service, he states: "Directly the candles are extinguished, they all cry out together 'Chaos!' and each one lies with her who first comes to hand."[58] Guibert further relates that if a baby is thus conceived, after its birth it is brought to a service, burned, and bread made from its ashes and pieces of the bread then shared as a sacrament. "Once that has been eaten, it is very rarely that one is brought back to his senses from that heresy."[59] Shades of the early tales told about first century Christians meeting behind closed doors! Needless to say, such language and tales can lead to lynch law violence and in this case they did.[60] Peter of Vaux-de-Cernay appropriated Augustine's description of an error of the Paterniani—"No one can sin from the waist down"—and blasted the Cathars for immorality.[61] Peter then reduced Cathar diet to ridiculing laughter by stating that if a *perfectus* ate a small morsel of forbidden food, those who had been consoled by that *perfectus* fell from heaven![62] Even Bernard of Clairvaux, the apostle of love, fell into this error of quick and false association.[63] In Moneta of Cremona's *Summa* the

57. For suggestions concerning renewal and the concept of "house churches" among the Cathars see le Goff, op. cit., pp. 130ff., 198ff.

58. Wakefield and Evans, op. cit., p. 103.

59. Ibid.   60. Ibid., p. 104.

61. Ibid., p. 240.   62. Ibid.

63. Ibid., p. 135ff. W. Nigg, *The Heretics* (New York, 1962), p. 189, erroneously takes one of these paragraphs out of context and makes of it a compliment by Bernard of the Catharists. In context, it is actually an exposé of the hypocrisy of the Catharists by Bernard. Also see Wakefield and Evans, p. 240ff.

peak of Catholic polemical literature was reached,[64] while the *Summa* of Rainerius Sacconi became the most widely circulated piece of literature against the Catharists.[65] At points the latter reads something like "for seventeen years I was a Watchtower slave" (Rainerius was a Cathar for seventeen years) and Rainerius finally says: "But why say more? It disgusts me to record. . . ."[66] It can hardly be said that here could be found objective reporting.

Several thousand questionnaires mailed out by a medieval Jeffrey Hadden[67] early in the twelfth century to churchmen and laity in southern France would certainly have revealed gathering storms in the churches which could perhaps have been avoided by clerical and church renewal procedures. There was a crisis in confidence in southern France. Flight from important issues raised even by persons with illusory and false assumptions is never redemptive for the church. An interesting exception to such flight merits specific mention. It is the *Summa* of James Capelli, a Franciscan who took great care to present the Cathars as they really were and did not appeal to popular rumor and false association.[68] Such orthodox reaction was unfortunately rare.

An important part of the "plus" response to Catharism was the emergence of the mendicant orders with a common touch among the people on the grass-roots level as well as with a genuine interest in a thorough-going renewal of the church in line with evangelical and apostolic interests. A most important additional reaction was the development of a relevant and vivid natural theology. Lynn White poses the question: "Why did the idea of an operational natural theology emerge in the thirteenth century and in the Latin West alone?"[69] It is suggested by him that this may have been one of the results of the Catharist struggle. Out of the milieu of opposing a heresy and counter church which committed itself to the intrinsic evil nature of the universe, natural theology emerged with its commitment to uphold the created order as a good act of the one good God. If this be true, because of the Cathar episode the church made a major contribution to the foundations of science in the West.[70]

But what of the lack of "staying power" by the Catharists? The

64. Ibid., p. 307ff.   65. Ibid., p. 329ff.
66. Ibid., p. 339.
67. See his *The Gathering Storm in the Churches* (New York, 1969).
68. Wakefield and Evans, p. 302ff.
69. *Machina Ex Deo*, p. 101.   70. Ibid., 102.

blood of their martyrs was not seed in any quantitative sense in this case. Were the Crusade and Inquisition successful? Doubtless they were successful, but there must have been other reasons which include not only the "plus" reactions of the church but also the "minus" content or thrust of Catharist faith. In addition to the extreme sectarianism and lack of organization among Cathars, at this point in the history of the dynamics of cultural change in the West, there was really no final place for a religion which was basically antinature; its death warrant was already written even before the earliest skirmish of the Crusade or the first burning in the Inquisition. Certainly, there were left-over pieces of sectarianism, anticlericalism, and anti-Romanism to be fit back together in Reformation centers at a later time.[71] But by no stretch of the imagination was this Catharism. As a counter culture or counter church, Catharism suffered a fatal flaw—it negated body and took nature far less than seriously.

We live in an age of darkness, anguish, desperateness, and presently, extreme anxiety. The Catharist drama must at least call historians to deep introspection concerning such anxiety in every man. As Lynn White states:

> In our time we are subject not only to individual but also to group anxiety, and this seems to be related to a velocity of change which is hard to assimilate emotionally. There have been hideous episodes of irrational slaughter of scape-groups in this century. More such tragedies are inevitable unless each of us ponders more deeply the surge forward of a new culture in which we are involved as were the men of the late Middle Ages and Renaissance. Only by understanding ourselves can we tame the wolf in our hearts.[72]

71. See Daniel Walther's fine article "Were the Albigenses and Waldenses Forerunners of the Reformation?" *Andrews University Seminary Studies*, VI, no. 2 (1968), 181ff. and also Lagarde, op. cit., I, 86.
72. Lynn White, *Machina Ex Deo*, p. 179.

Nicholas of Cusa and the reconstruction of theology: the centrality of Christology in the coincidence of opposites

H. LAWRENCE BOND

When Nicholas of Cusa is treated as a reformer, discussion is usually limited to his efforts to reform church practice and ecclesiology.[1] He primarily views himself not as a philosopher or as a conciliarist—as he so often is characterized—but as a reformer of theology who attempts to restore the doctrine of reconciliation as formative for every legitimate theological method.[2] Beginning with *Of Learned Ignorance* (*De docta ignorantia*), his writings commonly reveal: (1) a disaffection with the applications of scholastic logic to theological problems; (2) a recall to certain methodological lessons of Christian and classical antiquity; (3) an appeal to Christology as the prime resolution of theological problems; and (4) a vision of the coincidence of opposites as the way of the Infinite in the workings of the universe.[3]

This essay limits itself to Cusa's attempt to reconstruct theology by

1. For treatment of the considerable body of literature failing to acknowledge the primary importance of theology in Cusa's thought, see R. Haubst, "Nikolaus von Kues als theologischer Denker," *Trierer Theologische Zeitschrift*, LXVIII (1959), 129–145; "Nikolaus von Kues und die Theologie," *Trierer Theologische Zeitschrift*, LXXIII (1964), 193–210; and "Die leitenden Gedanken und Motive der cusanischen Theologie," *Mitteilungen und Forschungsbeiträge der Cusanus-Gesellschaft*, IV (1964), 257–277.

2. Recent literature surveying Cusa's thought in English indicates the need for viewing him in this fashion. What this study considers fundamental in Cusa's writings—the theological placing of *coincidentia oppositorum* that is fundamentally Christocentric—is generally overlooked; the overwhelming tendency is to delineate his ideas from the wrong starting point and to mishandle the proper relevance that philosophical notions actually hold in Cusa's scheme. Cf. J. H. Randall, *The Career of Philosophy from the Middle Ages to the Enlightenment* (New York: Columbia University Press, 1962), pp. 177–190; F. Coplestone, *A History of Philosophy*, 7 vols. (Westminster, Md.: Newman Press, 1953), III, 233ff.; A. A. Maurer, *Medieval Philosophy* (New York: Random House, 1954), ch. XX; and E. Gilson, *History of Christian Philosophy in the Middle Ages* (New York: Random House, 1955), pp. 534–540.

3. Two of the most useful and most complete studies of Cusa's theology are by R. Haubst: *Die Christologie des Nikolaus von Kues* (Freiburg: Herder, 1956) and *Das Bild des einen und dreieinen Gottes in der Welt nach Nikolaus von Kues* (Trier: Paulinus, 1952). See also E. F. Jacob, "Cusanus the Theologian," *Bulletin of the John Rylands Library*, XXI (1937), 406–424. However, they deal little with his method and almost altogether neglect the effort Cusa makes to employ *coincidentia oppositorum* as a device for theological reform.

appeal to Christology, the paradox of Christ's person, as the norm for theological method.

Christology is the prime resolution of the problem of theology for two reasons: (1) the distinction between the infinite God and the finite, fallen creature and (2) the incapacity of the finite mind to grasp Infinite Truth. Since Christ is the only means by which these two contradictories are reconciled, Cusa argues it is only reasonable we should turn to the work and person of Christ for an answer to the problem of theological discourse. The very word theology implies contradiction. Discourse about God inevitably fails because God is unnameable, indescribable, indefinable, while language is naming, enclosing, defining, that is, giving limitations. This dilemma is solved only by Christ, the divine mediator of opposites.[4]

Cusa's reconstruction of theology may be limited to two main considerations: (1) how the coincidence of opposites through Christ provides the only true knowledge of God, which is the epistemological basis for all theologizing, and (2) how the coincident nature of Christ's person provides criteria and models for right theologizing.

I

Cusa unfolds a program for theological reformulation in the separate parts of his *Learned Ignorance*. It rests on the primary lesson that a reform of epistemology must precede any reconstruction of method.[5] Every attempt at theological reform will fail unless it results

4. Three sermons preached in 1438–39, just prior to *De docta ignorantia*, reveal Cusa's earliest efforts to redefine basic theological problems and the task of theology itself. In them he seems especially preoccupied with the awesome gulf between the infinite God and the finite ways of knowing. As in the treatise that follows a year later, he stresses ignorance enlightened through Christ as the one solution to the dilemma of human knowledge. Unlike the longer work, the sermons do not pursue detailed applications of the *coincidentia* motif but celebrate the light of the divine Word piercing the darkness. His preaching from this period on reveals the confessional nature of his theologizing and the basis of the Cusan theology of the Word: Sermons 13, 14, and 15 in *Predigten 1430– 1441*, tr. J. Sikora and E. Bohnenstedt (Heidelberg: F. Kerle, 1956), pp. 335–368.

5. This is the central theme that ties together the several parts of the work. To stress only Books One and Two, as Johannes Wenck, a scholastic opponent, in his attack on Cusa, is to fail to consider the resolution of the dialectic that Cusa develops in his final part: see *Le "De ignota litteratura" de Jean Wenck de Herrenberg*, ed. E. Vansteenberghe (Münster: Aschendorff, 1910), pp. 38ff. Likewise, to view the role of Book Three on Christ as divorced from the other two parts and thus as a mere appendix for orthodoxy's sake, as T. Whittaker has suggested, is to deny the significant context in which Cusa unfolds and concludes his arguments; see "Nicholas of Cusa," *Mind*, XXXIV (1925), 439–440. An especially harsh treatment from this and a decidedly Thomistic view is V. Martin, "The Dialectical Process in the Philosophy of Nicholas of Cusa," *Laval théologique et philosophique*, V (1949), 213–268.

from a proper resolution of the dilemma of knowing. For this reason, Cusa says, the present state of the theological discipline is a stumbling stone both to truth-telling and to the critical practice of tradition.[6]

The only wise theologian, and hence the only one worthy of the name, is the theologian who recognizes his own ignorance and who comes to terms with the fundamental contradiction of his discipline: that the object of his inquiry cannot be known.[7] The theologian as fool is a favorite topic of Cusa's dialogues on wisdom and is the only antidote to the foolish theologian.[8] There is a fundamental contradiction in theology because there is a fundamental contradiction in all knowing, which is that the end of every intellectual being is the knowledge of God, who cannot, however, be known in himself. Our natural longing for knowledge is not without a purpose, but the immediate goal, the object of knowledge, is our own ignorance or *Deus absconditus*. This is the conclusion arrived at in the first two volumes of *Learned Ignorance*, which deal with God and the universe.[9] Redemption from the darkness of that ignorance, the fulfillment of knowledge and not its object, *Deus revelatus*, is the subject of the third and concluding volume, which is Cusa's major Christological statement.

Three particular features of his epistemology are importantly prefatory to his discussion of Christology. In the first place, all rational beings move toward knowledge, and this natural inclination is not thwarted, even notwithstanding the divine obscurity.[10] In the second place, all knowledge that is true comprehension of the nature of things also has its beginning and end from God.[11] And in the third place, knowledge of God, and thus the true knowledge of all things, comes through his revelation of himself.[12] Recognition of our own ignorance

6. *De docta ignorantia, Opera* I, I, i, 6 (hereafter referred to as DDI) and *Apologia doctae ignorantiae, Opera* II, 6. Where possible, references to Cusa's *Opera omnia* are from the edition by the Heidelberg Academy (Leipzig-Hamburg: F. Meiner, 1932–).

7. It is the *Deus absconditus* which is the subject of the first book of the DDI. All we know of Absolute Truth through cosmology is that it is beyond our reach: I, iii, 9. It is this acknowledgement of ignorance that brings us closer to the truth: iv, 9.

8. There is a fundamental crisis of knowledge which must be acknowledged in every valid attempt to realize the way of wisdom: it is simply that the mind cannot attain what it must know. In this manner the *idiota* of the dialogues explains the dialectic that escapes the scholastic and appears absurd to the uninstructed in the theological lessons of ignorance: *Idiota: De sapientia* I, *Opera* V, 9–10.

9. For Cusa, God is not such that can be the object of knowledge, for he operates as subject on our intellect. The only proper object of knowledge, therefore, is one's ignorance: DDI I, i, 6.

10. DDI I, i, 5.

11. DDI II, xiii, 113.

12. DDI II, xiii, 114.

bids us to find ourselves in him. But this too is beyond the ways of human intelligence, for God is known but not comprehended, disclosed but not discovered.[13]

Cusa endeavors to explain how God as Absolute Maximum or the Perfection of Being may be known, experienced, discussed by man, who is limited being, mere being. The problem is serious for one engaged in debate with both Aristotelians and Platonists who from a variety of vantage points use this terminology but fail, according to Cusa, to construct the problem correctly much less to resolve it.[14] Consequently, he sees contemporary, that is, fifteenth-century, theology to be in shambles. Both the scholastics and their critics are guilty of misconstruing the problem of knowledge and of confusing logical and linguistic distinctions and the priority of different considerations over others in the work of the theologian.[15]

It is here that Cusa attempts to correct what he considers to be the abortive attempt to unite by analogy natural knowledge or metaphysics with divinely revealed wisdom as complementary aspects of the same reality.[16] He argues that analogy of being or of proportional relationships starts from the wrong epistemological premise: it fails to grasp the incomprehensibility of the Infinite and the radical gulf between divine wisdom and the finite ways of knowing. Dialectic utilized by discursive logic is empty and distorting.[17] The only valid dialectic is the coincidence of opposites. But this dialectic is the epistemological given and is not the product of logic. The appropriate dialectic is the paradox of the Christ-maximum who makes himself known in learned ignorance.[18]

13. The books of the DDI correspond, therefore, to the three important contexts for the Cusan statements about knowledge: (1) *Deus absconditus*; (2) the universe of knowable things; and (3) the mysteries of faith through Christ. It is only through the last, however, that we can understand the first two: DDI I, xxvi, 56: ". . . ut ipsum ex omni nostro conatu de hoc semper laudare valeamus, quod nobis seipsum ostendit incomprehensibilem."

14. DDI II, viii and ix.

15. In Cusa's judgment, many of his contemporaries have distorted tradition to mean a sacrosanct attachment to a school of thought (*secta*); consequently, such a discipleship imprisons the intellect as it divorces tradition from critical reexamination and confuses the eternality of the Truth with the perennial relativity of the human perspective. See the opening remarks in his *Apologia*, pp. 2–3.

16. *De quaerendo deum*, *Opera* IV, *Opuscula* I, 221–222.

17. Ibid., pp. 20–21; *Apologia*, pp. 18, 32.

18. It is available to men only because the Father took pity and revealed himself in a sense-form adapted to human capacity (the hypostatic union of the two natures in Christ): DDI III, v, 134. See also DDI III, ix, 153; *Apologia*, pp. 14–15; Sermon no. 133, *Vier Predigten im Geiste Eckharts*, ed. J. Koch, *Cusanus-Texte* I, *Predigten* 2/5 (SB, Heidelberg, Phil.-hist. Kl., 1936–37, Abh. 2), pp. 72–74; and *Über den Ursprung (De principio)*,

Cusa refers to analogy in a special way. He is usually speaking of the analogy of proportion and of predication. For Cusa, analogy is legitimate only in a very general sense as a way of speaking about God subject to certain guidelines but not as the means of knowing God or as a logical device for theological method. Analogy should not be the basis on which predication can be made, that is, ascribing to God qualities found in his creation. Far better is negation, the use of negative names, e.g. *In*finite, *No*-Other, *Un*knowable, *Im*mortal, *Im*mutible, etc.[19]

He thereby rejects the discursive or syllogistic reasoning on which he implies analogy is based. First of all, discursive reasoning requires a comparison of terms. For that reason alone, it is unsuitable for discourse about God, the *Non-aliud*, for whom there is no other with which to make comparison.[20] Secondly, discursive logic is a contradiction in logic, for it requires a deduction that contradicts epistemology.[21] We cannot know the range of relationships that discursive logic requires for the resolution of problems. The deductive process requires an infinite number of middle terms and an infinite series of premises, and this exceeds the capacity of the finite mind.

These epistemological concerns lead us then to Cusa's description of the role of Christ in knowing. Christ is the mediator of knowledge by being simultaneously the limited and absolute Maximum, that is, Creator and creature. He is the nexus both in the coincidence of the Infinite and the finite and in the coincidence of knowledge and ignorance. The only sufficient and adequate way to the knowledge of God, accordingly, is learned ignorance made effective through Christ. Learned ignorance may be defined on two levels: (1) as the acknowledgement of one's inability to know God and (2) as the reconciliation of human ignorance and divine knowledge through God's self-disclosure in Christ.[22]

---

tr. M. Feigl, ed. J. Koch, *Schriften des Nikolaus von Cues* (Heidelberg: F. H. Kerle, 1949), p. 67.

19. DDI I, xxvi. Cf. Dionysius, the pseudo-Areopagite, *Mystica theologica* (PG Migne, vol. III) III, col. 1033 c d and V, col. 1048 a b. See Cusa's explanation of his use of the title *Non aliud* in *Directio speculantis seu De non aliud, Opera* XIII/1, pp. 13f.

20. The Aristotelian logic of the schools, according to Cusa, fails to grasp even the first assumption of theological truth—that "finite et infinite nulla proportio," DDI, I, i, 6.

21. In his *De coniecturis*, Cusa attempts to explain the special validity of logic properly understood as *ars coniecturialis*. See J. Koch, "Der Sinn des zweiten Hauptwerkes des Nikolaus von Kues *de coniecturis*," *Nicolò da Cusa* (Florence: G. C. Sansoni, 1962), pp. 101–123 and *Die Ars coniecturialis des Nikolaus von Kues* (Koln: Westdeutscher Verlag, 1956).

22. DDI, III, ix, 152–153.

Learned ignorance, as the knowledge through Christ, and Christology, as the knowledge about Christ, are necessarily prior to metaphysics and to all other theological and philosophical considerations. (The Cusan metaphysics, in turn, may be described as his Christology or Christocentric view of the universe.) For Cusa, therefore, Christology is the sole legitimate matrix in which one is able to theologize in an appropriate manner. Christology and not the negative or affirmative way is the clue to the knowledge of God.[23]

Learned ignorance, as the knowledge of faith in Christ, is the epistemological datum for theologizing. It is the necessary route by which we come to the coincidence of opposites (*coincidentia oppositorum*) as the appropriate theological method. Theological problems and theological problem-solving should be reconstructed in terms of the logic of concidence as opposed to the scholastic method of affirmation or double-truth and the Platonist way of remotion and negation.[24] Cusa insists that this is no arbitrary matter. The coincidence of opposites is the most appropriate way in which one can speak about the divine because it is the way and work of the reconciling Christ and the means of our knowledge of God.[25] The very activity of Christ which brings us into union with the ineffable is the coincidence of ignorance and knowledge by which one can know God even in finitude.

There is, then, a clear pattern in the relationship of the coincidence of opposites to the way we can truly know God: (1) the paradoxical nature of God forces us to admit our ultimate ignorance, for he is simultaneously the beginning of all and the end to which all things move; yet, in himself, he remains infinite, absolute, and hidden; (2) learned ignorance, the only mode of knowing accessible to finitude, likewise, teaches us that what we do discover about the divine nature we are unable to reconcile rationally; and (3) oblique knowledge gives way to effective knowledge in the ignorance-enlightened-through-Christ, the self-revelation of the God otherwise hidden.

Only the fool or layman (*idiota*) can truly be a theologian, for he alone knows that he does not achieve his own knowing. One is truly

---

23. *De filiatione dei, Opera* IV, *Opuscula* I, 56ff.

24. DDI I, xxvi, 55–56; Letter to Gaspard Aindorffer, *Autour de la "Docte ignorance,"* ed. E. Vansteenberghe (Münster: Aschendorff, 1915), pp. 113–114.

25. On *docta ignorantia* as the coincidence of affirmative and negative theology as of all methods of knowing God, see DDI I, i, 5f. and xvii, 35; *Apologia*, pp. 8–9, 20–21; *De non aliud*, p. 16; *De deo abscondito, Opera* IV, *Opuscula* I, 3.

a doctor of theology (*doctor theologiae*), learned in theology, only when he is first a doctor of ignorance (*doctor ignorantiae*).[26]

II

What then of the theologian's method? For Cusa, theology's subject matter is the infinite God's reconciliation of the world, and this subject matter determines the nature of theology as proclamation and disclosure and its method as coincidence. Proportional analogy and predication are conceptual blind alleys without the light of divine self-disclosure, that is, without the Christ-maximum as the model coincident.[27]

Given the necessary conceptual starting point and the proper set of premises, the theologian labors to declare the truth under the duress of both contemporary relevance and linguistic fidelity to his subject matter. Again and again Cusa reveals his own sense of this particular burden-bearing. He is no less the insatiable researcher for right language than for knowledge, and he finds the publication of knowledge equally compelling. This too is a curious feature of the protagonist of his *Dialogue on Wisdom*, the fool, purportedly unlettered in academic ways, but whose conceptions are so refined that they frequently exceed the grasp of the academician. The *idiota* bemoans the inescapable need to speak. But who can speak the unspeakable? He is struck by his own "idiocy," not struck dumb but gifted with the capacity to speak. Why the fool can say things which the scholar cannot is due to the emancipation of learned ignorance, to disclosure from on high. He feels compelled yet free to describe at length the full ramifications of the knowing given him.[28]

Cusa has the fool explain to the orator or scholar how theologizing is no mere academic enterprise but is conceived by the very coincident work assumed by the Infinite himself. The following series of propositions emerge in the course of a lengthy dialogue.

---

26. *Idiota: De sapientia* II, 29. The learned *idiota* in Cusa's dialogues is not to be taken as the lay scholar of natural reason who has brought into mature refinement an innate wisdom in natural man. He is the *doctor ignorantiae* simply because he is the recipient of the revealed knowledge of the divine; he is susceptible because he knows that he does not achieve his own knowing. As Cusa explains the mystery surrounding the notion of learned ignorance, which apparently eluded his critics, man is able to know nothing perfectly for the end of knowledge is hidden in God. *Apologia*, p. 3.

27. *Apologia*, p. 28.   28. *De sapientia* II, 29.

1. Although unattainable, ineffable, and interminable, the infinite God is the source by which, in which, and of which every intelligible thing is understood, every speakable thing spoken, and every terminable thing determined and limited.[29]

2. God is presupposed in every theological inquiry and in every question of being and essence, "for God is the absolute presupposition which presupposes all else."[30]

3. The divine Word is the ideal form of all conceivable things, the absolute concept, which contains all things, and the absolute reason, which alone provides a concept of conception itself.[31]

4. The disclosure of the divine in the Word is the only effective source of human knowing and is the illumination of the principle of coincidence by which one is able to describe both the nature of the Infinite and the finite. The truly learned theologian is learned in the word of the self-disclosing Word, to which the fool attributes his capacity to theologize and his use of the logical model of coincidence.[32]

The theology of coincidence provides the only connection between the need for silence and the theologian's irresistible urge to speak. His office is to reconcile the human word to the divine. This is the burden that Cusa presumes to bear inasmuch as the central problem to be resolved by the theologian is not knowledge—for that has been resolved in Christ—but how that knowledge is explicated in method and language.

As Christ the incarnate Absolute resolves the problem of the knowledge of God, so Christ the incarnate Word resolves the problem of discourse about God. Cusa defines the theological enterprise as essentially iconography by virtue of the Incarnation providing the gross metaphor for all coincidences, including the coincidence of finite language with the ineffable God.[33] And the icon of icons is the incarnate Christ; the hypostatic union of his person is the prime and model coincident.[34]

In a series of declarations in the *Vision of God*, Cusa demonstrates the manner in which the coincidence of the Incarnation is the basis and validation for the human word, for discourse about God. He stresses that Christ's reconciling work itself verifies the meaning of

---

29. *De sapientia* I, 9.
30. Ibid., 26–27.
31. Ibid., 30.
32. Ibid.
33. DDI III, vii, 141–142.
34. This idea runs throughout Book Three of DDI; for an explanation of the meaning of the hypostatic union for faith, see chs. II–IV.

creatureliness, which is the source and limit of language. The Incarnation makes possible the discernment of the real value of the created order and the validation of creaturely models (or iconography) in theological language.

1. The Incarnation is the affirmation of humanity and creatureliness, for God showed himself as creature (the begotten Son) in order to disclose himself and to draw men to him.[35]

2. As man, Creator, and the bond between the two, the incarnate Christ demonstrates the importance of the divine similitude in humanity through his work of reconciliation; he embraces in himself the roles of the divine lover, the loveable object, and the bond of love.[36]

3. Christ's sonship is the perfection of creaturehood, the definition of humanity, and the means for effecting true creaturehood and humanity, because every being is enfolded in him and fulfilled by him.[37]

4. Christ is himself the coincidence of the creature and the Creator, and his human sonship subsists in divine sonship. For as Son of Man and Son of God the coincident Christ discloses the divine and validates the creature.[38]

5. Knowledge of the incarnate Son is the means to the vision of the Father; by the coincidence in the Incarnation the Infinite is disclosed in the finite and the divine in humanity.[39]

6. The coincidence of humanity and divinity in the Incarnation provides the sole way to learned ignorance, the acknowledgement of divine self-disclosure and the filiation which is the ontological foundation for knowing.[40]

Theological method, therefore, is incarnational; it makes the word incarnate and takes its point of departure from the Christ-event. The crux of his argument once more is the dialectic between the Infinite and the finite. Because language, as verbal conceptualization, is limited to the measurable and comparable, the Infinite by definition is ineffable and inexplicable. But just as the Infinite is known by coincident knowledge (*docta ignorantia*), so the truths that pertain to the Infinite may be described in the language of coincident theology.

Cusa dismisses comparison and proportion as prime factors in theologizing and relies instead on coincidence, for it both preserves the

35. *De visione Dei, Opera omnia*, ed. F. Stapulensis (Paris, 1514), fo. 107 r.
36. Ibid., fo. 108 r.
37. Ibid., fo. 110 v. 38. Ibid.
39. Ibid., fo. 110 r. 40. Ibid., fo. 111 v and 113 v.

utter transcendence and mystery of the Infinite and places before finite knowing appropriate and "disclosure models."

This expression is taken from I. T. Ramsey, *Models and Mystery* in order to distinguish Cusa's use of theological models—founded on coincidence—from analogical language and models that imply proportion. While not referring to Cusa, Ramsey designates this kind of model, applicable to the intent of Cusa, as distinct from other models. For a disclosure model implies "some sort of echo between the model and the phenomena it enables us to understand, while at the same time denying . . . sheer reproduction, replica picturing. But it is precisely such similarity-with-a-difference that generates insight, that leads to disclosures when (as we say) 'the light dawns.' "[41]

Cusa uses coincidence of opposites to develop a picturing theology. This is his alternative to the compromising descriptions of predication and scholastic analogy and to the apophasis and silence of the *via negativa*.[42] Coincidence is the fundamental model of disclosure. It is the gross metaphor in determining ancillary models. He thus works the coincidence of opposites as the central and unifying logical model in order to demonstrate a similitude or echo between appropriate models and the divine reality but one which does not involve sheer proportion.[43]

In this fashion, coincidence of opposites as theological method directs reliable theological understanding and articulation. The theologian must avoid mere scale-models or miniatures and instead use coincident models that point to mystery and do not violate the paradoxical nature of Christian truth. The Incarnation, as the prime coincidence, sets limits for logical models and determines which inferences are reliable, that is, those picturing both distinction and reconciliation.[44]

From this basis Cusa would sharply reform contemporary efforts to theologize. The striking claim in his reassessment of theological language is his assertion that the hidden, infinite God has provided men with the icon, the model icon for all theological iconography, that illumines the abscondite God and that makes the Creator visible in his creation. He intends not only to reform scholastic methods but also to surpass the central achievement of negative theology, which can only

41. *Models and Mystery* (London: Oxford University Press, 1964), pp. 10ff.
42. As Cusa explains in his *Apologia*, pp. 16–17, positive and negative have no meaning in the Infinite where opposites coincide.
43. Ibid., p. 28.   44. DDI III, iii, 124ff.

declare the distance between infinity and finitude and remove the characterizations of perceptual language. The theology of coincidence provides its own critique of predication, but unlike negative theology, it also affirms the capacity of language to evoke appropriate understanding. Cusa intends that it communicate meaning beyond remotion, beyond the description of God by what he is not.[45]

Two main points summarize Cusa's arguments for a redirection of theological method: (1) theology's subject matter requires a language of coincidence or paradox that discloses both the mystery and the knowable about the infinite God and (2) the coincidence of opposites, as theological method patterned after the Incarnation, enables us to use linguistic models that disclose God-as-he-relates-himself-to-men and that preserve the essential mystery and transcendence of his person.

His theology of coincidence incorporates a succession of metaphors and models. They fall into three general categories: biblical, mathematical, and complicative or enfolding.

He explains in *The Search for God* that the biblical writers use models of disclosure not designating God but the manner of our knowing. This too is a guideline for right theological language. An example of the first category of Cusan models is *Theos*. *Theos* suggests contemplative (*theoreo*) searching (*theo*), and it symbolizes the inaccessibility of the Infinite to names and to conceptualization. However, the coincidence of the two ideas (contemplation and searching) discloses at the same time the essential coincidence of opposites in knowing and the self-disclosing nature of God. *Theos* is not removed from *theoria*, the avenue of coincident knowledge, the sole end of all being and knowing. The name *Theos* signifies the unknown God as he-who-makes-himself-available-to-knowing-in-intellectual-intuition by the light of his grace. As name and as model, it preserves the notions of transcendence and reconciliation, for it discloses God as the subject of illumined wisdom and not as the contrivance of knowledge. By using *Theos*, the theologian designates God as the Subject acting on human knowing.[46]

Mathematical models, the second category, have a certain advantage over other kinds of metaphors. They picture without violating distinction, provide coincidence without composition, and preserve the

45. DDI I, x, 21; *Idiota: De mente, Opera* V, ch. II; *De beryllo, Opera* XI/1, p. 35.
46. *De quaerendo deum*, pp. 14–15, 27–28.

necessary distinction between symbol and reality. The language of mathematics is symbolic and graphic; yet, in Cusa's view, it is the most abstract discipline, most nearly evoking pure intellection. The notions of infinity and coincidence are especially well articulated in mathematics.[47] The whole realm of contradictories gives way when in this discipline one introduces the concept of infinity. For example, as finite figures the polygon and the circle are contradictory and incongruent, but when the notion of infinity is applied to them, they coincide and all contrariety desists. When the number of the sides of any polygon is multiplied by infinity, the polygon coincides with the circle, and their objective opposition resolved. However, though they coincide, "no multiplication of its angles, even if infinite, will make the polygon equal with the circle."[48] All geometric figures are reconciled by the mathematical idea of infinity. This appropriately signifies without implying composition of particulars the coincidence of all multiples and opposites in the infinity which is God.

Complicative models, the third category, are models that enfold two or more terms. A favorite is *possest*, the title of one of Cusa's treatises. It signifies the coincidence of all potentiality (*posse*) and every being (*esse*) in the Absolute Maximum. Literally translated as he-who-is-all-that-is-able-to-be, *possest* denotes both actuality and possibility, for God is the Absolute Being whose entire potency is actuated in all potency and all being. His omnipotence embraces the actuality of all possibility. Cusa, once again, cautions that such an expression discloses coincidence and as all other terms does not name God in himself. This verbal identity of potency and actuality is to be understood as equivalent to the biblical confession of coincidence: "I am who I am." The Absolute Maximum is Absolute Possibility and Absolute Being, for he is free of all limitations, includes all, and never exhausts himself in actualizing all being. He alone can never be what he is not, and *possest* means that he is all that he can be.[49]

Whatever metaphors may be applied, the rules for theological language are the same: the transcendence and radical distinction of the Infinite must be preserved, and the coincidence (without composition)

47. DDI I, xvii, 33; chs. XI–XII present Cusa's summary of the significance that mathematical figures hold for theology.
48. DDI I, iii, 9.
49. *De venatione sapientiae*, tr. and ed. F. Wilpert, *Schriften des Nikolaus von Cues* (Hamburg: F. Meiner, 1952), XII, p. 52; *Vom Können-Sein (De possest)*, tr. E. Bohnenstadt, *Schriften des Nikolaus von Cues* (Leipzig: F. Meiner, 1947), IX passim.

not violated. Yet language exists for the purpose of communication, and the theologian must diligently seek language that enunciates the infinite God exceeding all, who enfolds all in himself. God in himself is beyond all language and knowing; the theologian, therefore, can only turn to language wrought out of the knowledge disclosed by the Infinite. The divine work of coincidence in the Word is the object of theological language and not God himself. Human words, as human knowing, are relational, and the ultimate reference point for both language and knowledge is God's action. Although it may appear that theology describes the divine person, the theologian articulates titles and names only as they are related to the divine self-revelation, and he speaks of God's person only in the very limited context of the finite mind's need for picturing and the Infinite's work of illumination in the finite world. The theologian, therefore, tells what God does and by that who he is.[50]

Furthermore, finite knowing requires picturing, that is, models and metaphors. Just as the redemption of broken men has required the union of the human and the divine in the work of Christ, so men in the condition of finitude need a portrayal of the Infinite in the language of time and sense. The means and the model for coincidence of the supernal with the temporal is the Incarnation. The truth of the hypostatic union is the only logical precedent for theologizing; the inexpressible, indeterminable God is declared in language as the divine Word is contracted to time, as Christ in real humanity. This Word is the source of language and the measure of theological truthfulness. "All created characters . . . are representative of the Word of God. Spoken word stands for the word of the mind; and this incorruptible word is reason; which is Christ himself, the incarnate Reason of all reasoning; for the Word was made flesh."[51]

As Luther and Calvin later turn to the doctrine of justification as the epistemological basis and controlling model for theology, so Cusa appeals to the reconciliation of opposites in the Incarnation as the

50. This theme, recurring so often throughout Cusa's later writings, is first delineated in his sermon on Luke 2:21: "His name was called Jesus." He introduces his exposition with a brief summation of the manner in which one may determine the name of Jesus. There are, he admits, an endless variety of names for Jesus in the functions of Word, Son, and Saviour. But a precise definition of *Ihesus in se* can never be achieved, for he is at once inexpressible and unknown. Such positive language is appropriate only for what he performs and not for what he is in himself: Sermon no. 14, *Predigten 1430–1441*, pp. 346–347.

51. *Of Learned Ignorance*, tr. G. Heron (London: Routledge and Kegan Paul, 1954), p. 162; DDI III, xi, 154.

basis for right theologizing and proper theological language. Cusa insists that God is hidden except as he reveals himself. In no case can one speak of a proportion between the Infinite and the finite; therefore, analogy and other logical devices inevitably misconstrue both the nature of God and the nature of God's relationship to man. Theological language like the doctrine of the Incarnation must communicate the union of the divine Word and the human word without commingling, without violating the integrity of each. The theologian can speak of the divine only in the language of paradox, of the reconciliation of opposites, which exceeds logical discourse, especially the analogy of being and the affirmative way of the scholastics. Theological method, consequently, should no longer be reduced to problem solving. It is descriptive rather than logical, declarative rather than academic. This bears considerable affinity with Luther's and Calvin's concept of the task of theology and of the role of the theologian. It is in this way most importantly that we may speak of Cusa as a reformer before the Reformation.

Jacques Lefèvre d'Etaples: principles and practice of reform at Meaux

JAMES JORDAN

"Let all hold firmly that which our forefathers and that primitive church, red with the blood of martyrs, decided: to know nothing besides the gospel, which is to know all." [1] With this appeal to the example of the early church, Jacques Lefèvre d'Etaples issued a clarion call for the church of the sixteenth century to return to a recognition of the authority, centrality, and absolute necessity of the Scriptures in the faith and life of all Christians individually and of the church in its totality. Lefèvre's call for a return to the Scriptures is the central and recurrent theme of the preface to his *Commentary on the Four Gospels*, which appeared early in 1522. About a year earlier, he had arrived in Meaux, probably on the initiative of Bishop Guillaume Briçonnet,[2] although it is possible that persecution of those with Lutheran leanings in Paris was an important factor in causing him to accept the bishop's invitation.[3] On August 11, 1521, Briçonnet placed him in charge of the hospital at Meaux,[4] but his duties in that position did not prevent him from participating actively in efforts then being made to revitalize and reform the church in that diocese.

Actually, thoughts of church reform were not new to the man from Etaples. More than a decade earlier, he took note of the serious shortcomings of the contemporary church in the preface to his first biblical commentary, the famous *Quincuplex Psalterium*, and he also sug-

---

1. Jacques Lefèvre d'Etaples, *Commentarii initiatorii in quatuor Evangelia* (Paris: Simon de Colines, 1522), f. aii r.: "Atque hoc firmissime teneant omnes, quod maiores nostri, quod primaeva illa ecclesia, sanguine martyrum rubricata sensit: extra evangelium nihil scire, id esse omnia scire." Cited hereafter as Lefèvre, *Quatuor Evangelia*. In the notes the text of Lefèvre's works is reproduced exactly as it appears in the original, including punctuation, orthography, the absence of accents, etc.

2. Nathanael Weiss, "La réforme du seizième siècle: son caractère, ses origines, et ses premières manifestations jusqu'en 1523," *Bulletin de la Société de l'histoire du protestantisme français*, LXVI (1917), 224–225. Also see a letter of Glareanus to Zwingli dated July 4, 1521, in Aimé Louis Herminjard, *Correspondance des Réformateurs dans les pays de langue française*, 9 vols., 2nd. ed. (Geneva and Paris: H. Georg, 1878–97), I, 71, 71 n. 10.

3. Charles Schmidt, *Gérard Roussel, prédicateur de la reine Marguerite de Navarre* (Strasbourg: Schmidt et Grucker, 1845), p. 11.

4. Toussaints Du Plessis, *Histoire de l'église de Meaux*, 2 vols. (Paris: Julien-Michel Gandouin and Pierre-François Giffart, 1731), I, 327.

gested the means by which the required reform could be accomplished. He wrote:

> I have frequently visited monasteries, and those who did not know this sweetness [the study of the Scriptures], I have considered to be wholly ignorant of the true food of souls; for spirits live by every word that proceeds from the mouth of God, and what are those words if not the sacred Scriptures? Therefore, those who are of that kind have dead spirits. And from that time in which those pious studies ceased, monasteries have perished, devotion has died, and religion has been extinguished, spiritual things have been exchanged for earthly things, heaven abandoned and the earth welcomed—certainly a most unhappy sort of trade.[5]

Unfortunately, the condition of the church had improved very little, at least in France, during the intervening years. Therefore, when Lefèvre wrote the preface to his *Commentary on the Four Gospels* in 1521, he outlined a program of church reform which was in strict accordance with the preliminary suggestions he had made in the *Quincuplex Psalterium*. The need for change was transparent and the means were to be found in the example of the early church. On that basis two things were required: "Would that the model of faith should be sought in that primitive church which consecrated to Christ so many martyrs, which knew no other rule except the gospel, which indeed had no other goal except Christ, and which rendered its worship to none except to God, the one in three."[6] In these words, Lefèvre distinguished the two fundamental characteristics of true worship: one is that all worship must be directed toward God alone, the triune God, and not adulterated by the elevation of creatures to the level of

---

5. Jacques Lefèvre d'Etaples, *Quincuplex Psalterium: gallicum, romanum, hebraicum, vetus, conciliatum* (Paris: Henri Estienne, 1509), f. a r.: "Frequens coenobia subii: at qui hanc ignorarent dulcedinem veros animorum cibos nescire prorsus existimavi. vivunt enim spiritus ex omni verbo quod procedit de ore dei. et quaenam verba illa: nisi sacra eloquia? mortuos igitur qui eiusmodi sunt spiritus habent. Et ab es tempore quo ea pietatis desiere studia: coenobia periere, devotio interiit et extincta est religio, et spiritualia pro terrenis sunt commutata, caelum dimissum et accepta terra, infoelicissimum sane commercii genus" Cited hereafter as Lefèvre, *Quincuplex Psalterium*.

6. Lefèvre, *Quatuor Evangelia*, f. aiii r. : "Et utinam credendi forma a primaeva illa peteretur ecclesia: quae tot martyres Christo consecravit, quae nullam regulam praeter evangelium novit, quae nullum denique scopum praeter Christum habuit et nulli cultum praeterquam uni trinoque deo impendit."

the Creator; the second is the indispensability and centrality of the Scriptures, for through his Word, God acts to redeem and sanctify men and to cleanse and reform his church.

Lefèvre's concern for the unadulterated worship of God alone seems to have been prompted by his growing uneasiness about the contemporary emphasis on the veneration of the Virgin Mary and of the saints. His own views on this practice had only recently undergone a transformation. At least as early as January, 1519, he was busily collecting the histories of saints with the intention of preparing a series of volumes on that subject,[7] and during that same year he took the first step toward accomplishing that goal by publishing a volume containing the lives of those saints whose festivals were celebrated in the month of January.[8] By 1522, however, the tendency for the veneration of the saints to become adoration and worship in the minds of many had become clear to him and, besides, he had been unable to discover any scriptural basis for the practice.[9] In the *Commentary on the Four Gospels*, therefore, while he did not reject completely the veneration of the saints and prayers to the saints, he did describe both practices as of secondary significance, to say the least, as unnecessary for the most part, and as definitely harmful at times.[10] His firm conclusion was that the worship of God alone is pure worship; worship rendered to any other cannot be pure.[11]

Actually, Lefèvre was much more concerned with the second characteristic of true worship, the restoration of God's Word to the place of central significance in the lives of individuals and in the corporate life of the church. The Bible is the very Word of God to man, Lefèvre was convinced, and it is the means through which God acts to redeem, guide, empower, and transform.[12] This is the real message of his preface to the *Commentary on the Four Gospels*. As a result, he repeats his call for a return to the Scriptures time after time. Thus, addressing himself to "kings, princes, nobles, and people of every race," he declared: "They ought to think of nothing else, embrace nothing so

7. Herminjard, *Correspondance*, I, 41–42.

8. See the letter from Lefèvre to Jean de la Grève in Symphorien Champier, *Que in hoc opusculo habentur. Duellum epistolare: Gallie et Italie antiquitates summatim complactens* (Lyons, 1519).

9. Herminjard, *Correspondance*, I, 41, n. 1.

10. Lefèvre, *Quatuor Evangelia*, John 12, f. 323 r. Also see Luke 21, f. 241 r., and Mark 16, f. 163 v.

11. Ibid., f. aii v.   12. Ibid.

much, aspire to nothing as much as Christ and the life-giving Word of God, his holy gospel." He continued: "And this should be for all the sole study, comfort, and desire, to know the gospel, to follow the gospel, to advance the gospel everywhere." [13] What was needed, then, was to confront the church and its people with the Scriptures in order that God might perform his redemptive and reformative work in them.

One means of confronting the church with the life-giving, transforming Word of God was readily available—the sermon. The structure of the mass provided an opportunity for the priest to preach without necessitating any changes in the liturgy whatsoever. In the preface to his *Commentary on the Four Gospels,* Lefèvre not only urged all members of the hierarchy to seize this opportunity, but he also suggested that they should deliver truly biblical sermons. [14] Furthermore, he insisted that the major responsibility of the priesthood was the proclamation of the Word of God and the instruction of the faithful in its true meaning. He even suggested that the higher one rose in the ecclesiastical hierarchy, the greater ought to be his love for the gospel of Jesus Christ. In fact, he felt that the basic requirement for attaining the papacy was that the candidate should have the deepest and most spiritual love for God's Son and God's Word. [15]

Turning his attention to the episcopal office in particular, the man from Etaples employed the figure given in the fourteenth chapter of Revelation in order to describe the primary duties and essential activities of a good bishop. "And surely," he wrote, "each one of the bishops ought to be similar to that angel which John, in the sacred Apocalypse, saw flying through the midst of heaven, bearing the eternal gospel toward every nation, tribe, tongue, and people, shouting: 'Fear the Lord and give him glory.' " [16] The similarity of a bishop to that angel means that he will preach only the Word of God, Lefèvre believed, and the fact that the angel was soaring in the sky suggested that the bishop's thoughts should always be directed toward heavenly things. There was also significance in the fact that the angel carried the eternal gos-

13. Ibid., f. aii r.: "Deinde reges, principes et magnates omnes, et subinde omnium nationum populi: ut nihil aliud cogitent, nihil adeo amplectantur, nihil aeque spirent ac Christum et vivificum dei verbum, sanctum eius evangelium. Et hoc sit cunctis unicum studium, solatium, desyderium: scire evangelium, sequi evangelium ubique promouere evangelium."

14. Ibid., ff. aii r.–aii v.   15. Ibid., f. aii r.

16. Ibid.: "Et certe quisque pontificum similis esse debet illi angelo quem Joannes in sacra Apocalypsi vidit per medium caelum volantem, habentem evangelium aeternum, super omnem gentem et tribum et linguam et populum vociferantem, Timete dominum: et date illi honorem."

pel, for it meant that the bishop would confine his interests and concerns within the limits prescribed by the Word of God. "Finally," he said, "since the angel is proclaiming to every nation, tribe, tongue, and people, and indeed with a loud voice, the bishop ought never to cease from preaching and summoning to the true worship of God." [17]

As a matter of fact, the bishop of Meaux, Guillaume Briçonnet, had taken the initiative in utilizing this means of church reform even before Lefèvre arrived on the scene. Briçonnet took possession of the diocese in 1518,[18] and his first act was to make a general visitation to determine the spiritual condition of both the clergy and the laity within the borders of his see. This investigation revealed that the situation in the diocese was deplorable. Of the 127 priests in the bishopric, only fourteen were worthy of the unqualified approval of the new bishop. The majority of the others did not even live in their parishes but entrusted the care of their flocks to ignorant and inept vicars, while they resided in Paris.[19] In addition, there was almost no preaching in the diocese because that responsibility had been entrusted to the Franciscans, and they preached only at certain special seasons of the year and then only in the more prosperous churches.[20] At Briçonnet's trial before the Parlement of Paris seven years later, the bishop's defense lawyer also said of the situation in 1518 that the Franciscan preachers "used only the sermons of Brother Robert, who was a Franciscan and who in the space of ten years had never more than one sermon which he preached in all the collections that he made."[21]

Bishop Briçonnet was anxious to remedy this situation, and he immediately initiated a number of procedures designed to suppress the abuses he had discovered and to provide more adequate spiritual care

17. The sentences preceding this quotation as well as the quotation itself are from Lefèvre, *Quatuor Evangelia*, ff. aii r.–aii v.: "Nam quia angelus: nihil debet nisi quod deus mandat, nunciare. quia volans: debet iugiter aciem mentis ad sublimia intendere. quia evangelium habens aeternum: nihil quod sit extra evangelii limites, curare. quod quia aeternum est: quid aliud quam immortalitatem promittere potest? denique quia omni genti, tribui, linguae et populo clamans, et magna quidem voce: nunquam a praedicatione, et provocatione ad verum dei cultum cessare."

18. Du Plessis, op. cit., I, 326.

19. Jean Henri Merle-d'Aubigné, *History of the Great Reformation of the Sixteenth Century* (tr. from the French; Philadelphia: James M. Campbell, 1846), p. 388.

20. Du Plessis, op. cit., I, 326.

21. Cited by Samuel Berger, "Le Procès de Guillaume Briçonnet au Parlement de Paris, en 1525," *Bulletin de la Société de l'histoire du protestantisme français*, XLIV (1895), 10: ". . . ne faisoient que les sermons de frere Robert qui estoit cordelier, et par l'espace de dix ans n'eut jamais que ung sermon qu'il preschoit à toutes les questes qu'il faisoit."

for the people of his diocese. In the very year of his arrival in Meaux, therefore, he convoked a synod to deal with these problems, and on October 31 the synod approved a decree requiring that all parish priests reside in their own parishes.[22] Unfortunately, the decree seems not to have been very effective, for there is ample evidence that the secular clergy of the diocese regularly ignored its key provisions. A second synod issued an even stronger statement regarding the residence of parish priests on January 7 of the following year; but in October, 1520, the problem had not yet been solved, for a third episcopal council also promulgated a regulation dealing with the same matter.[23]

Briçonnet was especially concerned about the dearth of preaching which prevailed in his diocese since preaching was one means of confronting the church and the people with the Scriptures, the Word of God. Once again, the bishop's defense lawyer of 1525 described his efforts in this regard:

> He divided his diocese, containing about two hundred parishes, into thirty stations and appointed in each station a preacher for the whole year, and especially for Lent and Advent. And to satisfy the said Franciscans, the defendant, before assigning any of the aforesaid stations, at least sent for their superior, presenting to him the list of the stations in order to know how many he could provide for according to the number of preachers in his monastery—in which he caused to be done what they wished . . . and the remainder he delivered to monks of other monasteries, as much of the aforesaid order as of others, and to several doctors, licentiates, and bachelors trained in theology, to whom he would have given a large salary, amounting to nine hundred pounds for the first year, seven hundred for the second, and five to six hundred for the third. . . .[24]

It was in this context of attempted reform that Lefèvre and a number of his students and associates answered the call of Bishop Briçon-

22. Du Plessis, op. cit., I, 326.   23. Ibid., I, 327.

24. Cited by Berger, op. cit., p. 10: "il divisa son diocese, contenant environ deux cens parroisses, en trente stacions, et ordonna en chascune stacion ung predicateur pour tout l'an, speciallement pour le caresme et l'advent. Et *morem gerens* ausdictz cordeliers, l'intimé, auparavant que baillir aucunes desdictes stacions, a tousjours envoyé querir leur guardien, luy presentant le rolle des stacions pour scavoir combien il en pourroit avoir selon le nombre des prescheurs de son couvent, auxquelz faisoit expedier ce qu' ilz en voulloient . . . et le surplus les bailloit à religieux d'autres couvens tant dudict ordre que d'autres et à plusieurs docteurs, licenciez et bacheliers formelz en theologie, ausquelz il auroit baillé gros sallaire, montant pour la première année neuf cens livres, la second sept cens et la tierce de cinq à six cens . . . ."

net to fill places of responsibility and service in the diocese of Meaux.[25] Lefèvre was placed in charge of the hospital, and most of the others were installed in the unoccupied preaching stations. One of these "imported preachers" was Gérard Roussel, noted at the University of Paris for his unusual knowledge of Greek, who became a canon of the cathedral of Meaux, and another was the great Hebraist, François Vatable. There were also two who held doctorates in theology, Martial Mazurier, who had been principal of the Collège Saint-Michel in Paris, and Pierre Caroli, a canon of Sens. Apparently, the Augustinian monk, Michel d'Arande from Dauphiné, joined the group about this time as did another native of the same French province, Guillaume Farel, who was later to become a leading exponent of the Protestant cause.

Thus, when Lefèvre arrived in Meaux, Bishop Briçonnet had already initiated a reform program with special emphasis on requiring the residence of priests in their parishes and on providing regular preaching throughout the bishopric. No doubt, then, some of the inspiration for these efforts of reform can be found in the widespread recognition in the early sixteenth century that the church was beset by serious abuses and shortcomings which literally cried out for amelioration. This recognition caused many different types of people to call for reform in one way or another. Some were humanists like Erasmus, others held high ecclesiatical office like Gian Matteo Giberti, bishop of Verona; some were outspoken Protestants, like the fiery Farel, and others, like Ignatius Loyola, were equally vigorous in their loyalty to the Roman Catholic church. The need for religious renewal and revitalization was apparent to a number of people, but their individual perspective and the methods they espoused often differed widely.

That Guillaume Briçonnet shared these desires for religious reform is indisputable. As early as 1507 he had been supported in his bid to succeed his father as abbot of the monastery of Saint Germain des Prés by the reform party in French monasticism.[26] Nor did the new abbot disappoint his supporters, for no sooner had he entered upon his duties at the abbey than he issued a series of directives intended to

25. Nathanael Weiss, "La réforme du seizième siècle: son caractère, ses orgines, et ses premières manifestations jusqu' en 1523," *Bulletin de la Société de l'histoire du protestantisme français*, LXVI (1917), 224–225.
26. Augustin Renaudet, *Préréforme et humanisme à Paris pendant les premières guerres d'Italie* (Paris, 1916), p. 453.

inaugurate a reformation of abuses within the monastery.[27] His reputation as a partisan of reform was already well established when he went to Italy as a special envoy of King Francis I to Pope Leo X,[28] and although he may have come in contact with those in Rome who shared his spirit and perhaps may even have been encouraged by those contacts, there is no evidence which suggests that those associations actually gave rise to his reform efforts at Meaux.[29]

In fact, the major inspiration behind the reformative work of Bishop Briçonnet at Meaux and the chief guide in implementing those activities was Jacques Lefèvre d'Etaples. In Meaux after 1518, Briçonnet repeated a pattern which is first discernable at Saint Germain des Prés about a dozen years earlier. When the new abbot undertook to reform that monastery in 1507, the response of some of the monks was to leave the monastery rather than submit to the changes which were being made.[30] Briçonnet then invited Lefèvre, his former teacher, to join him at the abbey, and with the resources of the monastery library at his disposal, the man from Etaples wrote his first two biblical commentaries, the *Quincuplex Psalterium* and the *Commentary on the Epistles of Paul.*[31] The latter volume, which contains many of the same principles of reform which were so eloquently expressed in the *Commentary on the Four Gospels* in 1522, was dedicated to Briçonnet and was presented to him when he returned from the antipapal Council of Pisa in 1513. Before the end of that same year, Briçonnet renewed his efforts to reform Saint Germain des Prés and appealed to other monasteries for help in carrying out his plans.[32] Once again some of the monks fled the monastery and this time their vacated cells were filled with some disciples and students of Lefèvre, who continued their studies under his direction and helped him in his own scholarly endeavors.[33] Some of these were the same ones who came to Meaux as preachers some five or six years later.

When Briçonnet brought Lefèvre to Meaux in 1520 or 1521, then, he was retracing the pattern already developed at Saint Germain. As

27. Ibid.   28. Du Plessis, op. cit., I, 326.

29. See Lucien Febvre, *Au coeur religieux du seizième siècle* (Paris: Sevpen, 1957), pp. 153–161, for a comparison of the work of Giberti as Bishop of Verona with that of Briçonnet as Bishop of Meaux. The similarities are numerous and Febvre's discussion suggests many interesting possibilities, but evidence of actual influence is lacking.

30. Renaudet, op. cit., p. 454.

31. Ibid., p. 503, n. 5; and Charles-Henri Graf, *Essai sur la vie et les écrits de Jacques Lefèvre d'Etaples* (Strasbourg: G. L. Schuler, 1842), p. 21.

32. Renaudet, op. cit., pp. 563ff.   33. Graf, op. cit., p. 13.

before, Lefèvre's coming was proceded by some initial efforts at reform, but these were renewed and intensified after his arrival on the scene and after his publication of a new outline of the principles of a reform program in his *Commentary on the Four Gospels*. Once again, also, Briçonnet sought additional help from outside, this time enlisting the services of Lefèvre's students and associates, many of whom he already knew personally. No doubt he felt that their principles and methods of reform would be those of their master and, therefore, they would all share a common aim and common means in their joint undertaking. Finally, on May 1, 1523, Briçonnet named Lefèvre his vicar-general in spiritual matters for the entire diocese of Meaux,[34] thereby putting him in a position to give more effective direction to the reformation of the bishopric.

While Lefèvre's friends were busy proclaiming the gospel from the pulpits of the diocese so that God might act through his Word to redeem and transform, Lefèvre was making an indirect contribution toward the same end. Sermons are a means of explaining the Scriptures but since he did not preach, Lefèvre used another method, that of writing commentaries on the text of Holy Writ. Without question, this was his aim in the publication of the *Commentary on the Four Gospels* in 1522 and in the publication of his other commentaries, as well. Of course, these commentaries were not intended for the people of the diocese because they could not read Latin, but they were intended for the priesthood whose major responsibility was the proclamation of the Word of God and the instruction of the faithful in its true meaning.[35] Thus, he sought to help priests better to understand the gospel themselves in order that they might more effectively aid the people in doing likewise. Even if most priests ignored both this responsibility and his efforts to help them meet it, he could count, no doubt, on the "imported preachers" at Meaux to utilize his work to improve their grasp of the real meaning of the Scriptures and to improve their preaching at the same time. Briçonnet certainly relied upon Lefèvre in interpreting the Scriptures as he indicated in his correspondence with Marguerite d'Angoulême, the sister of Francis I. She wrote to Briçonnet on one occasion confessing her inability to understand many passages of Holy Writ.[36] The bishop responded that

34. Weiss, op. cit., p. 225.   35. Lefèvre, *Quatuor Evangelia*, ff. aii r.–aii v.
36. Herminjard, op. cit., I, 108–109.

he also had difficulty discovering the true meaning of the Scriptures at times but he was fortunate in having three men at Meaux with him who were more able than he in that regard. He promised to consult those men about Marguerite's problems. The only one of the three whom he named in the letter was Lefèvre.[37]

In his *Commentary on the Four Gospels,* and in all of his commentaries, for that matter, the man from Etaples sought to lay bare the true meaning of the gospel, and in order to accomplish that he felt compelled to seek the guidance of the Holy Spirit alone. In fact, he explicitly declared in the preface to that work: "Therefore we have zealously performed the work of preparing new commentaries on the Gospels . . . , having followed only that grace which we have expected from God. . . . Nor have we rested upon the works of others so that, being more completely helpless, we should depend upon God."[38] One reason for his reliance upon the guidance of the Holy Spirit alone in the interpretation of the Scriptures was his deep conviction that the Word of God is sufficient in itself to provide redemption and reformation.[39] The teachings of men could only distort and adulterate the true meaning of the gospel; they could add nothing of value to God's Word. This was true even of his own efforts to explain the Scriptures, he admitted, unless he was directed by the Spirit of God. Thus, he said of his own commentaries: "If anywhere we were left to ourselves, we have intermingled something of ours, which we confess to be ours and by no means to be valued; but that which is not such, we owe to God."[40] Therefore, his summons to make the Bible central was a call to receive the gospel in all its purity, to seek its meaning under the guidance of the Holy Spirit, and to forsake completely the opinions of men.

Lefèvre had another reason, however, for relying solely upon God in his attempts to understand and explain the Scriptures. His study of the Bible had led him to conclude that the Scriptures are susceptible to two interpretations.[41] One of these is the historical and obvious

37. Ibid., I, 109–111.
38. Lefèvre, *Quatuor Evangelia,* f aiiii r.: "Iccirco operam navavimus parandis novis in evangelia commentariis . . . , solum eam quam a deo expectavimus secuti gratiam. . . . Neque aliorum laboribus incubuimus: ut inopes magis a deo penderemus."
39. Ibid., ff. aii v.–aiii r.
40. Ibid., f. aiiii r.: "Sicubi nos nobis ipsis relicti, nonnihil nostri admiscuimus quod: nostrum fatemur, et nequaquam magnifaciendum. quod autem tale non est: deo acceptum referimus."
41. Lefèvre, *Quincuplex Psalterium,* ff. a r.–a v. Relying solely upon Lefèvre's *Quin-*

meaning of the words which he called the "literal sense." The other one is an attempt to discover the deeper meaning of a passage by discerning the intention of the Holy Spirit who inspired the author and who, therefore, was responsible for the authentic meaning of the words. Since this latter interpretation emphasized the role and intention of the Spirit of God, Lefèvre called it the "spiritual sense."[42] Moreover, the spiritual sense alone has value for the spiritual life of the individual and the church, and only God himself, through the indwelling Holy Spirit, can reveal this meaning to the mind and soul of man. The spiritual sense of the Scriptures is not available to the unaided reason, as he said: "For it was not hidden from me that diligence which is given to study and to the reading of books cannot provide an understanding of these Sacred Books, but it is to be expected by a gift and a grace which are wont to be granted . . . as a result of the pure liberality of the One who gives."[43]

Lefèvre was not suggesting that human efforts were totally valueless in the study of the written Word of God, for his commentaries would have been a ludicrous exercise in futility if that were true. Rather, he felt that good commentaries can serve two useful purposes. First of all, they can aid in the proper interpretation of the literal sense, which is of no little significance since the literal sense underlies the spiritual and must be properly understood before the spiritual meaning can be grasped.[44] In addition, good commentaries may point to the spiritual meaning beneath the literal even though they cannot impart a genuine understanding of the spiritual sense of a biblical passage.[45] His conclusion was that commentaries are not absolutely necessary for understanding the spiritual meaning of the Scriptures, but by God's grace they may be useful in preparing for receiving such an understanding; and he fervently hoped that his own volumes would have some value in that regard.

Lefèvre, then, was seeking to reform the church at Meaux by making the Scriptures available to all as the means through which God

---

cuplex Psalterium, James Samuel Preus reaches a somewhat different conclusion in his *From Shadow to Promise* (Cambridge, Massachusetts: The Belknap Press of Harvard University Press, 1969), pp. 137–142.

42. Ibid., f. a v.

43. Lefèvre, *Quatuor Evangelia*, f. aiiii r.: "Et enim me non latebat, diligentiam quae studio et evoluendis libris praestatur, horum sacrorum aferre non posse intelligentiam: sed eam dono et gratia esse expectandam . . . pro mera largientis liberalitate concedi solet."

44. Ibid., Matt. 13, f. 56 r.; f. aiiii r.   45. Ibid., f. aiiii r.

acts to redeem, guide, nourish, and empower. His commentaries were an attempt to help priests and preachers better to understand the Word of God and more effectively to proclaim the gospel to the people. There are some bits of evidence, moreover, which suggest that Lefèvre and his associates took an additional step toward achieving that goal —they established a school at Meaux.[46] Apparently its major purpose was to give instruction to the uneducated clergy of the diocese and to train young men for ecclesiastical careers.[47] In March, 1522, Marguerite d'Angoulême wrote to Bishop Briçonnet saying that she was sending a young man "in order that he might be able to study at the school of your company" because she wanted him "to learn the way of truth."[48] No doubt, then, biblical studies were an important part of the curriculum, and the school was one more means of helping the clergy take the Word of God to the church and to the people.

These efforts at church reform had continued in the diocese of Meaux for about two years when Lefèvre acted to take the Word of God directly to the people. His aim had ever been to confront the people and the church with the actual text of Holy Writ; his own commentaries and the sermons of the preachers in the diocese were only intended to help them grasp the authentic meaning of the text by God's grace and to make that spiritual significance active in their lives. The basic need, therefore, was to make the Scriptures available to the people in the language which they knew and understood. In the preface to his French translation of the Gospels, Lefèvre declared that the purpose of those translations was that "the ordinary members of the Body of Jesus Christ, having them in their language, may be able to be as certain of the evangelical truth as those who have it in Latin."[49] In accordance with that purpose he undertook a whole series of French translations of the Bible. The first to appear was his version of the four Gospels, which came from the presses of Simon de Colines on June 8,

46. Merle-d'Aubigné, op. cit., 388.

47. Maurice Mousseaux, *Aux Sources françaises de la Réforme: La Brie protestante* (Paris: Librairie protestante, 1967), pp. 30–31.

48. Ph.-Aug. Becker, "Marguerite, duchesse d'Alençon et Guillaume Briçonnet, évêque de Meaux, d'après leur correspondance manuscrite," *Bulletin de la Société de l'histoire du protestantisme français*, XLIX (1900), 419–420: ". . . affin qu'il puisse aprendre a l'escolle de vostre compaignie."

49. Jacques Lefèvre d'Etaples, tr., *Les choses contenues en ce present livre: Une epistre exhortatoire. Le S. Evangile selon S. Matthiew—S. Marc.—S. Luc.—S. Johan. Aucunes Annotations* (Paris: Simon de Colines, 1523), f. aii v. : ". . . affin que les simples membres du corps de Jesuchrist ayans ce en leur langue: puissent estre aussi certains de la verite evangelique comme ceulx qui lont en latin." Cited hereafter as Lefèvre, *Les Evangiles*.

1523.[50] The remainder of the New Testament was printed in three installments later in the same year, with a combined edition of all the books of the New Testament except the Gospels appearing on November 6.[51] One other portion of Lefèvre's French translation of the Bible was published before his forced departure from Meaux. That was the vernacular version of the Psalms which was published on February 16, 1524.[52]

Apparently, the man from Etaples was encouraged in his preparation of a French translation of the Bible by Marguerite d'Angoulême and perhaps even her brother, King Francis I,[53] and their mother, Louise of Savoy. Early in January, 1523, after Marguerite had bemoaned her inability to understand many passages of Holy Writ,[54] Briçonnet replied that he was aware that her problem stemmed from "bad translations of the Holy Scripture."[55] He suggested that Lefèvre and two of his associates were capable of remedying that situation, and within six months they had begun to do so. Lefèvre took note of the initiative and support in this undertaking which emanated from Marguerite and her mother in the preface to the last part of his French translation of the New Testament. He wrote: "And now it has pleased the Divine Goodness to incite the noble hearts and Christian desires of the highest and most powerful ladies and princesses of the realm to cause the New Testament to be printed again for their edification and consolation and for that of the realm."[56]

Although Lefèvre was grateful for the initiative and encouragement which he received from the royal family, his chief reason for translating the Bible into French was to place the Word of God in the hands of the people. In his vernacular version of Holy Writ, he sought to give the people the pure text of the Scriptures without additions or distortions because God speaks and acts through his Word to redeem

50. Maurice Villain, "Le message biblique de Lefèvre d'Etaples," *Recherches de science religieuse*, XL (Jan.–April, 1952), 253.

51. Ibid.

52. Philippe Renouard, *Bibliographie des éditions de Simon de Colines, 1520–1546* (Paris: E. Paul, L. Huard, et Guillemin, 1894), p. 53.

53. Herminjard, op. cit., I, 85, 85 n. 2.

54. Ibid., I, 108–109.　　　　　　　　　55. Ibid., 110.

56. Jacques Lefèvre d'Etaples, tr., *Ceste second partie du N.T. contenant les epistres de S. Pol, les epistres catholiques, les Actes des Apostres, l'Apocalypse de S. Johan l'Evangeliste* (Paris: Simon de Colines, 1523), f. Aii v.: "Et presentement il a pleu a la bonte divine inciter les nobles cueurs et chrestiens desirs: des plus haultes et puissantes dames et princesses du royaume de rechief faire imprimer le nouveau testament pour leur edification et consolation et de ceulx du royaume." Cited hereafter as Lefèvre, *Seconde partie*.

and reform. As a result, he rejected the use of paraphrases and glosses "for fear of giving another meaning than the Holy Spirit had suggested,"[57] and because human words can add nothing of value to the Word of God.[58] Furthermore, Lefèvre declared that it was necessary to give the Scriptures to the people as a means of correcting "the defects of Christianity." In fact, he suggested that the Turkish threat to Europe was a divine summons to the people of that continent to turn back to God in Christ and forsake all faith in creatures and human traditions.[59] He summed up his argument with a ringing confession of faith: "Let us understand that men and their doctrines are nothing, except insofar as they are corroborated and confirmed by the Word of God. But Jesus Christ is everything. He is wholly man and wholly deity, and no man is anything except in him. And no word of man is anything except in his Word."[60]

Even with his deep conviction regarding the urgent and absolute necessity for all men to have direct access to the Word of God, Lefèvre was not so naive as to think that his vernacular Bible would be welcomed by the ecclesiastical authorities in France. In fact, there seems to have been serious opposition to his work of translation from the moment that it became known, for in a letter to Farel a year later, the man from Etaples credited King Francis I with smoothing the way for the publication of his French New Testament.[61] Actually, in the preface to his first published translation, Lefèvre tried to anticipate some of the objections which would be raised and to refute them in advance, while at the same time offering some counsel to the people on how to read the Scriptures with the greatest benefit to themselves. "Some will say," he wrote, "that by offering the Gospels to them [the common people] in this way, many things will be difficult and obscure, which ordinary people will not be able to understand, and they will be able to become the cause of error."[62] If this be the case, said Lefèvre, then

---

57. Lefèvre, *Les Evangiles*, f. aiiii v.: "ce ne on voulu faire ne aucunement user de paraphrase, se autrement a este possible expliquer le latin: de paour de bailler autre sens que le sainct esperit navoit suggere aux evangelistes."

58. Ibid.   59. Ibid., ff. aii v.–aiii r.

60. Ibid., f. aiiii r.: "Sachons que les hommes et leurs doctrines ne sont riens, sinon de autant que elles sont corroborees et confermees de la parolle de dieu. Mais Jesuchrist est tout: il est tout homme, et tout divinite. et tout homme nest riens: sinon en luy. Et nulle parolle dhomme nest riens sinon en la parolle de luy."

61. Herminjard, op. cit., I, 220–221.

62. Lefèvre, *Les Evangiles*, f. av r.: "Secondement diront que en leur baillant ainsi les evangiles: maintes choses seront difficiles et obscures: lesquelles les simples gens ne pourront comprendre: mais pourront estre cause de erreur."

it was not fitting that the Greeks have the New Testament in Greek nor the Romans in Latin, for the difficult passages were difficult for those people, too.[63]

A second reason offered by Lefèvre for giving the Bible to the people in the vernacular was that the Scriptures and even Jesus Christ himself approve this procedure. As supporting evidence he cited the words of Jesus in Luke 11:52 concerning "doctors of the law who have taken away the key of knowledge." Since the Word of God is the key to divine knowledge, those who would withhold the Scriptures from the masses are guilty of keeping them out of the kingdom of God.[64] In addition, after recalling Christ's commands for the evangelization of the whole world, Lefèvre asked this question: "And how will they preach the gospel to every creature, how will they instruct in observing all things that Jesus Christ has commanded, if they do not want the common people to see and read the gospel of God in their language?"[65]

Lefèvre further suggested that the danger of falling into error as a result of misunderstanding the Scriptures was not nearly so great with the common people as it was with the learned and powerful who already have the Bible available to them. He reminded his readers that history has shown that those who have fallen into error in the past were very often the most learned men, such as Arius and Sabellius, rather than ordinary Christians.[66] According to the man from Etaples, this was because the ecclesiastic, the noble, and the scholar are too often characterized by pride, and an arrogant spirit cuts men off from the grace of God. Yet, understanding of the spiritual meaning of the Scriptures is a gift of the grace of God to the humble and trusting, Lefèvre insisted, and in humble prayer and sighs "can be obtained more grace, understanding, and knowledge of God and of his Holy Scriptures than by reading the commentaries and writings of men concerning them, for the anointing by Christ, as Saint John says, teaches all things."[67]

63. Ibid.   64. Ibid., f. av v.

65. Ibid.: "Et comment prescheront ilz levangile a toute creature, comment enseigneront ilz a garder toutes choses que Jesuchrist a commande, se ilz ne veulent point que le simple peuple voye et lise en sa langue levangile de dieu?"

66. Ibid., f. av r.

67. Lefèvre, *Seconde partie*, f. Aiii v.: "Et en iceulx peult on obtenir plus de grace: dintelligence: et de congnoissance de dieu et de ses sainctes escriptures, que en lisant les commentaires et escriptures des hommes sur icelles, car lunction de Christ comme dit sainct Jehan enseigne de toutes choses."

Lefèvre's insight into human nature was revealed as he tried to guide the common people in their use of the Scriptures. He wanted them to know that they could read the Bible themselves and could understand it spiritually and beneficially with the aid of the Holy Spirit, but at the same time he did not want to provide them with an occasion for pride and self-confidence, for this would make them incapable of a proper relationship with God. He admitted that they might be able to understand the Scriptures even better than the more learned and more powerful, but he reminded them that this was true only insofar as they remained humble and receptive before God.[68] He concluded his warning with this injunction: "It is necessary, therefore, to honor the Holy Scripture in what one understands, while giving thanks to the One who gives the understanding; and in what is not understood, to believe it according to the interpretation of the Spirit of God."[69]

In the preface to his French translation of the last part of the New Testament, Lefèvre laid the groundwork for going beyond the regular preaching ministry of the church in his effort to confront the people of the diocese of Meaux with the Word of God and to help them understand and apply it. He compared ordinary Christians in their relation to the church and the Bible with monks and nuns in their relation to their monastic orders and rules. He pointed out that those monastics who do not understand Latin are given their rule in the vernacular in order that they might have it in their possession, study it, and have it explained to them in their chapters. Lefèvre concluded that, in like manner, every Christian should have the "rule" of Christianity, "which is the Word of God, the Scripture full of grace and mercy," in a language which he can also understand.[70] The Christian should have his rule in his possession, too, should study it, and should have it explained to him "not just once but customarily in the chapters of Jesus Christ, which are the churches where all people, simple as well as learned, ought to assemble to hear and honor the holy Word of God."[71]

68. Ibid., f. Aiiii r.

69. Ibid., f. Avi v.: "Il fault doncques honnorer la saincte escripture en ce que on entend: en rendant graces a celuy qui donne lentendement. Et en ce que on nentend point: en le croyant selon le sens de lesperit de dieu. . . ."

70. Ibid., f. Aviii r.: ". . . les simples de la religion chrestienne, seule necessaire . . . doibvent avoir leur reigle, qui est la parolle de Dieu, escripture pleine de grace et de misericorde. . . ."

71. Ibid., f. Aviii v.: ". . . non une fois mais ordinairement es chapitres de Jesuchrist, qui sont les eglises ou tout le peuple tant simple comme scavant se doibt assembler a ouyr et honnorer la saincte parolle de dieu."

Without detracting in any way from the importance of preaching as a means of transmitting the Word of God to the people, therefore, Lefèvre also pointed up the need for the clergy to exercise its proper didactic function as well. The people should be instructed in the meaning of the Scriptures and guided in their own personal study of Holy Writ. Lefèvre recalled that the great Chrysostom had followed this procedure by encouraging his people to study the Scriptures carefully at home in order that they might be able to profit more fully from his own biblical preaching and teaching.[72] The clergy of Meaux were encouraged to follow his example, which was now possible because the people of the diocese had the Scriptures available in the vernacular. The man from Etaples jubilantly described to Farel in a letter of July 6, 1524, the results of his efforts in this regard:

> After the French books of the New Testament were published, you would scarcely believe with what ardor God excited the minds of the simple folk in several places to embrace his Word. . . . Now in our whole diocese on religious holidays and especially on Sundays, the Epistle and the Gospel are read to the people in the vernacular language and if the priest has any word of exhortation, he adds it to the Epistle or to the Gospel or to both passages.[73]

In the same letter, Lefèvre reported that Bishop Briçonnet had charged Gérard Roussel with the responsibility of giving the people daily instruction in the Epistles of Paul. Lefèvre also said that the bishop had sent preachers to other parts of his diocese to provide the same kind of teaching ministry in those places.[74] Roussel himself described his activities in a letter to Farel of the same date, saying that all of his time was consumed in preaching and teaching. In addition to his lectures on the Epistles of Paul, he was also instructing the common people in the Gospels and the better educated in the Psalms.[75] Some of the charges brought against Roussel in the hearings conducted by the Parlement in 1525 involved these very activities. The examiners were told that after his sermon, Roussel was accustomed to meet with "wool-combers, carders, and other people of the same

---

72. Ibid.

73. Herminjard, op. cit., I, 220–221: "Vix crederes, posteaquam libri gallici Novi Organi emissi sunt, quanto Deus ardore simplicium mentes, aliquot in locis, moveat ad amplexandum verbum suum. . . . Nunc in tota diocesi nostra, festis diebus, et maxime die dominica, legitur populo et epistola et evangelium lingua vernacula; et si paroecus aliquid exhortationis habet, ad epistolam aut evangelium, aut ad utrumque adjicit."

74. Ibid., I, 222.   75. Ibid., I, 237–238.

stamp" to discuss the Epistles of Paul, the Gospels, and the Psalms in the vernacular and that these people actually brought those books with them.[76] Briçonnet's support of these efforts can be seen especially in the fact that he distributed copies of Lefèvre's French translation of the New Testament and of the Psalms, without charge, to all the people of his diocese who were too poor to purchase them.[77]

Lefèvre's goal in all of these endeavors, then, was to bring about reformation in the lives of the people and in the life of the church by a return to the centrality and indispensability of the Scriptures. He was prepared to make one more major contribution toward attaining that goal. Having given the Bible to the people in their own language, he recognized the need of providing them with some assistance in interpreting the Scriptures in order that they might perceive the spiritual meaning of the text under the guidance of the Holy Spirit. That was the motive behind his preparation of biblical commentaries for those who could use Latin; and surely, if the educated could profit from suggestions regarding the proper interpretation of Holy Writ, the average Frenchman, who had had little or no previous contact with the Scriptures, needed such help desperately. In order to meet this further need of the common people of France, in 1525 Lefèvre published a kind of commentary in French upon the Scripture passages which were a part of the regular liturgy of the mass in the diocese of Meaux.[78] Actually, no edition of the *Epistles and Gospels,* as the little work was called, bears the name of the author, but there is little doubt that the man from Etaples was largely responsible for it. The Sorbonnist Noel Béda, in his attack upon Lefèvre written in 1526, attributed the volume to "Jacques Lefèvre and his disciples."[79] Another witness was Jean Lecomte d'Etaples, who wrote:

There already exists, to be sure, some short *Exhortations for the Fifty-two Sundays of the Year.* I myself collaborated on it, the fourth one to do so, when I was at Meaux under the evangelical episcopacy of Guillaume Briçonnet .... Those exhortations, composed in rela-

76. Charles Schmidt, "Gérard Roussel, inculpé d'hérésie à Meaux," *Bulletin de la Société de l'histoire du protestantisme français,* X (1861), 220.

77. Du Plessis, op. cit., I, 331.

78. Jacques Lefèvre d'Etaples, *Les Epistres et Evangeles pour les cinquante et deux sepmaines de lan* (Meaux: n.p., 1525). This work has been recently republished by M. A. Screech under the title Jacques Lefèvre d'Etaples, *Épristres et Évangiles pour les cinquante et deux sepmaines de l'an* (Geneva: Librairie Droz, 1964).

79. Cited by Screech, op. cit., pp. 11, 18 n. 9.

tion to the circumstances of that place and time, were revised and corrected by my patron and fellow-citizen Lefèvre, the ornament not only of our town of Etaples but of all the French and even of the entire world. . . .[80]

The preparation of the *Epistles and Gospels*, then, was an attempt to help the ordinary Frenchman understand those passages of Scripture regularly read in the mass and hopefully to point him to an understanding of the spiritual sense which alone would be beneficial to him. There may well have been another motive behind the publication of that little volume, however, and it certainly was used to serve an additional purpose. Under pressure from the Sorbonne and the Parlement of Paris, on October 15, 1523, Bishop Briçonnet issued two synodal decrees, one addressed to "the faithful of the diocese of Meaux" and the other to the clergy, in which he sought to stop the spread of Lutheran ideas in his bishopric.[81] Then on December 3 of the same year, he acted again not only closing the pulpits of the churches of Meaux to those with Lutheran leanings but also revoking the preaching licenses which he had granted, including those which he had given to the "imported preachers" two years earlier.[82] Admittedly the date of the latter decree raises some problems, especially because Gérard Roussel and some others not only continued to preach but also began giving instruction in various portions of the Bible to the people with Briçonnet's knowledge and support, as is indicated by the previously cited letters of July 6, 1524.[83]

Nevertheless, it is clear that at least some of the "imported preachers" were silenced, and a few, like William Farel, seem to have left Meaux at about this time.[84] The net result was that the responsibility for preaching fell once again upon the parish priests or, more exactly,

80. Cited by Screech, op. cit., p. 11: "Il existe déjà à la vérité, de courtes *Exhortations pour les cinquante—deux dimanches de l'année*. J'y ai moi-même collaboré, moi quatrième, quand j'étais à Meaux, sous l'épiscopat évangélique de Guillaume Briçonnet. . . . Ces exhortations, composées en rapport avec les circonstances du lieu et de l'époque, étaient revues et chatiées par mon mécème et concitoyen, Lefèvre, ornement non seulement de notre ville d'Etaples, mais de toutes les Gaules et même de l'univers entier. . . ."

81. Those decrees are given in Herminjard, op. cit., I, 153–155, 156–158. The question of the influence of Luther's ideas upon Lefèvre and his associates at Meaux is as difficult as it is tantalizing. The available documents are usually rather vague on this point. At any rate this question would require extensive research and is beyond the scope of this essay.

82. Ibid., I, 171–172.   83. See above, nn. 73, 74, 75.

84. Herminjard, op. cit., I, 178–181; and *Guillaume Farel* (Neuchâtel et Paris: Editions Delachaux et Niestlé, 1930), pp. 115–116.

upon their inept and ignorant vicars. Briçonnet's secretary, Lermite, later reported that the bishop attempted to ameliorate this situation by requiring the vicars at least to read the Scripture passages of the day, the Epistle and the Gospel, to the people in the vernacular.[85] He felt that this practice would provide a little spiritual food for the people committed to the care of such ecclesiastics. Moreover, the publication of the *Epistles and Gospels* would enable those vicars to go one step further by providing them with brief homiletical explanations of the biblical passages which could also be read to the people, and apparently the bishop commanded that this be done.[86]

In all these ways, the man from Etaples sought to rescue the Word of God from neglect and obscurity and to release its redeeming and reforming power in the lives of individuals and in the common life of the church. He was convinced that if the gospel were only made available and made known, the whole world would be transformed by Jesus Christ working through his Word. This was, to him, the one great need of his day, and he gave himself unsparingly to meet that need. If he suggested changes in doctrine, practices, and customs along the way, it was no more and no less than what was required by his attempt to know the Scriptures in their purity and to apply them as accurately and completely as possible to men and to the church. He was no rash iconoclast. He never sought to destroy, only to build; and to build in strict accordance with the requirements revealed in the pages of Holy Writ.

What result his many efforts might have ultimately achieved will never be known. The opposition to Lefèvre, which had begun even before his arrival in Meaux,[87] became more intense after the publication of his *Commentary on the Four Gospels* in 1522,[88] and ended in vigorous attacks upon him and all of his associates at Meaux by the Sorbonne and the Parlement of Paris in 1525.[89] The result was that the program of reform in the diocese of Meaux was violently crushed,

85. Cited by Screech, op. cit., p. 10.

86. Charles-Henri Graf, *Essai sur la vie et les écrits de Jacques Lefèvre d'Étaples* (Strasbourg: G. L. Schuler, 1842), pp. 109, 113.

87. See Richard Cameron, "The Attack on the Biblical Work of Lefèvre d'Étaples, 1514–1521," *Church History*, XXXVIII, no. 1 (March, 1969), 9–24. Also see Richard Cameron, "Charges of Lutheranism Brought Against Jacques Lefèvre d' Etaples, 1520–1529," *Harvard Theological Review*, LXIII (Jan., 1970), 119–149.

88. Carolus Du Plessis d'Argentré, *Collectio judiciorum de novis erroribus*, 3 vols. (Paris: Andreas Cailleau, 1725–36), II, x–xi.

89. Du Plessis, op. cit., I, 332–333; II, 283.

and the active agents of that reform, with the exception of Bishop Briçonnet, were forced to flee from France.[90] Apparently, amidst the shrill exchanges of the theologians and the furious religious conflicts which characterized the second quarter of the sixteenth century, there was no place for the quiet evangelical reform attempted at Meaux by Jacques Lefèvre d'Etaples.

90. Herminjàrd, op. cit., I, 404, 406 n. 5, 408.

Part IV. History, eschatology, and the contemplative life

Orderic Vitalis on Henry I: theocratic ideology and didactic narrative

ROGER D. RAY

The old assumption that the medieval chronicler's religious rhetoric is mere convention and expresses little of his purpose is now perishing; but it certainly dies hard. Many German scholars have set it fully aside. In *geistesgeschichtliche* studies of medieval historiography, which over the last four decades have almost poured forth, one most easily finds serious discussions of the part theology played in the actual making of narrative.[1] Historians elsewhere have been slower coming around, though recent publications suggest that there may at last have come a general breakthrough.[2] The new research has everywhere proceeded

1. Johannes Spörl did most to catalyze this new study; see especially his seminal methodological essay, "Das mittelalterliche Geschichtsdenken als Forschungsaufgabe," which first appeared in *Historisches Jahrbuch der Görres-Gesellschaft*, LIII (1933), 281–303, and has since been reprinted as the lead article in Walther Lammers, ed., *Geschichtsdenken und Geschichtsbild im Mittelalter* (Darmstadt: Wissenschaftliche Buchgesellschaft, 1965), pp. 1–29. The Lammers anthology is an excellent showcase of the vigorous line of research Spörl helped to begin; see pp. 460–475 for an extensive bibliography, compiled by Sibylle Mähl, listing publications from 1933 through 1959. In this tradition the most fertile methodological discussion still goes on; see, e.g., Helmut Beumann's introduction to Siegmund Hellmann, *Ausgewählte Abhandlungen zur Historiographie und Geistesgeschichte des Mittelalters*, ed. H. Beumann (Darmstadt: Wissenschaftliche Buchgesellschaft, 1961), esp. pp. x–xvii. By far the best overview of the history of medieval historiography is also the product of *Geistesgeschichte*; see Herbert Grundmann, *Geschichtsschreibung im Mittelalter* (Göttingen: Vandenhoeck and Ruprecht, 1965).

2. For particularly noteworthy evidence of this, see R. W. Southern, "Aspects of the European Tradition of Historical Writing: The Classical Tradition from Einhard to Geoffrey of Monmouth" (Presidential Lecture, Annual Meeting of the Royal Historical Society, 1969), *Transactions of the Royal Historical Society*, 5th ser., XX (1970), 173–196, esp. 173f. Southern notes, with proper gratitude, that nineteenth century editors like Bishop Stubbs had "little concern with the minds of the men" who wrote the texts they prepared for publication; this article is also distinguished for giving notice of the *geistesgeschichtliche* research in an early footnote, an acknowledgement one rarely finds in an English language publication. A few studies similarly sensitive have come from French scholars. In fact, Paul Alphandéry was a pioneer in "Les citations bibliques chez les historiens de la première croisade," *Revue de l'histoire des religions*, XCIX (1929), 139–157, but he has had few successors like Jacques Chaurand, "La conception de l'histoire de Guibert de Nogent," *Cahiers de civilisation médiévale, Xe–XIIe siècles*, VIII (1965), 381–395, and, very recently, Jean Leclercq, "Monastic Historiography from Leo IX to Callistus II," *Studia monastica*, XII (1970), 57–86. In this country the article-length studies of T. E. Mommsen have been especially forward looking; see several of them now collected in *Medieval and Renaissance Studies*, ed. Eugene F. Rice (Ithaca: Cornell University Press, 1959), pp. 265ff. See also the incisive work of Charles W. Jones, *Saints' Lives and Chronicles in Early England* (Ithaca: Cornell University Press, 1947), and the useful monograph of Robert W. Hanning, *Vision of History in Early Britain* (New York: Columbia Univer-

from the belief that we have too long tended to judge medieval chroniclers by modern standards, and must now attempt to view them less from the front than from behind, that is, in terms of their own scholarly reasons and resources. It has become clear that since medieval historiography is throughout didactic, we should study it with interest in the pedagogical interaction of all narrative elements—which requires openness to the possibility that apparently platitudinous religious matter may in fact signal what the author thought was the burden of his story. Nonetheless, it has lately been once more asserted that clerical chroniclers were almost never "engaged in presenting a religious picture of the world," and now the seemingly ubiquitous opinion comes not from a positivistic editor but from an avowed intellectual historian.[3]

It is of course true that medieval authors often had interests and anticipated audiences that would seem to make religious sentiment almost inappropriate. Even in these instances, however, one must be on guard against anachronism; for it is we, not the chroniclers, who feel the need to distinguish between rhetoric and reality. They surely knew the difference, too. Yet they were always concerned to treat their subjects in ways that best drew the reader back into the authority of Christian and classical antiquity. In other words, they wanted to teach traditional values through an impressive deployment of traditional literary means. Helmut Beumann has incisively shown that just when an author seems to put together a mere patchwork of commonplaces, he may actually be expressing authentically personal thoughts in the most efficacious and relevant way; Donald J. Wilcox's study of fifteenth-century Florentine historians even leads one to suspect that ever since antiquity historical authors may have perceived reality in ways inseparable from their rhetorical ability to represent it.[4] In a word, things

sity Press, 1966). To the short study of Ray C. Petry, "Three Medieval Chroniclers: Monastic Historiography and Biblical Eschatology in Hugh of St. Victor, Otto of Freising, and Ordericus Vitalis," *Church History*, XXXIV (1965), 282–293, I owe the beginnings of my interest in the history of medieval historiography.

3. William J. Brandt, *The Shape of Medieval History: Studies in Modes of Perception* (New Haven: Yale University Press, 1966), p. xviii.

4. See "Topos und Gedankengefüge bei Einhard," now in H. Beumann, *Ideengeschichtliche Studien zu Einhard und anderen Geschichtsschreibern des früheren Mittelalters* (Darmstadt: Wissenschaftliche Buchgesellschaft, 1962), pp. 1–14; another article reprinted in this volume, "Die Historiographie des Mittelalters als Quelle für die Ideengeschichte des Königtums," pp. 40–79, was in several ways methodologically influential in the preparation of this study. For Wilcox, see *The Development of Florentine Humanist Historiography in the Fifteenth Century* (Cambridge: Harvard University Press, 1969).

that look lifelessly formalistic to us may in truth partake of the narrative essence.

This study will present an example of narrative largely controlled by ideas ultimately expressing values of its author's experience of Benedictine monasticism. The case in point will be the account of Henry I of England given in the *Historia Ecclesiastica* of Orderic Vitalis (1075–1142), the English-born historian who spent all but his first ten years as a Black Monk in the Norman Abbey of St. Evroul and more than three decades writing his now renowned lifework.[5] The narrative is strewn through the last four books of the thirteen that eventually made up the huge text; though it is intermixed with large sections on other subjects and is prone to move along by a version of the nonchronological *ordo artificiosus*, it sustains its own kind of didactic unity. How the author's pedagogical intent influenced the making of his narrative will be the major interest, but there will be no possibility of adequately treating important didactic devices such as his resourceful use of several ancient rhetorical strategies.

First, however, a terminological comment seems due. I have decided to use the word "ideology" with reference to the framework of ideas expressing the necessities out of which Orderic responded to his subject matter. It seems better than terms like "philosophy" or "theology" since we usually prefer it today in order to speak of a network of thoughts that make intelligible not only personal and communal goals but also the experiential needs from which they arise. It thus allows one to organize many of Orderic's own requirements, for it has the advantage of making room for both theoretical and practical kinds of religious interest in the world. It helps, for example, to communicate the interrelatedness of what at first glance seem disparate things, like Orderic's distinctly moral reactions to history and his ostensibly material concern for such matters as feudal landholding. Since I will focus on Orderic's presentation of Henry I, the political aspects of his

5. The standard text is *Orderici Vitalis Historiae Ecclesiasticae Libri Tredecim*, ed. Auguste Le Prévost with Léopold Delisle ("Société de l'histoire de France," 5 vols; Paris: J. Renouard, 1838–55). Hereinafter: Le Prévost. A superb new edition is now in progress, and one volume has so far appeared: *The Ecclesiastical History of Orderic Vitalis*, ed. and tr. Marjorie Chibnall ("Oxford Medieval Texts"; Oxford: Oxford University Press, 1969), vol. II; it contains books three and four of the *Historia*. Hereinafter: Chibnall. The indispensable introduction to Orderic and his work remains L. Delisle, "Notice sur Orderic Vital," which is printed in Le Prévost, I, i–cvi. A helpful recent study is Hans Wolter, *Ordericus Vitalis, Ein Beitrag zur kluniazensischen Geschichtsschreibung* (Weimar: Franz Steiner, 1955). For an introduction to books three and four of the *Historia*, see Chibnall, pp. xii–xliii.

working ideology will predominate, so other sides of his entire frame-work of meaning will perforce not figure. It might also be best to ex-plain in advance that I will not claim any communal validity for Or-deric's political ideology. He repeatedly points out that he writes for the religious delectation of his own monastic readers there at St. Evroul; it might therefore seem reasonable to assume that the *Historia* reflects the ideological basis of his claustral society. In many ways it no doubt does, but since the first half of the twelfth century was full of ideological change, and since there is evidence in his work that Orderic was having some trouble gaining the favor of his living audience, it is probably best to take it that he speaks only for himself.[6]

In a first section I will now try to piece together hints of political ideology and interpret them against a backdrop of relevant contem-porary thought; then in a second I will trace out the narrative role of ideology in Orderic's account of Henry I.

I

From Heinrich Böhmer onwards, students of Orderic have observed that his outlook remained deeply theocratic even while many in the twelfth century were beginning to think along more pragmatic, post-Gregorian lines.[7] This view seemed to take on dramatic new possibili-ties when in 1951 George H. Williams argued that a very good candi-date for the authorship of the largely proroyalist writings usually called *The York Tractates* was Archbishop Bonne-Ame of Rouen, a prelate quite well known to Orderic and maybe even a personal friend.[8] Soon thereafter Hans Wolter reasonably wondered whether

6. Orderic's difficulties with his own monastic readers underlie the agitated prefaces to books six (Le Prévost, III, 1–3) and eleven (IV, 159–161). In "Orderic Vitalis and His Readers," *Studia monastica*, XIV (1972), 15–34, I have shown that many other aspects of the developing text may be understood in light of the author's apparent problems with those who were trying to make a religious use of the *Historia* even while he pressed on writing it.

7. See Böhmer, *Kirche und Staat in England und in der Normandie im XI. und XII. Jahrhunderts* (Leipzig: Dieterich, 1899), p. 278. Also Wolter, *Ordericus Vitalis*, pp. 130–131. I have learned in communications with Marjorie Chibnall that she concurs with this longstanding view. It has not been, however, without occasional exceptions; see Heinz Richter, *Englische Geschichtsschreiber des 12. Jahrhunderts* (Berlin: Junker and Dunn-haupt, 1938), pp. 151f., who argues that Orderic embraced the incipient secularism of his time and rather put his Christian view of history in brackets; also Hanning, *Vision of History*, pp. 126–135 and notes, who presents him as the exemplar of a new Anglo-Norman historiography which leads soon to the classicism of Geoffrey of Monmouth.

8. *The Norman Anonymous of 1100 A.D.* (Cambridge: Harvard University Press, 1951), pp. 102–127. For Orderic's account of Archbishop William, see Le Prévost, II, 64–65, 213, 313–315 (here Orderic assesses William's character), 374; III, 250–251, 379, 470–473; IV,

some features of Orderic's historical thought might be explicated by reference to the anti-Gregorian tractates. After all, Wolter pointed out, Orderic criticizes the reform papacy, shows great "devotio" to the English kings, and in the structure of his first two books leaves the impression that the temporal authority may know a preferable participation in the divine kingship of Christ, since spiritual rulers partake only of his human priesthood.[9] Although Williams's case for Archbishop William of Rouen is not in all ways conclusive, scholarly criticism has not destroyed its basic plausibility. David Douglas wrote in 1964 that the tractates "are now generally believed to have been compiled in Rouen about the end of the eleventh century, and it is not impossible that their author was William Bonne-Ame."[10] In any event, it stands unchallenged that these writings gather up many traditional themes of Anglo-Norman theocratic monarchy and represent what Norman Cantor has described as "a convenient source-book for the historian of early medieval political ideas."[11] On all these accounts the tractates still seem a possible reflector of Orderic's ideological heritage.

Wolter's question certainly deserves another asking, for beyond the evidences he noticed there are others that these anonymous writings promise to illumine. It will therefore be useful to state some of the pertinent ideas in the central Tractate 24a.[12] The work is titled *De consecratione pontificum et regum et de regimine eorum in ecclesia sancta,* and its aim is to show that the royal sacring is better than the episcopal unction. To this end the author quotes at some length from

---

42, 78, 98, 116–117, 297f., 299–300 (epitaph). This prelate ordained Orderic to the priesthood (V, 135–136) and had a web of relationships throughout the neighborhood of St. Evroul.

9. Wolter, *Ordericus Vitalis,* pp. 130, 229 (nn. 604–605).

10. *William the Conqueror, The Norman Impact on England* (Berkeley: University of California Press, 1964), p. 257. For a critique of Williams's views see Norman F. Cantor, *Church, Kingship, and Lay Investiture in England, 1089–1135* (Princeton, N.J.: Princeton University Press, 1958), pp. 174–197. The text of the tractates will be cited in the recent edition of Karl Pellens, *Die Texte des Normannischen Anonymous* (Wiesbaden: Franz Steiner, 1966). Hereinafter: Pellens. This is the only complete printing of the tractates. It should be used with care, for several aspects of Pellens's work on it have been sharply attacked; see, for instance, the review of Walter Ullmann in *Historische Zeitschrift,* CCVI (1968), 696–703, which in addition notes the durability of Williams's book.

11. *Church, Kingship, and Lay Investiture,* pp. 195f.

12. Pellens, pp. 129–180. For an able analysis of the ideas on kingship running throughout the tractates, see Williams, *The Norman Anonymous,* pp. 155–174. On Anglo-Norman theocratic kingship see also Ernst Kantorowicz, *The King's Two Bodies, A Study in Medieval Political Theology* (Princeton: Princeton University Press, 1957), pp. 42–86; Böhmer, *Kirche und Staat,* pp. 177–269; D. C. Douglas, *William the Conqueror,* pp. 247–264.

actual *ordines*, including the profoundly theocratic Edgar Ordo by which the later Anglo-Saxon kings and William the Conqueror were anointed. But before the Anonymous gets around to the juxtaposition of texts, he explains in detail that the consecration of the king mystically transforms him into a man of unique value.[13] He becomes a "sanctus," sacramentally set apart from other men "quasi extra terram." Even though he remains "naturaliter" just a man, he becomes through grace "christus Domini." This term plainly means something more than "the anointed of the Lord," for throughout Tractate 24a it is paralleled with the proper name "christus" applied to Jesus, with of course the qualification that only he is "christus per naturam."[14] The king holds an almost messianic place in history, so he may licitly be called "messias." On him the right movement of salvation history depends, till the Lord comes. He is a new Solomon. As such he is "rex pacificus," and in this role he is nearest God. Since Christ was "rex et sacerdos," the earthly monarch rules "populus Dei" with a similar authority. "Sacerdotium" is taken up into "regnum," not by accidents of history but by the example of Christ, for his royalty subsumed his sacerdotality. In all the king rules by grace rather than by nature or heredity, and is to worldly regime what Jesus is to heavenly order.

The Edgar Ordo liturgically embodied this theory, and the practice of singing *laudes regiae*, the royal litanies chanted by the people both at the coronations and on stated days during the liturgical year, reinforced it. In regard to the *laudes* it is worth mentioning that typical surviving texts from Normandy are distinct from those of other places due to their strong emphasis upon the theme "Christus vincit, Christus regnat, Christus imperat," which in one eleventh century text of Rouen leads the song along in a crescendo until the people finally shout "Regnum Christi veniat."[15] The *laudes*, in other words, were well equipped to sustain what might be called a Christ-centered social consciousness.

In this context of thought certain remarks Orderic makes become rich with ideological significance. These loci usually fall, by the way,

13. Pellens, esp. pp. 134–161.

14. See, e.g., ibid., p. 137. This relationship must be even more striking in the best MS, since it never capitalizes "christus." See the comment of Pellens, p. xxiv.

15. For this see E. Kantorowicz, *Laudes Regiae, A Study in Liturgical Acclamations and Mediaeval Ruler Worship* (Berkeley: University of California Press, 1958), pp. 166–168.

in his account of Henry I; few appear in the earlier sections on the two Williams or in the short later one on Stephen. Several things perhaps explain this. First, Henry I and Orderic flourished together, and Orderic naturally felt that his own needs and aspirations were more bound up with Henry than with the others. He saw Henry at close range; in 1113 the king stopped at St. Evroul to celebrate the Feast of Purification and on that occasion secured the abbey's possessions by the grant of a royal charter. Orderic was delighted by all this, and came away impressed that Henry had profound interest even in the renunciatory life.[16] Then, too, the king ruled for thirty-five years, and after completing his conquest of Normandy, kept a reasonably good peace for much more than two decades. On the whole Orderic saw in Henry what he thought was the reality of true monarchy, so there easily came to mind ideas which articulated his sense of relative well-being as a monk of St. Evroul and a royal subject. In William I, Rufus, and Stephen most of these factors were lacking; their histories thus did not bring to life the positive influence of ideology on the making of didactic narrative. However, it might be argued that some of Orderic's demurrers as regards these three kings stemmed from their failure to fit his special viewpoint.[17]

Orderic is keenly interested in the significance of the coronation rite. He notes that the two Williams and Henry I were all crowned by a proper ceremony, and even in the case of Rufus he asserts that the king ruled by grace and not by mere hereditary right.[18] Of course given the succession questions that in different ways bothered the Conqueror and his sons, the traditional ideas of nature and grace were especially handy, but for this study it only matters that Orderic thought these notions preserved the true interests at stake. He liked William I over Harold and certainly preferred Henry I, probably even Rufus, to Robert Curthose. In the case of Henry alone, though, does he follow up with the thought that the coronation effected an important change

16. Le Prévost, IV, 301–303.

17. E.g., Orderic's famous account of the Conqueror's dying moments includes a speech in which the king evaluates his reign in primarily theocratic terms; see ibid., III, 228–248. The reservations Orderic had about Rufus seem to have derived from the king's tendency to be a theocratic monarch more in the breach than otherwise; see III, 384, IV, 37–38, esp. 83–86. Orderic's poem eulogizing Henry seems about as much a judgment upon Stephen as praise of his predecessor; see V, 53–54.

18. For William I, see ibid., II, 156–157 (Chibnall, pp. 182–186), 239; Rufus, III, 242, 256; Henry, IV, 91.

in the person crowned, and placed a new and unique value upon him. This comes out as Orderic narrates a battle that happened at Brémule in 1119.[19] Henry was able to handle the French well enough, but the disaffected Norman baron who had stirred up the trouble to begin with turned on his monarch and got off a blow of the sword to the head, which was fortunately protected by a strong hauberk. The assailant was quickly dealt with, but Orderic observes how brash it was in any case that someone should dare to raise his hand against the head "that had been besmeared with the sacred chrism by episcopal ministry and burdened with the royal diadem, the people rejoicing and giving thanks and praise to the Lord God."[20] It is in this clear that Orderic thought Henry did undergo true sacring; some recent historians have been less sure about this. From his word "delinitum" it is tempting to conclude that he had in mind the crossing of the head called for in the *ordo* by which Henry was apparently crowned.[21] It is certain that his reference to the popular response indicates *laudes regiae* and not the voice of approval perhaps given by the people in the actual ceremony, for the *laudes* alone were supposed to follow the anointment. It therefore appears that Orderic understood Henry's coronation as theocratic in the old style, and believed the ceremony put into the king a numinous, inviolable quality.

In another place Orderic gives his monarch one of the highest sacramental titles of liturgical kingship, and this comes in a text the students of Orderic seem always to have overlooked. In 1119 Henry had to suppress an uprising of Eustace of Breteuil whose wife, Juliana, was one of the king's illegitimate daughters.[22] It turned out that she was left alone to withstand the siege her father had set up, so without the aid of her husband Orderic says she was reduced to sheer "fraus feminae." She trumped up a pretext for a conference and then took the occasion to send an arrow at the king's heart, which missed. What scandalizes Orderic about this is not the attempted patricide but the

19. Ibid., IV, 360–361.

20. "Nefariam enim temeritatem inchoaverat, qui dextram cum framea ferientem super caput levaverat, quod per pontificale ministerium sacro chrismate delinitum fuerat, et regale diadema, populis gaudentibus, Dominoque Deo gratias et laudes concinentibus, bajulaverat." Ibid.

21. On Henry's coronation see Cantor, *Church, Kingship, and Lay Investiture*, pp. 135–146; P. L. Ward, "The Coronation Ceremony in Medieval England," *Speculum*, XIV (1939), 173–176. It would seem that Henry was crowned by an *ordo* acceptable to the English reformers, and not by the Edgar Ordo; the new ceremony still apparently included chrism, and so was something of a compromise.

22. Le Prévost, IV, 336–339.

assault on the royal body. Juliana's enormity lay only in her having taken thought to send her hand against "christus Domini."[23]

Orderic uses other terminology of early medieval theocratic theory. Recounting a very deteriorated Norman situation Henry faced in 1118, he laments that it was all worse than civil war.[24] The Norman rebels remind him of those Old Testament dissidents who deserted the king anointed by Samuel and joined themselves to Absalom. Thus the Norman traitors deserted "princeps pacificus" who, Orderic also points out, had been set apart by episcopal election and benediction.[25] In these terms Henry was a new David, one of the Anonymous' favorite "christi," set apart by ecclesiastical ritual as a "rex pacificus." All this is to Orderic's mind a very heavy judgement upon the Norman criminals.

After Orderic records Henry's death, he then includes a long poem he wrote about the chaos that everywhere seemed to break out once the king was gone.[26] It is throughout a very gloomy piece in which Orderic makes it plain that Henry I was essential to a viable human existence. Thus he speaks of the king not only as "amator pacis" but also as "tutor Ecclesiae." With reference to this last term it is worth noting that Tractate 24a enjoins the king to teach ("docere"), instruct ("instruere"), nourish ("enutrire"), and defend ("munire") the church.[27] Orderic prays that the deceased king will now enjoy deserved association "forever with Christ the King of kings." Towards the end of the poem he affirms the unbreakable continuity of divine law and therefore expresses assurance that God will give another "patronus Ecclesiae." Finally he asks, "Christ, grant a leader who will desire and hold fast peace and justice, and will guide your people." For, he goes on, only when the obdurate are dealt with by such a person can the faithful perform their Christian service.[28] The implication is that the church cannot otherwise adequately operate—which leaves but a short step to the belief that the king plays a virtually salvific part in history, since the church's sacramental machinery will at best run slow without

23. "... manum suam in christum Domini mittere praecogitavit." Ibid., 338.

24. Ibid., 328–329.

25. "Tunc plurimi Achitophel et Semei, aliosque desertores in Neustria imitabantur, et operibus illorum similia operabantur, qui, relicto rege per Samuelem divinitus ordinato, Absalon parricidae jungebantur. Sic nimirum plerique faciebant, qui pacificum principem, pontificali electione et benedictione consecratum, deserebant. . . ." Ibid.

26. Ibid., V, 53–54.   27. Pellens, p. 158.

28. "Christe ducem praebe, qui pacem justitiamque / Diligat ac teneat, populumque tuum tibi ducat. / Justitiae virga turgentum percute dorsa, / Ut secura tibi tua plebs possit famulari." Le Prévost, V, 54.

his protection. Thus on these practical grounds Orderic seems to correlate the redemptive interests of Christ with monarchy.

II

It is by now sufficiently clear that Orderic was indeed intellectually old fashioned, and that he plainly employed theocratic notions similar in typical themes to some of the more traditional ideas of Tractate 24a. How this political theology functions ideologically to pressure, inflect, and shape his narrative is never more apparent than in Orderic's long account of the general council held in 1119 at Reims and presided over by Pope Callixtus II.[29] This meeting very much jogged Orderic's thought; several scholars have in fact suspected he must have been there. I doubt this, however. Orderic took few trips, and when he did get to make one, he usually found some way to mention it in his text, if for no other reason than to enhance his admittedly thin credentials as an eyewitness researcher.[30] In any case, his narrative shows profound interest and considerable self-conscious technique. It is, for one thing, full of contrived oratory, deliberate to the point that he once uses textbook rhetorical terminology.[31] Of course the speeches function to present the great matters of the occasion in terms of what seemed suitable ideas and motives. But before Orderic gets going with the proceedings he takes care to develop the attitude of Henry I towards them. This he does in a portrait of the king haranguing his assembled bishops to the effect that they should be dutiful to the pope but should bring home no "superfluous inventions," for his kingdom would remain, as ever, altogether competent to do its own justice. With this prefaced, other circumstances set, and the principal participants named, Orderic strings together narrative and discourse recounting first a complaint of the French king against certain Norman bishops; next, a wife's cause against an unfaithful husband; then a conflict between the bishop of Evreux and a noble layman who successfully charged the prelate with being a liar. In this last matter feelings grew so hot between French and Norman parties that violence broke out on the floor. When things settled down, the pope rose and delivered a florid speech about the painfully demonstrated need for peace among the people of God. The discourse belabors this theme but eventually

29. Ibid., IV, 373–393.
30. For Oderic's trips see Wolter, *Ordericus Vitalis*, pp. 64–65.
31. Of one speech he says he will first give the "prooemium." Le Prévost, IV, 387.

works in comments about the pope's plans to make a short trip away to meet with Henry V of Germany. The speech makes it seem that the kind of trouble on the council's floor was all very much the same as that about which the pope wished to speak with the emperor. Then in just a few sentences Orderic remarks that the trip was a flop and that the pope in fact returned to Reims never having even seen Henry V. A report of the fiasco was made to the council by a cardinal who notably fails to mention the great issues that were never talked over. Orderic concludes the cardinal's speech with the words, "About this I have now said enough," and one gets the feeling that it was likely the author who had gotten his fill. For he goes on to something else, to narrate a litigation involving Abbot Pontius of Cluny, the upshot of which was that the papal jurisdiction over the abbey seemed at bay. A cardinal again speaks for the pope, and the forthcoming defense of the papal governance of Cluny turns out to be not so much a vote for general papal authority as an effort to protect the abbey's traditional interests. On the last day of the council the bishop of Barcelona delivered a long speech on the royal and sacerdotal powers, and Orderic, elsewhere quite ready with reconstructed oratory, little more than remarks that all paid attention. He does report that the pope at last excommunicated the German emperor, but again there is no especially interested comment. The whole narrative concludes with a transcript of the council's decrees. They are of course Gregorian every one.

The point is, the reforming decrees rather represent conclusions that do not follow from Orderic's narrative premises. This becomes all the more impressive if one compares this account with the other principal narrative of the council, one written by a certain canon of Strasbourg named Hesso.[32] In this work several things depart from Orderic's version, but nothing so much as the main issues discussed: simony and lay investitures. Of course Hesso too is interested in peace, but he has a very different notion of what the war is. For instance, though his first major speech is about conflict among the people of God, the symbolic chief offender is Simon Magus, not the devil stirring up a rambunctious feudal aristocracy in violation of the Truce of God,

32. *Hessonis Scholastici Relatio de Concilio Remensi, MGH*, SS, XII, 422–428. Hesso claims to have been an eyewitness (428). On the council see C. J. Hefele, *Histoire des Conciles*, tr. and rev. H. Leclercq (Paris: Letouzey and Ané, 1912), V, pt. 1, 576–592; Stanley A. Chodorow, "Ecclesiastical Politics and the Ending of the Investitures Contest: The Papal Election of 1119 and the Negotiations at Mouzon," *Speculum*, XLVI (1971), 613–640.

which is clearly most on Orderic's mind.[33] On the whole Hesso's narrative makes the decrees seem a good summation of the council's substantive business. In Orderic, by contrast, they simply dangle at the end. It is certainly not that Orderic was slow to perceive the council's reforming import. Early on in his narrative he makes prominent his awareness of what Henry I had at stake in the proceedings. Nor does Orderic argumentatively resist what Gregorian matter he could not pass over in silence. As for the nearly startling decrees, it would no doubt have been unthinkable to leave them out. Orderic thus put a kind of benign ideological de-emphasis upon them, and this gives his narrative its odd shape compared to Hesso's.

In his entire report of the council Orderic is plainly working hard to keep inviolate certain attitudes towards Henry I, and on many other occasions narrative materials come out with the same sort of bearing. His account of Anselm, for instance, is heartily affirmative, but it is manifest that Orderic appreciates him primarily for his work at Bec, not at Canterbury.[34] It pleases Orderic to record his death with that of Abbot Hugh of Cluny; the careers of the two men had similar importance to him.[35] He never mentions Anselm's struggle with Henry I. The English investitures controversy figures little in the *Historia*, but although Orderic never explicitly takes sides, there can be no doubt where he stood. Even when he records Rufus's troubles with Anselm, he only deplores them and never really says what they were.[36] As for the German investitures contest, Orderic favors the pope, but his support is very much of the traditional sort classically associated in the monastic world with Cluny.[37] Nothing in the oratory Orderic puts into the mouths of the pope and his spokesmen at Reims would lead an otherwise uninformed person to suspect that the Gregorian reform had altogether broken out. When he describes a conference between Henry I and Callixtus shortly after the council, he makes the pope call

33. *Relatio*, 424; cf. Le Prévost, IV, 381–382.

34. An account of Anselm runs in usually small installments from late in Book IV through Book XI. Orderic's warmest appreciation comes in the notice of Anselm's election as abbot of Bec (Le Prévost, II, 245–246; Chibnall, pp. 294–296), and this passage was written long after his death.

35. Le Prévost, V, 297–299. But Orderic devotes far more space here to Hugh.

36. Ibid., IV, 13–16, 54–56. In the latter place (p. 56) Orderic tells his readers that if they want to know more about Anselm's grief over Rufus and Ranulf Flambard, they should go to Eadmer's book.

37. Ibid., III, 163–164, 461; IV, 4, 221. See also Wolter, *Ordericus Vitalis*, p. 131; of course the thesis of Wolter's study is that Orderic represents rather a "Cluniac" historian (38–40, 148).

the king a "true heir of Solomon," an old favorite among theocratic ascriptions.[38] In his account of a legatine appeal to a royal council held in 1118 at Rouen, Orderic even suggests criticism of the reforming papacy. He tells how the papal agent complained of Henry V, the antipope, and the exile of Gelasius II, but then points out that the legate more desired the help of money than prayers.[39]

Throughout his treatment of Henry I Orderic's major theme is how the king tried to keep peace for the church. There is one important variation on it: how Henry's pragmatism and apparent Midas touch made him the greatest and wealthiest of occidental monarchs.[40] Though this motif has especially interested modern scholars, it was only important to Orderic insofar as it helped to explain his first premise, for the king could certainly not have pacified the church's circumstances if he had not possessed savoir-faire in both politics and finances. In other words, if raising up new counselors "from the dust," as he says in a famous phrase,[41] was of value in establishing social quiet; if wealth lent to Henry's reign economic stability—then all the better for those, like Orderic, who only wanted peace. Yet Orderic certainly does not write as an ideologist in his account of "rex pacificus." It is simply that theocratic ideology comported well with personal and communal needs which are in the *Historia* obvious enough. For instance, he needed peace for the easily overlooked reason that much of the violence he chronicles transpired not far from his abbey, often within a radius of about thirty miles at places like Laigle, Breteuil, Sées, Argentan, Alençon, Almenèches, Evreux, Lisieux, or hard by home at Gacé; and this is not to mention that hostilities sometimes became grievous interruptions right at St. Evroul.[42] What bothers Orderic most about all this is that feudal warfare hurt the church, and he particularly deplores obstructions to liturgical regularity. In a memorable passage, for example, Orderic relates that just before Tinchebray Henry visited the church at Sées and heard a long speech from the

38. Le Prévost, IV, 399. Henry's long reply is entirely consistent with a theocratic notion of kingship (399–403). In this whole passage the reforming program is especially conspicuous by its absence.

39. Ibid., 329–330. "Retulit etiam Gelasii Papae, qui jam cis Alpes venerat insurgentibus procellis, exilium, et a Normannica Ecclesia subsidium petiit orationum, magisque pecuniarum."

40. Ibid., 92, 164, 236–239.

41. Ibid., 164. On this often-quoted remark see R. W. Southern, "King Henry I," in his *Medieval Humanism and Other Essays* (Oxford: Blackwell, 1970), pp. 211–212.

42. When Robert de Bellême was finally imprisoned, Orderic felt great relief, for, as he says, peace came at last to the region of St. Evroul. Le Prévost, IV, 307.

pious Bishop Serlo.[43] The prelate explained that his church was so far cluttered with possessions brought there for safekeeping by terrified little people that one could hardly bend the knee at the altar. As he listened the king was also viewing the alleged jumble, and finally getting the point, he blurted out that he would soon go forth to reclaim Normandy for the church. Then on the eve of Tinchebray Orderic portrays Henry making a prayer which expresses the piety of "princeps pacificus."[44] Henry's entire struggle against Duke Robert and Robert de Bellême Orderic construes as the king's care of the church, and this is no less the line of interpretive thought in the following sections in which he narrates how the monarch tried to preserve the gains hammered out in the first decade of the century. All along Orderic finds ways to underscore his thesis. Once he has the count of Maine give a speech arguing that opposition to the king is in reality defiance of God, for social disorder hits the church hardest of all.[45] In other places Orderic reminds his readers what havoc conflict causes for decent worship. He laments, for instance, the inordinate circumstances created in his own monastery when some nuns from nearby Almenèches, driven by force from their cloister, took refuge for several months in the chapel of St. Evroul.[46] Orderic bears in mind larger interruptions of divine service. He notes that things one time were in such disarray at Evreux that Divine Office was canceled there for an entire year.[47] Rehearsing a long tangle of troubles that happened at Alençon in 1118, he finally comes down to sums, and prominent among them is that the faithful thereabout were not that year able to celebrate properly the season of Advent.[48]

In a word, feudal warfare threatened the sort of human activity that was closest to Orderic's heart, namely, liturgical practice, so it was quite natural for him to locate his king in the midst of a fundamentally religious context of problems. Orderic was no monastic man of affairs; he never even held a claustral office higher than librarian. We must assume that his life was therefore organized more closely around

43. Ibid., 204–206.
44. "Novit omnipotens Deus, in quem credo, quod pro desolatae plebis subventione hoc certamen ineo. Ipsum Factorem nostrum intimo corde deposco ut illi det victoriam in conflictu hodierno, per quem suo tutelam et quietem decrevit dare populo." Ibid., 228. A message from Henry to Duke Robert, given in the text just above this prayer (227f.), states that the impending battle would be fought for the sake of ecclesiastical quiet.
45. Ibid., 235–236.   46. Ibid., 181–183.
47. Ibid., 331.   48. Ibid., 331–334.

the liturgical *horarium* than were those of other monastic historians, who, like Suger of St. Denis or Robert of Torigni, felt the multidirectional pull of many administrative duties. Orderic lived so close to the liturgy that he easily thought his own text an expression of its piety. Many have noticed that the *Historia* is full of its author's spirituality, and no one, so far as I know, has ever raised a question about its authenticity.[49] There is about the text a spontaneous and almost infectious emotional quality. Marjorie Chibnall has suggested that the *Historia* may have sunk into its medieval unpopularity because of its intensely personal nature.[50] We must therefore believe that Orderic represents at least one medieval monk who really wrote his book for the glory of God and thus as a part of his day-to-day worship. There is in fact a passage in which he remarkably puts monastic scholarship in the intellectual sphere of the *Opus Dei*. In his account of St. Evroul's great Abbot Thierry Orderic reports that some resented the abbot's constantly insisting they "pray, read, chant, write"; these monks thought Thierry paid too little attention to abbatial finances and too much to prayer. With all the topological authority of the Rule Orderic assails these critics "who put worldly cares before Divine Office" and thus caused distress to this exemplary abbot who practiced his monastic principles "as much in praying as in writing."[51] The same view of scholarly work undoubtedly went for Orderic. John Benton has recently suggested that Guibert of Nogent became rather a "monastic personality," an individual in whom the values of claustral discipline were genuinely internalized.[52] If this was true of Guibert, it was more so of Orderic, for he was earlier and longer a monk and never came close to being the monastic businessman abbots had to be. It seems accurate to say that the *Historia* evidences throughout a monastic sensibility which especially becomes a cultic way of interpreting all hu-

49. Orderic's great editor Le Prévost did once rebuke his friend Léopold Delisle for overlooking what seemed to him the outstanding trait of the *Historia*: the liveliness and veracity with which it describes the Christian life and reflects its author's own religious sentiment. See this in a letter quoted at the end of Delisle's "Notice sur Orderic Vital" (ibid., I, cvi).

50. "Orderic Vitalis and Robert of Torigni," in *Millénaire monastique du Mont Saint-Michel* (Paris: P. Lethielleux, 1966), II, 133–139.

51. Le Prévost, II, 50 (Chibnall, p. 52). The Rule's enjoinder "nihil operi Dei praeponatur" (Ch. 43) is unmistakably mirrored in Orderic's attacks on those "qui mundiales curas divinis praeponebant officiis."

52. *Self and Society in Medieval France, The Memoirs of Abbot Guibert of Nogent*, tr. with an introduction by Benton (New York: Harper and Row, 1970), pp. 21–22.

man experience. After all, if living in the liturgy was truly being a man, then all people might readily seem under a proportionally similar necessity to fulfill themselves through some liturgical means.

The world, then, had to be kept safe for worship. On this premise theocratic ideology came straight home, for unless the king was out there living up to his own liturgical self-understanding, then no one could be sure of a proper chance at blessedness. To Orderic this much was risked in monarchy, so he prepared his text according to political notions that promised to meet the need for, and aspiration towards, liturgical perfection. Thus at the beginning of his history of Henry I he argues that the king's success was chiefly evidenced in the increase of liturgical activity during his reign; at the end, when he was already beginning to undergo the ordeal of the early "Anarchy," Orderic prays that the church may have another like him, so that divine service may go on.[53] In the narrative interim Orderic proceeds with what often seems a strong empirical sense, but even in the most downrightly concrete passages there frequently occur tips, as we have seen, that he thinks the true significance of his text religious. His entire account of "christus Domini" reassures him that there is the possibility of a life sufficiently free from chronic disturbance to permit Benedictine peace, and this is his message to others.

Modern scholars have often had their doubts about the *Historia* as a narrative source for the career of Henry I, and have sometimes even blamed Orderic for not having raised questions that were really several centuries beyond him. This study will certainly not redress his image among these critics; it may, in fact, confirm their assessment by clarifying what they have long known is somehow wrong. On the other hand it may help to remind readers that the *Historia* was after all a true product of its author's own subjectivity, of his own personal predispositions and historical commitments. In all kinds of study it should therefore be interpreted with sensitive awareness of the religious problems Orderic hoped it would illumine.

---

53. Le Prévost, IV, 91–92; V, 54.

Historia fundamentum est: the role of history in the contemplative life according to Hugh of St. Victor

GROVER A. ZINN, JR.

Of the several themes which give a conceptual unity to the writings of Hugh of St. Victor (d. 1141) there are two which stand out. First, there is the Hugonian sense of the importance of history to the Christian and his religion, for Christianity is based on "deeds done in time." Second, there is the formulation and systematic exposition of the ideal of ascetic contemplation which gives such a distinctive mark to the writings of the Victorine school as represented by Hugh and his disciple Richard of St. Victor. Hugh's sensitivity to the essentially historical nature of the Christian religion set him apart from contemporary masters teaching in the schools of Paris and Laon, where logic and reason as opposed to a sense of the historical nature of Christianity were emerging supreme in the conceptualization and exposition of the truth of Christian doctrine. In exegesis Hugh insisted upon the role of history as a "foundation" for all worthwhile Biblical interpretation, while in the field of *divinitas* (we would say theology) Hugh took history as the framework for the exposition of theological *quaestiones* in *De sacramentis christianae fidei*, the first of the medieval *summae*. The Victorine conception of the contemplative life, particularly systematization of its stages and incorporation of elements from the mystical theology of Dionysius the pseudo-Areopagite, marked a new departure in the mystical literature of Western Christendom. The Victorine program was of fundamental importance in the history of later Christian mysticism, especially through the influence of Hugh and Richard upon the early Franciscan movement and above all upon one of St. Francis' most brilliant sons, St. Bonaventure.

To say that history and contemplation are distinctive unifying themes within the Victorine synthesis is not sufficient. History and contemplation are themselves brought into close correlation, one might even say union, in Hugh's thought. On the level of literary proximity of themes, M.-D. Chenu has noted that some of Hugh's most important and penetrating comments on history and its significance are found in mystical *opusculae*, especially *De arca Noe morali*.[1] The appearance of a concern with history in a treatise on the contemplative life is not incidental. It is characteristic of the basic orientation of Hugh's thought. For the Victorine canon, fulfillment of the mystic's desire, which finds fruition in the restoration of the effaced *imago Dei* and ultimately in the celestial *visio Dei*, is rooted fundamentally and necessarily in the phenomenon of salvation history, centered on the Incarnation of the Word and extending through time from the Creation of the world to the Consummation of all things in the Last Day. Given the actual situation of man's present existence, qualified by the fact of sin and its fruits, it is only through history that man can begin to overcome the temporality, finitude, instability, and death-ward movement of life. As the result of this conviction, Hugh's theology unites in an intimate manner that which is most inward, the renewal of the *imago Dei* at the innermost core of the human person, and that which is preeminently outer, namely the succession of deeds done in time (*ordo rerum gestarum*) which comprises the divine "work of restoration."

The profoundly interior and individual experience of the contemplative life as envisioned by Hugh of St. Victor was pursued and nurtured in the climate of the particular corporate style of life which characterized the community of Canons Regular at the Abbey of St. Victor near Paris. The climate of St. Victor was marked by a firm commitment to intellectual discipline, devotion to the regularity of liturgical celebration, and dedication to the spiritual quest. Jean Châtillon has characterized the Victorine atmosphere as notable above all for a profound love of Scripture and tradition, joined with an extraordinary intellectual curiosity and an equally ardent desire to place the many facets of human knowledge at the service of the Christian faith and the knowledge of God.[2] To this perceptive judgment must be added the element of liturgical regularity and homiletic practice which shaped the rhythm and vision of life at St. Victor with an equal force:

> The regulation of the daily life applies the great principles of common life, charity, and equality. The canonical hours and the cele-

1. *Théologie au douzième siècle* ("Etudes de philosophie médiévale," Vol. XLV; Paris, 1957), p. 68 n. 1.
2. "De Guillaume de Champeaux à Thomas Gallus: Chronique d'histoire littéraire et doctrinale de l'école de Saint-Victor," *RMAL*, VIII (1952), 139–162, esp. 146. On the history of the Abbey, cf. F. Bonnard, *Histoire de l'Abbaye royale et de l'ordre des chanoines réguliers de St-Victor de Paris*, 2 vols. (Paris, 1905–7)

bration of the eucharist mark the rhythm of each day. The religious feasts and anniversaries so cherished by the Victorines mark out the course of the year: such as those of Sts. Augustine and Gregory. Men preached during these liturgical solemnities. They preached frequently at St. Victor, and we have numerous manuscripts to show it.[3]

The works of Hugh of St. Victor reflect the Victorine climate: open to the currents of intellectual life stirring in the Parisian schools yet maintaining steadfast fidelity to the ancient traditions of *lectio divina* and monastic spirituality.

The life of contemplative asceticism was thus nurtured in a community oriented toward the recollection and celebration of the work of restoration in a regular round of liturgical observance. Victorine spirituality is set, as Châtillon has observed, within the church—within the church conceived as a mystery rather than an object, as a dynamic rather than static phenomenon, as an economy of action rather than an institution of juridical structure. Victorine spirituality is ecclesiological and liturgical, and in turn, Victorine ecclesiology turns out to be a spirituality.[4] However, Châtillon's observation needs expansion. The Victorine conception of the church includes a dynamism and "economy" (*dispensatio*) extending *in time*. Victorine ecclesiology and Victorine spirituality are oriented toward a positive appreciation of the work of restoration carried out in history. History, eschatology, and contemplation fuse in the Victorine vision.

It is the purpose of this essay to explore the basis for this correlation of history and contemplation in the thought of Hugh of St. Victor.[5]

3. G. Dumeige, *Richard de Saint-Victor et l'idée chrétienne d l'amour* (Paris, 19152), p. 19.

4. J. Châtillon, "Une ecclésiologie médiévale: l'Idée de l'Eglise dans le théologie de l'école de Saint-Victor au XIIe siècle," *Irénikon*, XXII (1949), 113, 115, 410f.

5. For the most recent study of Hugh's thought, see R. Baron, *Science et sagesse chez Hugues de Saint-Victor* (Paris, 1957) and *Etudes sur Hugues de Saint-Victor* (Bruges, 1963). Hugh's commentary on Dionysius' *Celestial Hierarchies* has been studied by R. Roques, "Connaissance de Dieu et théologie symbolique d'après l' 'In Hierarchiam coelestem sancti Dionysii' de Hugues de Saint-Victor" in *Structures Théologiques de la Gnose à Richard de Saint-Victor: Essais et analyses critiques* (Paris, 1962), pp. 294–364. The various studies by H. Weisweiler remain invaluable, esp. "Die Arbeitsmethode Hugos von St. Viktor. Ein Beitrag zum Entstehen seines Hauptwerkes De sacramentis," *Scholastik*, XXXV (1949), 59–87, 232–267; "Die Ps.-Dionysiuskommentare 'In Coelestem Hierarchiam' des Skotus Eriugena und Hugo von St. Viktor," *RTAM*, XIX (1952), 26–42; "Sacramentum fidei. Augustinische und ps.-dionysiche Gedanken in der Glaubenauffassung Hugos von St. Viktor," in *Theologie in Geschichte und Gegenwart* (Schmaus-Festschrift), ed. J. Auer and H. Volk (München, 1957), pp. 433–456; "Sakrament als Symbol und Teilhabe. Der Einfluss des Ps.-Dionysius auf die allgemeine Sakramentenlehre Hugos von St. Viktor," *Scholastik*, XXVII (1952), 321–343; and *Die Wirksamkeit der Sakramente nach Hugo von*

The study will focus primarily on two treatises, *De arca Noe morali* and *De arca Noe mystica*.[6] These two treatises, written between 1125 and 1129/30 and therefore early in his career,[7] use the figure of the Ark of Noah floating upon the chaotic waters of the flood as the focus for an extended meditation on the nature of time and history and on the manner of man's restoration, the latter conceived in terms of a life of contemplative asceticism. Before turning to these treatises specifically, we shall consider Hugh's conception of history as represented by his hermeneutic and *De sacramentis christianae fidei*.

Historia fundamentum est. This phrase sums up Hugh of St. Victor's attitude toward the role of history and the literal, historical sense of Scripture in biblical exegesis.[8] The metaphor came from Gregory the Great's comparison of exegesis to the building of a house. The historical sense lays the foundation; allegory erects the walls; tropology beautifies the house with an overspread of color.[9] For Gregory this sequence referred to the relation of the senses in exposition of a given

St. *Viktor* (Freiburg, 1932). Weisweiler's perspective has been continued by H.-R. Schlette, *Die Nichtigkeit der Welt*: *Der philosophische Horizont des Hugo von St. Viktor* (München, 1961) and "Die Eucharistielehre Hugos von St. Viktor," *Zeitschrift für katholische Theologie*, LXXXI (1959), 67–100 and 163–210. Fundamental for Hugh's sense of history is Chenu, *La théologie*, pp. 62–89.

6. The text of *De arca Noe morali* is in *PL* 176:617–680. An English translation will be found in *Hugh of St. Victor: Selected Spiritual Writings*, tr. a Religious of C.S.M.V., with an Introduction by Aelred Squire (London, 1962). The division of the treatise into chapters in the translation differs from that of Migne and has been adopted here. Further citations will be by the title *A. mor.* followed by book and chapter according to the tr., then the Migne reference, and finally the page of the tr., cited as C.S.M.V. The text of *De arca Noe mystica* is found in *PL* 176:681–407; cited hereafter as *A. myst.*

7. Dating established by Damien van den Eynde, *Essai sur la succession et la date des écrits de Hugues de Saint-Victor* ("Spicilegium Pontificii Athenaei Antoniani," Vol. XIII; Rome, 1960), p. 80. On matters of dating, the conclusions of van den Eynde are to be preferred to those of Baron, *Sci. et Sag.*, pp. xliii–l, and *Etudes*, pp. 69–89. The essay on authenticity in *Etudes*, pp. 31–67, is useful.

8. The basic study of Hugh's exegesis is B. Smalley, *The Study of the Bible in the Middle Ages*, 2nd ed. rev. (Oxford, 1952), esp. ch. 3. Cf. H. de Lubac, *Exégèse médiévale: Les quatre sens de l'Ecriture* ("Théologie," Vols. XLI, XLII, LIX, Paris, 1959–62), II, i, ch. 4 (partly a reply to Smalley's interpretation). Also see H. P. Pollitt, "Hugh of St. Victor as Biblical Exegete" (unpublished Ph.D. dissertation, University of Sheffield, England, 1960). There is a good section on Hugh's hermeneutic in R. Wasselynck, "L'Influence des *Moralia in Job* de S. Grégoire le Grand sur la théologie morale entre le VIIe et le XIIe siècle" (unpublished Ph.D. dissertation, Lille, Faculté de théologie, 1956).

9. See Gregory, *Mor.*, *Ep. miss.*, iii, *PL* 75:513C. Hugh's use in *Didascalicon*, IV, 2. Cf. Charles Henry Buttimer, *Hugonis de Sancto Victore Didascalicon De Studio Legendi: A Critical Text* ("The Catholic University of America. Studies in Medieval and Renaissance Latin," Vol. X; Washington, D.C., 1939), p. 4. English tr. Jerome Taylor, *The "Didascalicon" of Hugh of St. Victor* ("Columbia University. Records of Civilization Sources and Studies," No. LXIV; New York, 1961), p. 45. Hereafter cited as *Did.*, book and chapter, with ed. Buttimer by page, and tr. Taylor by page.

text. Hugh retains this meaning. But more important is a new significance he derives from the construction motif. Hugh conceives of each
of the Biblical senses—history, allegory, and tropology—as a distinct
discipline. The proper method of Bible study is a process of construction, because a series of disciplines must be mastered:

> First of all, the student of Sacred Scripture ought to look among
> history, allegory, and tropology for that order sought in the disci-
> plines—that is, he should ask which of these three precedes the oth-
> ers in the order of study.
>
> In this question it is not without value to call to mind what we
> see happen in the construction of buildings, where first the founda-
> tion is laid, then the structure is raised upon it, and finally, when
> the work is finished, the house is decorated by the laying on of
> color.[10]

In the older Gregorian sense of foundation, Hugh insists that the
interpreter must have a thorough grasp of the literal sense of individual passages of Scripture, insofar as that is possible, before he seeks
to elicit the deeper allegorical and/or tropological senses of the text.
To this end all possible resources are mobilized. The *trivium* especially aids literal exegesis.[11] To grammar, rhetoric, and dialectic Hugh
would add such resources as the acquisition of languages, historical
knowledge, and shrewd observation on the part of the good exegete.[12]

The new meaning Hugh gave to history as a foundation in exegesis
is most important for our study, and for Hugh's thought. It marks
something of a new perspective in medieval hermeneutics, for Hugh
proposed that the historical exegesis of Scripture be considered a discipline. The student of Scripture begins by reading the Biblical narrative with an intention to understand the text *as history*, as the account
of an ordered series of events. Hugh's instructions in the *Didascalicon*
are explicit:

> First you learn history and diligently commit to memory the truth
> of the deeds that have been performed, reviewing from beginning

10. *Did.*, IV, 2, Buttimer, p. 113, Taylor, p. 135. See also Hugh's discussion of *historia*
in the preface to his *Chronicon*, ed. W. M. Green, "Hugo of St. Victor: De tribus maximis
circumstantiis gestorum," *Speculum*, XVIII (1943), esp. 491, ll. 3–34.

11. *De sacr. chr. fid.*, I, prol., v and vi, *PL* 176:185AC, tr. Deferrari, pp. 5f.

12. On resources for exegesis, cf. my article "Hugh of St. Victor and the Ark of Noah
—A New Look," *Church History*, XL, no. 3 (Sept., 1971). Hugh's program, and its necessity, are also there compared with Augustine's use of classical culture in *De doct. chr.*

to end what has been done, when it has been done, where it has been done, and by whom it has been done. For these are the four things which are especially to be sought for in history—the person, the business done, the time, and the place. Nor do I think that you will be able to become perfectly sensitive to allegory unless you have first been grounded in history.[13]

The exegete is not simply being trained with an adequate knowledge of grammar and other tools which will enable him to read the text and understand the sense of the words. Something more important is going on in Hugh's program of introductory studies. The student is being taught to examine the biblical text from a particular point of view: history.

This interpretation is supported by the biblical books Hugh suggests as most useful for the study of exegesis *ad litteram*. He lists: "Genesis, Exodus, Josue, the Book of Judges, and that of Kings, and Paralipomenon; of the New Testament, first the four Gospels, then the Acts of the Apostles."[14] The list concludes with a pointed comment: "these eleven seem to me to have more to do with history than do the others . . . ." The order in which the books are to be read is also significant, for Hugh declares that "the same order of (biblical) books is not to be kept in historical and allegorical study. History follows the order of time; to allegory belongs more the order of knowledge, . . ."[15] For the student of literal exegesis, Hugh consciously selected those books having the most to do with the unfolding history of the people of the Old Testament, the life of Christ, and the development of the early church. It is possible, Hugh notes, to take the meaning of "history" more broadly and construe it to mean "not only the recounting of actual deeds but also the first meaning of any narrative which uses words according to their proper nature."[16] In this sense all Scripture belongs to the study of history. The definition in *De sacramentis christianae fidei* synthesizes the narrative and literal aspects of the "historical" sense of Scripture: "History is the narration of deeds done, expressed by the first signification of the letter."[17] Nevertheless,

---

13. VI, 3, Buttimer, pp. 113f., Taylor, pp. 135f.
14. Ibid., Buttimer, pp. 116f., Taylor, pp. 138f.
15. Ibid., 6, Buttimer, p. 123, Taylor, p. 145.
16. Cf. n. 14, above.
17. *De sacr. chr. fid.*, I, prol., iv, *PL* 176:184D, tr. Deferrari, p. 5.

the sense of historical narrative and order remains the basic perspective for the discipline of *historia*. The Bible itself is primarily historical:

> as we run through the series of books in the Old Testament and the New, we see that the collection is devoted almost entirely to the state of this present life and to deeds done in time . . . .[18]

The foundation of history must be firmly laid, and that foundation consists of a narrative or series of events (*narratio* or *series rerum gestarum*).[19]

Hugh's sharp sensitivity to the historical dimension of the Christian faith emerges also in his doctrinal writings. In *De sacramentis christianae fidei* the sequence of topics under which theological *quaestiones* are grouped follows broadly the unfolding of divine initiatives in the course of biblical history rather than a strictly logical plan of grouping. Hugh begins with the work of creation and continues with chapters on the Trinity, God, the angels, man's creation, fall, and restoration, the institution of the sacraments, faith, the sacraments of the natural law, and the sacraments of the written law. The second book of *De sacramentis* considers the Incarnation of the Word, the church, the ecclesiastical hierarchy, sacraments and sacramentals, simony, vices and virtues, and concludes with a consideration of eschatological fulfillment and judgment. Thus *divinitas* (theology) is grounded in the Biblical text by more than the fact that it draws upon Scripture for insights. The very "economy" or dispensation of sacred history becomes the integrating structural principle of order in the exposition of the truth of the Christian religion.[20]

The role of history in the structure of *De sacramentis* is stated clearly by Hugh:

> And if we inquire into this carefully in all these works [of restoration] according to the sequence of time and the succession of generations, and the dispensations of precepts, we declare with confidence that we shall have touched upon the whole sum of Divine

---

18. *Did.*, IV, 1, Buttimer, p. 70, Taylor, p. 102.

19. See the excellent remarks by Chenu, *La théologie*, pp. 64ff.

20. On various approaches to the structure of theological method, see Y. M.-J. Congar, "Le Moment 'economique' et le moment 'ontologique' dans la sacra doctrina (révélation, théologie, somme théologique)," in *Mélanges offerts à M.-D. Chenu* ("Bibliothèque Thomiste," Vol. XXXVII; Paris, 1967), pp. 135–187, esp. 159ff.

Scriptures. But we must begin with the foundation of our first parents, and we must develop the story gradually as we proceed always to those works which follow in order.[21]

Sequence of time; succession of generations; dispensation of precepts; follow in order: all of these are expressions reflecting Hugh's understanding of history as an economy or dispensation of divine initiatives in time. History is not only the foundation of exegesis, but of the building up of doctrine as well. *De sacramentis* is "that foundation, so to speak, of the knowledge of faith, . . ."[22] The order and "shape," as it were, of the foundation are determined by history.

In the position taken on individual *quaestiones* Hugh's sense of history is clear. He rejects the Augustinian interpretation of the six days of creation in Genesis I. Hugh insists rather cautiously to be sure that creation took place over a period of time, and that "it does not seem at all derogatory to the omnipotence of the Creator, if He is said to have brought His work to completion through intervals of time, . . ."[23] The sequence of events is of benefit, interest, and example for man. The movable precepts of the written law are also viewed from an historical perspective: "according to dispensation they were added to the natural commands for the time either for exercise or for meaning."[24] One of the most telling examples is Hugh's discussion of the question "Whether faith was changed according to the changes of time." Hugh concludes that faith has been constant in that it has always been faith in the God who is Creator and Redeemer. Faith has grown and changed, however, with respect to the cognition of faith, that is with respect to knowledge of the manner of man's redemption. Before the law, redemption was hoped for. Under the law a Redeemer was promised, but whether God, angel, or man was unknown. Now, under grace, the faithful are enlightened with knowledge of the Redeemer. Just as different people have different capacities for cognition in faith, so, Hugh insists, "let us not doubt that from the beginning through the succession of the times faith has grown in the faithful themselves by certain increases."[25] Finally we have Hugh's theology of the sacra-

21. I, i, 29, *PL* 176:204C, tr. Deferrari, p. 27.

22. I, prol., "why he has changed the reading," *PL* 176:183/184, tr. Deferrari, p. 3.

23. Ibid., i, 3, col. 188BC, pp. 8f. Cf. ibid., ch. 2, col. 187C–188B, p. 8.

24. *De sacr. chr. fid.*, I, xii, 23, *PL* 176:360C, tr. Deferrari, p. 201. In the Migne text, the ch. is 9, not 23.

25. Ibid., x, 6, *PL* 176:339B, tr. Deferrari, p. 177. Much of this ch. is from a letter to

ments. Each historical period under the natural law, the written law, and grace has had its sacraments which effectively related the believers to God. With the passing of time and the transition from one age to the next the sacraments of the previous age lose their efficacy. But in their own time they were effective; they were not *merely* symbols of the true sacraments to come in the time of grace.[26]

In each of the foregoing examples an historical perspective is obvious. Hugh understands the divine economy of salvation to be a matter of change and development in time. The church has existed from the foundation of the world; yet it has not existed in one and the same form, nor with the same sacraments, nor with the same cognition of faith. Yet it has the same Lord. There is an inherent dynamism in the church when seen as the community of believers existing through all ages. It is this dynamic, communal nature of the church set in history and held in tension between Creation and the eschatological denouement of history which gives Hugh's theology and spirituality much of their distinctive character.

The sense of history which Hugh shows in his writings was characteristic of a particular segment of twelfth-century society: monks and canons regular. History had no place in the liberal arts and consequently in the later university curriculum. The classical *historiae* were read for moral *exempla* in connection with grammar and rhetoric. Hugh, reflecting traditional models, placed the *historiae* among the "appendages" to the arts linking prose composition, verse, fables, and histories.[27] The masters in the schools tended to move away from the practice of integral biblical reading in *lectio divina* with its historical frame to a program oriented around collections of *quaestiones* covering theological topics in a systematic, objective manner. Abelard's rational and anthropocentric framework for a doctrinal treatise —*fides, caritas,* and *sacramentum*—broke decisively with any notion of an historical economy for *divinitas*. Meanwhile, the dialecticians, Abelard and Peter Lombard included, were so defining the content of

---

Hugh from St. Bernard. On the distinction between cognition and affection in faith, cf. ibid., 3 and 4, cols. 331B–333D, pp. 169–171.

26. Ibid., I, xi, 1, *PL* 176:343BC, tr. Deferrari, p. 182: "If anyone, therefore, should deny that prior sacraments had the effect of sanctification, he would not seem to me to think rightly." In the same ch. Hugh points out that they are signs and figures of the later sacraments under grace.

27. *Did.*, II, 29; III, 3 and 4, Buttimer, pp. 45f. and 52–55, Taylor, pp. 80 and 86f.

faith and thus theological reflection that all sense of historical development was excluded. To be logically consistent, statements of faith must be constant through the ages, a position counter to that embraced by Hugh, as we have seen. For the dialecticians the tense of the verb was incidental, not essential.[28]

Several reasons for the birth of historical consciousness in monastic and canonical *milieux* have been advanced. The involvement of monks and canons in the political life of the day has been cited as one contributing factor.[29] Anselm of Havelberg and Otto of Freising belonged to the "unusual category of religious-men-of-politics" who were consciously attempting to relate the *vita activa* of political men and the *vita contemplativa* of the monastic life.[30] Anselm, a canon regular, was engaged in diplomatic activity which brought him into contact with the Eastern church. The resulting appreciation of a divergent tradition encouraged him to reflect upon the historical development of the church and her teaching. With Anselm we see a positive appreciation of mutations in structure and doctrine in the age of grace; sacred history is being extended from the Old Testament, through the New, and into the present age.[31] Otto of Freising, like Anselm, was involved in the movement of monastic reform which swept Europe in the twelfth century. He viewed the panorama of mankind's history from Creation to Consummation through the Augustinian "spectacles" of the Two Cities.[32] Both men, deeply involved in the historical events of their own day, viewed the sweep of history in biblical, eschatological categories.

Another suggestion for the origin of monastic concern for history lies close at hand in the life of the monastery and close to the heart of many a monk. R. W. Southern suggests that the rise of history-writing on the part of monastics was motivated by a desire to glorify the local community by recording its past and by the very practical community

---

28. For the various developments, cf. Smalley, *Study of the Bible*, pp. 73ff.; Chenu, *La théologie*, pp. 65ff., 93ff., and *Toward Understanding Saint Thomas*, tr. with authorized corr. and bibl. add. A.-M. Landry and D. Hughes (Chicago, 1964), pp. 302–304; Baron, *Sci. et Sag.*, pp. 235f.; and J. de Ghellinck, *Le mouvement théologique de XIIe siècle*, 2nd ed., aug. (Bruges, 1948), pp. 161ff.

29. Chenu, *La théologie*, pp. 63f.

30. Spörl, J., *Grundformen hochmittelalterlicher Geschichtsanschauung* (München, 1935), pp. 21ff.

31. Chenu, *La théologie*, p. 70.

32. Cf. Spörl, *Grundformen*, pp. 32–50, and Ray C. Petry, "Three Medieval Chroniclers: Monastic Historiography and Biblical Eschatology in Hugh of St. Victor, Otto of Freising, and Ordericus Vitalis," *Church History*, XXXIV (1965), 282–293.

need to preserve the records of the monastery, thus securing monastic rights in feudal courts and enhancing the reputation of the community in the eyes of men.[33]

Both of these suggestions have merit and find support in the monastic life of the eleventh and twelfth centuries. There is, however, another aspect of monastic and canonical communal life which provided not only an impetus for historical writings, but also furnished a framework within which history might be interpreted. This is daily participation in the liturgy as Dom Leclercq has pointed out.[34] For monastic writers the act of recording history, like the chanting of the liturgy, is a vital means of engaging in the praise of God for his mighty works.[35] "Ordericus Vitalis, . . . says several times that one must 'sing' history like a hymn in honor of Him who created the world and governs it with justice."[36] Hugh of St. Victor was in hearty agreement with the Benedictine historian at Saint Evroul.

It is true that the liturgy enveloped the monk in a world rich in symbols which pointed to transcendent spiritual realities.[37] Abbot Suger's narrative of the dedication of the new church of the Abbey of St. Denis, during which he suddenly saw in the earthly celebration of the Eucharist the reflection of the celestial *leiturgia*, is indicative of such a frame of mind. The same may be said of the whole of Suger's building activities at St. Denis.[38]

The liturgy has another aspect, however. The structure of the yearly cycle of the liturgy is a continual recapitulation of the history of the people of God, Hebrews and Gentiles both, moving through the vicissitudes of this life toward their ultimate eschatological destiny. The Lenten *agon* placed the recapitulation of the five ages of history from

33. *The Making of the Middle Ages* (New Haven, Conn., 1953), p. 192. J. Leclercq, *The Love of Learning and the Desire for God*, tr. C. Misrahi (New York, 1961), p. 197, agrees that this is one factor among several.

34. Ibid., pp. 159f.

35. On the liturgy as praise, cf. U. Berliere, *L'ascese bénédictine des origines à la fin du XIIe siècle* (Paris, 1927), pp. 151, 168.

36. Leclercq, *The Love of Learning*, p. 159. On Ordericus, cf. Petry, "Three Medieval Chroniclers," pp. 295ff., and H. Wolter, *Ordericus Vitalis: ein Beitrag zur kluniazensischen Geschichtschreibung* (Wiesbaden, 1955).

37. See Chenu, *La théologie*, p. 347.

38. See *Libellus alter de consecratione ecclesiae sancti Dionysii*, in *Abbot Suger on the Abbey Church of St.-Denis and its Art Treasures*, ed., tr., and annot. E. Panofsky (Princeton, N.J., 1946), pp. 119–121. On Suger's building program and the Dionysian light metaphysic which informed his attitude, cf. O. von Simson, *The Gothic Cathedral: Origins of Gothic Architecture and the Medieval Concept of Order*, 2nd ed. rev. (New York, 1962), chs. III and IV, esp. pp. 102ff.

Creation to the Incarnation before the brethren in dramatic form.[39] Biblical lessons accompanied by selections from the commentaries and writings of the great doctors of the church underscored the significance of Hebrew history and elucidated the foreshadowing of the life and history of the church in the history of the earlier people. Throughout the liturgical year the continuing history of the church in the sixth age, the age of grace, was recounted in the celebrations of the feast days of the saints.

Hearing the lives of the saints read in the context of the liturgy the individual was again plunged into the history of God's people and impelled to reflect not only upon the *magnalia Dei* recorded in the Bible, but also on God's active providence visible in the present age. Hagiography was overly credulous and burdened with legendary material. Nevertheless, it possessed an essential historical core and performed a crucial historical function within the structure of the liturgy.[40]

In the *Didascalicon* Hugh clearly connected the study of the Bible *ad historiam* with the liturgical praise of God. "You have in history the means through which to admire God's deeds . . . ."[41] Perusing the pages of Holy Writ the reader sees the way in which God has guided his people by patriarchs, judges, and kings through Exodus, prosperity, the Exile and return, how he sent his Son to restore mankind, and what the fruition of history will be in the Last Judgment. Such a reading of history concludes: "See how, from the time when the world began until the end of the ages, the mercies of God do not slacken."[42]

In the third and fourth books of *De vanitate mundi* the connection between a sense of history and a liturgical frame of reference is more pronounced. Recounting the *processus saeculi* through the stages of biblical history, culminating in the Incarnation of the Word and the sending of the twelve apostles, the narrator (*ratio*) repeatedly moves his partner in the dialogue (*anima*) to the praise of what God has done in history:

A. Greatly do I admire, and I am amazed (*Valde admiror, et stupeo*) within myself when I take notice to consider the divine disposition of passing things . . . .[43]

39. See O. B. Hardison, *Christian Rite and Christian Drama in the Middle Ages* (Baltimore, Md., 1965), pp. 8off. On the evolution of the structure of the liturgical cycle, cf. P. Batiffol, *History of the Roman Breviary*, tr. A. M. Y. Baylay, 3rd ed. (London, 1912).
40. See the judicious remarks by Leclercq, *The Love of Learning*, pp. 164–169.
41. VI, 3, Buttimer, p. 116, Taylor, p. 138.   42. Ibid., Buttimer, p. 117, Taylor, p. 139.
43. *De vanitate mundi*, III, *PL* 176:724D–725A.

A. How very great and amazing (*stupenda*) are the works of God in the universe, . . .[44]

In a striking linguistic parallel Baldwin of Ford describes his attitude in the presence of the Eucharist with words echoing Hugh: *stupor et admiratio*.[45] What Baldwin experienced in the presence of the sacrament *par excellence* was the same response that Hugh felt in the presence of history. History was, for our Victorine canon, equally sacramental. God has revealed himself in the Incarnation of the Word and in his sacraments which preceeded and follow him from Creation to Consummation. The response of one who considers this properly can only be one of praise, meditation, and wonder. Such is the response of liturgical piety.

In *De arca Noe morali* the significance of history and the work of restoration are firmly grounded in Hugh's theological position, especially in his epistemology and anthropology. Any appreciation of these aspects of his systematic thought must be based upon a proper perception of the Hugonian doctrine of the created perfection of man and the disastrous effects of the Fall upon man's noetic and volitional capabilities. Only from this perspective can the Victorine emphasis upon the work of restoration in its historical aspect be seen in its true light.

In the perfection of creation man experienced within himself the presence of his Creator by contemplation. Created *ad imaginem Dei* man "saw" in the image, as in a mirror, the reflected presence of God within him:

Man was created in the image and likeness of his Maker . . . . For the heart of man was so created that from it, as from His mirror, the divine wisdom should be reflected back and that which of itself could not be seen should in His image be made visible.

Great indeed was the honour of man, thus to bear God's image, always to see in himself the face of God, and through contemplation to have Him ever present.[46]

The experience of God possessed by the first man was neither an experience of the senses, nor a conclusion reached by reason over a

44. Ibid., 726B.

45. See *De sacram. alt., PL* 204:655 and 685, and the comments by Leclercq, *The Love of Learning*, p. 228.

46. *A. mor.*, IV, 6, *PL* 176:651D–652A, C.S.M.V., p. 102. Cf. *De sacr. chr. fid.*, I, vi, 14, *PL* 176:271D, tr. Deferrari, p. 103: ". . . through the presence of contemplation He was then perceived more manifestly by the knowing."

span of time spent in observation and reflection. Reason has its proper mode of knowing God, particularly through reflection upon the work of creation, but the experience being considered here is different. It was immediate and inward, with no possibility of doubt. Furthermore it was an integral part of the first man's created being, his natural state. As H. Köster has pointed out, it is impossible to understand Hugh's doctrine of the *visio Dei* from the standpoint of a dialectic of nature/supernature or nature/grace as these categories are used in Thomistic thought. From the Hugonian point of view contemplative knowledge of God is *natural*; it is the loss of this vision which is *un*natural.[47] As M. -D. Chenu has pointed out for the twelfth century in general, the function of grace was conceived as a restoration of nature. In short, grace had the effect of "re-naturing."[48] This means that the works of restoration are precisely what the name implies: the divine activity of restoring to man that which he has lost through sin. And, as part of man's natural endowment must be included the primal contemplative experience. Man is by his created nature a contemplative.

Hugh confesses the difficulty of giving a positive description of this contemplation enjoyed by the first man. Finally, he was content to insist that the knowledge of God possessed in primal contemplation was more than the knowledge men now have through faith (for God is "absent") and less than the future knowledge of God enjoyed by the saints in the celestial beatific vision.[49] By excluding two polar terms, Hugh managed to effect a sort of *via negativa* and thus defined a "region of experience" in which the primal contemplative experience might be located, despite the difficulty of adequately describing it.

The idea of progress and temporal change was inherent in the Victorine concept of this primal knowledge of God. Like faith which has also increased with the passing of time for fallen man, so also was the case for man in creation. His immediate, inward knowledge of God was perfect only in the sense of initial perfection. Increased knowledge of God with the passing of time was to be expected. "If the obedience of man had persisted, very much would have been added to that same knowledge through subsequent revelation."[50]

47. H. Köster, *Die Heilslehre des Hugo von St. Viktor: Grundlagen und Grundzüge* (Emsdetten, 1940), p. 42; also Schlette, *Die Nichtigkeit*, pp. 40f. "Natural" is used here in the first of three senses distinguished in *A. myst.*, V, *PL* 176:689A: "That integral and uncorrupted good in which the first man was created."

48. *La théologie*, p. 504, with refs.

49. *De sacr. chr. fid.*, I, vi, 14, *PL* 176:271CD, tr. Deferrari, p. 103.

50. Ibid., 271D.

Along with an inward sense of the divine presence man also was capable of perceiving the power, wisdom, and goodness of the triune God as manifest in the created universe. In the beginning the fabric of the universe was like a "book" or a "spoken, external word of God." Viewed rightly and understood as the symbol of a higher reality, the visible world was able to lead man to a knowledge of the invisible world of spiritual realities and God. The world was a *sacramentum*: *per visibilium ad invisibilium*. In *De tribus diebus* Hugh seeks to indicate the numerous manifestations of the trinitarian God in the world by using the book metaphor:

> The universe of the sensible world is like a book written by the finger of God, i.e. created by divine power. Individual creatures are like figures intended to manifest the wisdom of the invisible God; not figures invented by the consent of humans but instituted by the divine will.[51]

In the moral treatise on the Ark Hugh related the world as word and book to two other words and books in order to explore the relationship between God, man, and the world and between that which is unchanging and that which always changes.[52] The first book is the book written by man and made by human craftmanship. They last but a short time being made of the skins of animals or other corruptible material. The second book is the world which God has created out of nothing. It is marked by mutability, but it does not cease to exist. The third book is the Wisdom of God, the Word of God, the second Person of the Trinity. In contrast to the external, impermanent world of temporal reality, this book, or word, is immutable and eternal and is "internal" to God.

The fundamental role of the contemplative experience, complimented by the external perception of the divine in the fabric of the universe, emerges in several passages in *De arca Noe morali*. By means of this experience man had the knowledge of God which inspired love

51. Ch. III, *PL* 176:814B. The universe as a symbol is a major theme of Hugh's commentary on Dionysius' *Celestial Hierarchies*, cf. *PL* 175:1118CD: "The creature reveals the artisan, and the beauty of the admirable works commends the splendor of the author. . . . many goods were made by God, in order to disclose the one supreme good; and in a similar fashion many beautiful things were made and they represent (*demonstro*) the image of the one supreme beauty." Here Hugh moves within the bounds of the idea of "participation" which formed so prominent a feature of the Dionysian world view. Cf. Weisweiler, "Sakrament und Teilhabe."

52. II, 12–13, *PL* 176:643B–646A, C.S.M.V., pp. 87–92; cf. *De sacr. chr. fid.*, I, iii, 20 and vi, 5, *PL* 176:225AB and 267B–268B, tr. Deferrari, pp. 50, 97.

of God in his heart. From this adherence of love came the stability of life which the first man enjoyed and for which man searches now.

> The sight of Him [God] enlightened his mind with knowledge, and made him to rise up and to lie down with love.[53]

> The first man, then, was made in such way that, if he had not sinned, the power of contemplation would have kept him always in his Maker's presence. By always seeing Him he would thus have loved Him, by always loving Him he would always have cleaved to Him, . . . The human heart [would have] kept its stability in cleaving to divine love and remained one in the love of the One, . . .[54]

With the Fall and its effects man no longer has either knowledge or love of God. His life is now marked by their antitheses: ignorance and concupiscence, or blindness and instability. The creature created in the image of God, he who once beheld his Maker inwardly with an inner eye and heard Him with an inner ear, was no longer sensitive to the inward, spiritual dimension of life.[55] Having lost his spiritual senses man has also lost the stability of his created being, for he no longer adheres to God in love, nor orders through reason the desires of the body to their proper end. In the Augustinian sense of the Socratic injunction "know thyself" man no longer knows the proper relation of the self to either God or the world. Rather than the world serving his needs, man finds that he has become a slave, as it were, to the world.

> But after he was cast out from before God's face because of his transgression, he became blind and unstable, blind through mental ignorance and unstable through fleshly concupiscence . . . . Since men were thus subject to the darkness of ignorance and unaware of the existence of any other invisible good things, it was inevitable that they should lose control of themselves through the lust for earthly things which can be seen.[56]

53. *A. mor.*, IV, 10, *PL* 176:671A, C.S.M.V., p. 135.
54. Ibid., I, 2, cols. 619/620, p. 46; similar passage, ibid., IV, 10, col. 674AB, p. 136f.
55. "Before he sinned the first man had no need for God to speak to him outwardly, for he possessed an ear within his heart by which he could hear God's voice after a spiritual manner. But when he opened his outward ear to listen to the serpent's guile, he closed his inward to the voice of God." Ibid., 9, col. 669A, p. 132.
56. Ibid., 10, col. 671A, p. 135.

God alone being immutable and eternal, He only could be the source of unending joy and perfect fulfillment for man. By the adhesion of love man had participated in the goodness and beatitude of God, sharing also in his stability. Cast out from the vision of the invisible, able only to comprehend the visible world, man turned to the objects within his view in search of fulfillment for his desires. In so doing, the human heart, once unified in the love of God, the supreme Good, became divided through love of a multiplicity of objects:

> The human heart . . . was as it were divided into as many channels as there were objects that it craved, once it had begun to flow in different directions through earthly longings.[57]

The material world, impermanent and insufficient in itself to serve as the final good of man, failed man in his search for satisfaction:

> Failing to find what it longs for in those things which it has, its desire is always reaching out in pursuit of the unattainable; and so it never has rest. Therefore, from movement without stability is born toil without rest, travel without arrival; . . .[58]

In a passage from *De vanitate mundi*, a work which repeats many of the themes of the Ark treatises, Hugh broke forth in a lament which eloquently expressed his profound horror of time and the effect of total dissolution which the flux and impermanence of time has upon human life and the meaning of existence.

> R. It is a lengthy business to show the vanity of this world by going through particular cases. You do, however, realize that none of all the things that you are looking at abides. They all pass, and return to the place whence they arose. Just as they all have a beginning, so do they also have an end, . . . they are all alike passing away and going towards one place. O mighty flood, whither are you being borne away. . . . O stream that fails not, O water course never still, O whirlpool never sated! Whatever is subject to birth, whatever involves the debt of mortality, that does insatiable death gulp down. It never ceases to consume the one and ensnare the other, or to engulf them both. The present is always passing on, the future always following; and, since the continuity is unbroken, there is a belief that this is the permanent condition of things.[59]

57. Ibid., I, 2, cols. 619/620, pp. 46f.
58. Ibid., p. 47.   59. II, *PL* 176:711AC, C.S.M.V., p. 171.

The agony and despair of this passage have the sweep of the torrential waters of a flood. This is the world of which fallen man, if he be perceptive, is aware. What hope can be found within it? Before the Fall, time moved toward a *telos* which was the translation of each man to the *visio Dei*. With the rupture of this state by sin, man no longer experiences time as a succession of events moving toward a goal, apart from the work of restoration. Otherwise, time has become a flux. The seasons were ordered to renew and revive the world with offspring to provide unending sustenance by "renewing the old, re-establishing the fallen, and restoring the worn." [60] Now the passage of the seasons and years only brings the gnawing question:

> Where are our fathers? Where are those rich and mighty men . . . .
> Where, when all is said and done, are all those of whose friendship
> and intimacy we used to feel so sure? [61]

Such a heightened sense of the mutability of the material, temporal world as reflected in *De vanitate mundi* stood at the base of Hugh's thought in the Ark treatises: "Let us contemplate the vast and horrible confusion that prevails in that world down there, and the infinite distraction in the minds of men." Contrasted to this confusion and distraction is the "perpetual, unshakable stability" of God. [62]

Hugh saw the multiple and chaotic nature of man's disordered desires and the flux of time mirrored in the waters of the flood, upon which the Ark of Noah rode. The waters reflect the endless struggle and the futility of life lived in time under the conditions of the Fall. Man perceives life as mutable, passing away, never fulfilled, divided, and ultimately meaningless. This is the flood from which the Ark delivers man.

The flood has two aspects, one external, the other internal to man. Externally the flood symbolizes the flux of time, the ebb and flow of events, moving on endlessly without purpose in an ultimate sense. [63] Ultimately this perception of external disorder in the world is grounded in a disorder within man. This is the second reference of the flood symbol, for it points to the internal confusion and chaos gen-

60. *De arrha animae*, ed. Müller, p. 7, tr. Herbert, p. 17.
61. *De vanitate mundi*, II, *PL* 176:712B, C.S.M.V., p. 172.
62. *A. mor.*, IV, 4, *PL* 176:666B, C.S.M.V., p. 126.
63. This evaluation of the world always stands in tension with the Hugonian principle that the world as created and in itself can be qualified only as good.

erated by the divided desires of man as he seeks fulfillment in the present age.[64]

The Victorine valorization of the symbolic content of the flood waters ran counter to the traditional interpretation in medieval exegesis. For earlier exegetes generally, the flood had been a type for Christian baptism. The waters were waters of destruction, to be sure, but they destroyed evil in order to prepare for the rebirth of good. In the days of Noah the waters of the flood destroyed the evil humanity of that day, preserving only Noah and his family, and purified the world. So in the time of grace the sacrament of baptism, prefigured by the flood, cleanses man of sin.[65]

This destructive yet cleansing power of the waters of the flood was not present in the treatises on the Ark of Noah. Hugh viewed the flood totally under the aspects of destruction and chaos. There was no possibility of renewal or rebirth in the waters. The flood leads only to death and destruction. Here, in Hugh's use, we see a typological element "broken." But it was broken to be filled with a new content. The reference was shifted from sacramental typology to psychological and "existential" realities. Thus the flood became the vehicle for a profound and agonized sensitivity to the disorder which Hugh perceived in man and in man's relationship to the world and to God.

We have come to the central question of the Ark treatises: How is it possible for man to move from his present state of instability to some sort of stability? This was the question with which the moral treatise on the Ark opened. Ultimately the question and the answer come out in terms of time and eternity. How can that which is mutable and temporal relate to that which is immutable and eternal? Such had been the central metaphysical problem for Augustine; so it was also for Hugh. The Victorine canon, like his mentor the Bishop of Hippo, re-

64. See, e.g. *A. mor.*, IV, 12, *PL* 176:673A, C.S.M.V., pp. 138f.: "The desire of this world in the heart of man is as it were the waters of the flood, . . ." Also, ibid., 16, col. 675B, p. 143: "Let a man return to his own heart, and he will find there a stormy ocean lashed by the fierce billows of overwhelming passions and desires, . . . For there is this flood in every man, . . ."

65. For the traditional interpretation, cf. J. Danielou, *From Shadows to Reality: Studies in the Biblical Typology of the Fathers* (London, 1960). For an example in the tradition, see Bede, *Hexameron*, *PL* 91:94D and 97D. He also saw a prefiguring of the temptations of this life in the tumult of the flood. The symbolism of water as an element of destruction and regeneration has been presented in M. Eliade, *Patterns in Comparative Religion* (Cleveland, 1953), ch. V, esp. pp. 210ff., and *The Sacred and the Profane* (New York, 1961), pp. 129–132.

solved the dilemma within the dialectical structure of the two loves of man—or rather the one love which man may direct toward either of two objects: the world or God. The theme was *amor Dei / amor mundi.* And as the object of love is, so is the lover. To love that which is material, temporal, and finite is to partake of these qualities. To love God is to begin to partake of the immutability, unity, and peace of God:

> Let us then see what we can do to attain the love of God, for he will integrate our hearts, he will restore our peace and give us ceaseless joy.[66]

In a later opuscule on the subject of love Hugh summed up this polar theme of love with the recognition that it is one love which seeks either of two objects:

> A single spring of love, welling up within us, pours itself out in two streams. The one is the love of the world, cupidity; the other is the love of God, charity. The heart of man is in fact the ground from which, when inclination guides it towards outward things, there breaks that which we call cupidity; although, when its desire moves it towards that which is within its name is charity.
>
> There are then, two streams that issue from the fount of love, cupidity and charity . . . . So all that is good derives from it and from it every evil comes.[67]

The final tragedy of the Fall is that man is turned totally "outward." He is left with the material world, and even this world, intended in the wisdom of creation to serve man's needs and to function as a sacrament of spiritual reality, has ceased to fulfill its created purpose. The world has become an end, no longer is it a means, and all due to man's disorder.

Love and knowledge are closely linked in Hugh's theology of creation and redemption, but finally love achieves a certain primacy. In this sense, Hugh is at one with his Cistercian contemporaries in their concern with love and its dimensions. For Hugh love is, in the language of *De laude caritatis*, the road of God to man and the road of man to God. In the ecstasy of contemplation love makes the final thrust, penetrating into the nuptial chamber while the intellect remains outside, as Hugh comments in book VI of his commentary on

66. *A. mor.*, I, 3, *PL* 176:620A, C.S.M.V., p. 48.
67. *De substantia dilectionis*, tr. C.S.M.V., p. 187.

Dionysius' *Celestial Hierarchies.* It is the fire of divine love which transforms man and reforms the *imago Dei* within.[68] The theme of love, particularly the idea of the fire of love, would be developed with an especial power by Richard of St. Victor.

To renew knowledge and love of God a new approach of God to man is needed, taking into account the human situation conditioned by original sin. God has approached man in a new way, through the work of restoration, deeds done in time, centered on the Incarnation of the Word. Here lies the basis of Hugh's firm commitment to history—the eternal Word of God has become the Incarnate Word:

> The Wisdom of God Himself, except he had first been known corporally, never would have been able to illumine that blind eye of the mind [*mentis acies*] to that spiritual contemplation.[69]

Hugh introduces the Ark of Noah as symbolic of man's restoration. The keel signifies the sweep of salvation history from Creation to Consummation, centered on the Incarnation. The keel is immersed in the turbulent flood waters, yet it remains stable in their midst, cutting a true path. The superstructure of the vessel, shaped like a truncated pyramid, signifies the contemplative quest for it draws to the unity of a cubit at the summit. The details of this structure, a description of which is beyond the scope of this paper, portray in a complex iconographic scheme the stages of the mystic quest: awakening, purgation, illumination and union.

As a symbol the Ark also represents, like the flood, the "breaking" of a typological motif. Medieval exegetes followed Tertullian in viewing the Ark primarily, but not exclusively to be sure, as an ecclesiological type. The Ark which saves Noah and his family in the flood is the foreshadowing of the church "outside of which there is no salvation." The dominant emphasis was on the sacramental, hierarchical, and institutional aspects.[70] Hugh chose to shift the emphasis, focusing on a dynamic conception of the church. As noted previously, this idea of the church emphasized the community of believers which has existed throughout all the ages of the world, constantly growing in faith and charity while moving toward her eschatological destiny.

68. See *De laud. carit., PL* 176:969–976; *Comm. in hier. coel.,* VI, *PL* 175:1038D. The theme of the fire of divine love is found, e.g. *A. myst.,* IX, *PL* 176:697B and *In eccl. homil.,* I, *PL* 175:118.

69. *De scripturis et scriptoribus sacris,* V, *PL* 175:14D. Tr. via Smalley, *The Study of the Bible,* p. 94.

70. Cf. Danielou, *From Shadows to Reality,* for the tradition.

Hugh introduces another new motif in his exegesis of the Ark, for he associates it with the great "housebuilding" texts of the Old Testament. The Temple and the Tabernacle were traditional *loci* for exegesis bearing upon the contemplative life and its development. Hugh brings this perspective to the Ark treatises.

There are three houses of God: the world, the church, and the soul. Each he inhabits in a different way: king, head of household, bridegroom. As we have noted above, the relationship between man and God sustained externally through creation has been broken. The world is opaque. Likewise, the internal inspiration of the *imago Dei* is darkened. Of the three houses of God only one now sustains initially a positive relationship with fallen man: the house of the church. It has, however, become the locus in time and space for the restoring activity of the divine purpose and heals man, becoming in this way the place of preparation for the restoring of the house of God within the soul.[71]

When building one must know the place and the material. The Ark of Wisdom is built in the heart of man and the material is pure thoughts.[72]

The question of the nature of the thoughts out of which this Ark is built brings a prompt response from Hugh. The means for reintegrating man's thoughts and building them up into this stable and unified fabric is none other than the work of restoration. There is no order where there is no limit, and the works of restoration are the divinely provided focus for man's thoughts if he would begin the ascesis of the contemplative quest.[73]

The human mind, Hugh points out very sagely, cannot be forced to limit its attention to one object, although it had done this in the perfection of creation insofar as love of God absorbed one. Yet the mind must not willingly be attached to the manifold distractions and the infinite number of desirable objects in the world of common experience. The works of restoration, varied yet limited, provide the needed focus and the necessary variety to enable concentration, meditation, and withdrawal. And this is accomplished, as suggested above, in a

71. On the three houses, cf. *A. mor.*, I, 4, *PL* 176:621AC, C.S.M.V., pp. 49f. On Hugh's introduction of the housebuilding motif, cf. F. L. Battles, "Hugo of Saint-Victor as Moral Allegorist," *Church History*, XVIII (1949), 220–240.
72. *A. mor.*, IV, 1, *PL* 176:663B–665B, C.S.M.V., pp. 122–125.
73. Ibid., 17, col. 677A, p. 146.

liturgical context, providing both the necessary variety and the needed limitation.[74]

Every mystic must face the question of selecting a focus for concentration as he begins to practice meditative withdrawal and introversion. How does one still the "surface mind" as Evelyn Underhill has called the scattering of interests which typifies our usual waking consciousness of the world about us?[75] Each mystical tradition has its particular traditions and techniques in this respect. As Underhill has pointed out, there is a common approach. Recollection and introversion usually begin with "the deliberate consideration of and dwelling upon some one aspect of Reality . . . . The self, concentrated upon this image or idea dwelling on it more than thinking about it . . . becomes in the language of asceticism "recollected" or gathered together.[76]

Until the twelfth and thirteenth centuries and the rise of devotion to Jesus in the Bernardine and Franciscan mystical traditions, Western mystics seem to have spoken little of a specific focus for meditation and contemplation. Even the Victorines have been suspected of having no intense focus. K. E. Kirk finds the Victorines "jejune and uninspiring" when compared to St. Bernard and St. Francis on the matter of the "subjects of meditation, that shall lead to fruitful contemplation."[77] Kirk has reference to the use by the saints of the life of Christ as the greatest subject for meditation. He contrasts this with the Victorine "meditation upon the harmony of the universe" and their use of all knowledge for the ends of meditation. Kirk is symptomatic of a position which overlooks the specifically Victorine emphasis upon the works of restoration as the focus for meditation, and the liturgical setting of the contemplative quest. What we have with the Victorines is a vision which fuses the historic, personal, and cosmic dimensions of God's redemptive purpose. Meditation upon that purpose as manifest in time places the initiate in a context much wider than devotion to the life of Jesus.

Victorine contemplative life is liturgical, yet personal; a consciousness of history, yet a movement away from the flux of time toward the unity, stability, and peace which are found with God alone. The fruitful variety of the works of restoration is the voice of God calling man

---

74. On the objects of attention, see ibid., 4 cols. 665D–666C, pp. 125–127; also ch. 6.
75. *Mysticism*, p. 302.   76. Ibid., p. 315.
77. *The Vision of God; The Christian Doctrine of the Summum Bonum* (London, 1931), p. 376.

to unity through the warp and woof of history, through the space-time matrix of human existence. Here are the anthropological emphasis and the existential dimension of Hugh's spirituality. It speaks to the situation of fallen man in clear tones. Man must know himself as ignorant, estranged, distracted, and divided. Scripture speaks to him of this, and also offers the way of healing and restoration. History is the new mode of divine presence. The work of creation, by virtue of which man once beheld his Maker within and perceived his power, wisdom, and goodness without, is no longer capable of manifesting the divine presence. A new approach is necessary and it is found in the works of restoration—a series of events in time with historical reality which also, because of their transcendent reference, offer a point of mediation with the divine.

Further exploration of the use of the works of restoration as a focus for meditation and the initiation of contemplation must await the study of Victorine materials, especially sermonic, from this point of view. Meanwhile, the Ark treatises serve as an initial example. The Ark becomes the center of an extended meditation and moral allegory which both reinforces the Victorine sense of history in the Christian religion and opens out into the subtle and complex field of the stages of the contemplative life, with all of it done not for knowledge, but finally for virtue and the reformation of man in the *imago Dei*.[78] In the Ark, as in all of Hugh's thought, the central and primal point of mediation and meditation is the Incarnation, for there God has entered historical existence as a person, and from that reference point time again has meaning.

78. On the drawing of the Ark and meditation, cf. my article, "Mandala Symbolism and Use in the Mysticism of Hugh of St. Victor," *History of Religions*, XII (1972–73), and also "*De gradibus ascensionum*: The Stages of Contemplative Ascent in Two Treatises on Noah's Ark by Hugh of St. Victor," *Studies in Medieval Culture*, V.

Perspectives on Celtic church history

JOHN T. McNEILL

I use the word "perspectives" to suggest areas of the field that have been brought to clearer view by twentieth century scrutiny and research. Celtic church history still presents to the student many gaps in assured knowledge, amid which opinions contend. For a long time the variety of interpretations largely reflected the ecclesiastical affiliation or the national heritage of the researcher, but that obstacle to reliable history has been largely if not entirely overcome. About the beginning of this century, under the influence of German and French scholars such as Kuno Meyer, Heinrich Zimmer, Henri d'Arbois de Jubainville and Joseph Vendryes, there came a widened outlook and a primary concern for objective facts. It is in this temper generally that scholarship has since proceeded. If we discern in its products a few examples of extreme and fantastic opinions, these are in most cases personal to the author rather than contrived to defend a cause or a prejudice.

It is a field, too, in which vast labor has been expended in our time, though the fruits of this are slow to reach the general reading public. They have to be gleaned not only from scores of books but from countless studies appearing in serials and journals that serve the interests of specialists and are made available only in the ampler libraries. There has been industrious ransacking of literary sources already known; some manuscript material has been brought to light, and the growing body of archaeological findings has been eagerly studied.

1. *The Celts*

Problems regarding the early history of the Celts have received much fresh attention and among them some elements of certainty have come to be recognized. Although the actual place of origin of the Celtic race is still in doubt, the two centers from which they expanded and spread their culture in western Europe are known and have been archaeologically explored. The earlier of these is Hallstatt in Upper Austria about 50 miles southeast of Salzburg, where they flourished from about 800 B.C. The second is La Tène at the northeastern end of Lake Neuchâtel in Switzerland, roughly 300 miles westward from

Hallstatt, where a more refined and advanced art and workmanship appeared about 500 B.C. The Hallstatt smiths were pioneers in the use of iron for swords and implements while they also continued the use of bronze, which had long been common among the inhabitants of Europe and western Asia. Hallstatt lay at the heart of the Urnfield region, so-called from burial practices of a period beginning in the second millennium B.C. in which cremation was followed by the deposit of the ashes in urns that were collectively buried under mounds of earth. The territory in which the urn cemeteries are found lies north of the Alps and extends from eastern France to western Hungary. It is believed by some archaeologists that the urn burials were Celtic; if that were made certain a very early origin for the European Celts could be affirmed. Even this, however, would not foreclose the possibilty that their original home was in Asia, among the shifting and tumultuous peoples who from remote prehistorical ages struggled for existence in the area north of the Black Sea and on mountainsides of the Caucasus. Support for the latter view is based largely on the identification as Celtic of place names and tribal names and the more or less attested movements of these allegedly Celtic tribes westward into Europe. At the present stage of research, this view has not been convincingly demonstrated.[1]

The Hallstatt Celts show in their ornamentation borrowings from a wide range of sources including elements from the Sarmatians and Persians. Such influences cannot be traced in human contacts but belong within a general process of mutual exchange of arts and crafts that took place among primitive societies. The La Tène Celts were receptive to features of Greek and Etruscan styles of ornament which they treated with originality and incorporated in a distinctively Celtic art of great variety and charm. There is a remarkable continuity in Celtic art from the La Tène period into the medieval era, so that Christian Celtic art in stone and metal and in manuscript illumination

1. Henri Hubert, *Les Celtes et expansion celtique jusqu'à l'époque de La Tène* (posthumous work, ed. Marcel Mauss et al.; Paris, 1932), tr. M. R. Dobie, *The Rise of the Celts* (London, 1934); Jacques Moreau, *Die Welt der Kelten* (Stuttgart, 1958); Calvin Kephart, *Races of Mankind, their Origin and Migrations* (New York, 1960); Myles Dillon and Nora K. Chadwick, *The Celtic Realms* (London, 1967), esp. chs. 1 and 9, both by Dillon. Hubert discounts the suggestion of an Asiatic origin, and holds that the identification of the Cimmerians of antiquity with the Cimbri is part of a "confusion that has raged like a pestilence among modern historians." Kephart, however, uses this identification in course of an elaborate argument for the Caucasus region as the place of origin. Dillon treats the question of origins cautiously, but thinks the Celts emerged as a separate people about 2000 B.C., while he recognizes the evidence of certain affinities of ancient Celtic language with those of the Hittites and of the Tokharians of Turkestan.

repeats the patterns of antiquity, with infinite variation. Thanks to eager archaeologists, knowledge of the material remains of the pre-Christian and early Christian existence of the Celts has been greatly extended in our century with impressive evidence of a delicate skill of hand and an unfailing sense of beauty hardly paralleled elsewhere.[2]

The range of Celtic penetration and conquest in the ancient world has been freshly defined. We know that we are here dealing with a flourishing and aggressive branch of the Indo-European stock. During most of a millennium before the Christian era they were with great energy expanding their sway. At some unknown period of antiquity Celtic tribes began to make forays and settlements in Spain, Gaul, Britain and Ireland. If elements of this expansion go back, as some suppose, to an era beyond 1500 B.C., the tide of Celtic movement westward was repeatedly swollen by large migrations during the Hallstatt and La Tène periods. As a consequence the Celts established permanent sway over large areas, in varying degrees mingling with the native folk. Before the coming of the Romans most of what is now France, all of Britain, including the Pictish north, the Hebrides and other neighboring islands, and all of Ireland, that remote island which men thought of as the utmost west, had become homelands of the Celtic race and culture. Celts controlled too a large area in central and northern Spain where the term "Celtiberian" was applied to Celts and their Iberian predecessors in alliance or racial blend. And in Italy what the Romans called *Gallia Cisalpina*, Hither Gaul, roughly the Po valley, had been dominated by Celtic tribes from the fourth century B.C. It was in 390 B.C. that Brennus and his Gaulish tribes crushed a Roman army and occupied Rome but failed to take the well-provisioned fortress of the Capitoline hill and for a great ransom left the city to join their countrymen who were already spreading over the Po valley, and settled near Ravenna. Eastward too the Celts pushed their way with vigor. In 279 B.C. a Celtic army was active in Achaea and sacked Delphi, but soon met defeat and extinction. Three other strong tribes of Celts, numbering 20,000 in all, in 278 passed over into Asia Minor. After devastating other districts they carved out an area of dominance in the northern part of what was later to be the extensive Roman province of Galatia. Their greatest stronghold here was

2. P. Jacobstal, *Early Celtic Art* (Oxford, 1944); Dillon and Chadwick, op. cit., ch. 12, "Celtic Art," by Nora Chadwick (an illuminating treatment). For Ireland we now have the two superb volumes by Françoise Henry, of which Vol. 1, *Irish Art in the Early Christian Period* (Glasgow and Ithaca, N.Y., 1965), is of use here.

Ankara, the present capital of Turkey. In time these Celts learned Greek, but nearly 700 years later St. Jerome in his commentary on Galatians stated that in addition to Greek they were still speaking a Celtic language like that which he had heard during his four-year stay among the Treveri at Treves. Jerome's statement has been questioned on grounds of improbability; but the maintenance of a Celtic speech under alien rule over many centuries has numerous familiar parallels, as in Ireland, the Hebrides, the Scottish highlands and Brittany.

In course of the Roman expansion Cisalpine Gaul was subdued by 222 B.C.; Spain, with its Celtic and other peoples was finally wrested from the Carthaginians in 201 B.C. although Celtiberian revolts followed till 133; Transalpine Gaul (France) was absorbed into the Roman administration by about 50 B.C.; in 25 B.C. Galatia became an imperial province, and before A.D. 100 the Roman province of Britain took stable organization. Scotland, however, north of the Forth and Clyde, remained independent of Rome, and Ireland never saw the Roman banners. In these areas, and in Brittany where the original Celtic stock was later strengthened by migration from Britain, probably a larger admixture of Celtic blood than elsewhere has remained. The adoption of Christianity in these countries was to bring their people into the circle of Latin culture, but without destroying the Celtic cultural tradition. It is in these areas that we can speak of the history of a Celtic Christianity, marked by its own peculiarities and existing in structural detachment from the hierarchical Western church.

By Greek and Roman writers the Celts are depicted as tall, strong and daring warriors armed with long two-edged swords, coming into battle in chariots from which they would leap, often stark naked, upon their surprised and unnerved enemies, whose severed heads they hoped to carry back to decorate their rude dwellings. They were boastful, like Homer's heroes and those of Irish legendary tales, and they ostentatiously wore torques and bracelets of gold. Charged with practices of blood-curdling savagery, they were also credited with mental alertness and talent and with love of poetry and music. Gibbon calls the Celts of western Europe "a hardy race of savages." From the point of view of Graeco-Roman civilized men the Celts were barbarians, but at the same time candidates for civilization. It was observed, too, that they honored and obeyed the "philosophers and theologians" called druids, in whose presence ritual acts were performed. The druids were credited with a philosophical system which included some recondite doctrines, especially the transmigration of souls, but specific evidence for this is lacking. Certainly they were teachers, but what they taught was orally transmitted and we have no texts for it.[3] It has been suggested that the custom of putting Celtic youth to school for long years under the instruction of the druids was a factor in the later development of Irish and Welsh monastic schools.

2. *Issues in early Celtic church history: Ninian and Columba*

Traditionally it was supposed that Paul's Epistle to the Galatians was addressed to the Christians in the northern and Celtic part of the wide province of Galatia. Such was the opinion of Jerome, and of others of the patristic age. Only in the late nineteenth century was this view seriously challenged, but the evidence cited against it was so impressive that scholarly opinion became divided, and in recent discussion the tendency is to state the pros and cons but refrain from a decision. The "North Galatian theory" is thus still not excluded. We are permitted to suppose as a possibility that it was Celts who first read this very early fragment of the Christian Scriptures, perhaps mentally turning its stirring Greek phrases into their ancestral Gaelic. At any rate, since the Celtic stronghold of Ankara had been made the capital of the Roman province, it must soon have been visited by Christian preachers whose hearers would be largely Celts. But we know of nothing that would indicate what might be thought of as a Celtic church in Galatia.

Fantastic legends of the labors of the early Apostles and other New Testament personages in Galicia, a Celtic area of Spain, in Gaul, and in Britain have no historical basis, and the statement of Gildas that Christianity was introduced into Britain before the death of Tiberius (37 A.D.) is probably not based on any reliable tradition. Yet if we remember the crowded roads and busy harbors of the time, we must

---

3. The principal classical references to the Celts are: Herodotus, *History*, I, vii–xiii; II, xxiii; Xenophon, *Hellenica*, VII, i, 20, 31; Polybius, *History*, I, xvii, 4; lxxvii, 4–LXXX, 1; III, xvii–xxxv; Caesar, *Gallic War*, I, 30; III, 9, 10, 19; VI, 11, 16, 17; VII, 32, 63; Diodorus Siculus, *Historical Library*, IV, lvi, 3; V, 28–31; XXII, ix, xl; XXV, xii, xiii; Strabo, *Geography*, III, iv, 16, 17; IV, i, 13, 14; Livy, *History*, V, xxxiv–xlviii. James J. Tierney summarizes the testimony of classical writings in his essay, "The Celts in Classical Authors" in *The Celts*, ed. James Rafferty (Cork, 1964, 1968), pp. 23–34. Myles Dillon in Dillon and Chadwick, ch. 1, offers useful quotations from Strabo and Diodorus Siculus, both of whom were dependent in some measure upon Poseidonius, whose works are lost.

suppose a first century infiltration of Christian teaching and some presence of Christian believers in these areas. There are other wide areas of the Empire and places beyond it where Christianity comes to notice first with such strength that it must have been planted very early by persons who will forever remain anonymous. It is strange how widely this quite obvious fact is overlooked by historians. Our best hope of learning anything about the unreported beginnings is probably the study of ancient burial places in which Christians were buried with their heads to the west. Apart from statements by Tertullian and Origen for an earlier era, we may be sure that the presence of three British bishops and a presbyter from different parts of the province at the Synod of Arles in 314 is sound proof that there existed a Christian church in Britain adequately organized well before Constantine's liberation edict of 313.

The issues most vigorously discussed with regard to the rise of Christianity in Britain belong, however, within a later century, and have to do mainly with Scotland. I refer to the work of learned protagonists of Ninian and Columba as founders of the Scottish church. Since Ninian died about 432 and Columba in 597, there is no question of precedence in time. It must be kept in mind, however, that our chief source for Columba was written a century after his death by one of his ablest successors, while it was only about 1165, more than seven centuries after Ninian's death, that St. Aelred, Cistercian abbot of Rievaulx in Yorkshire, making use of some eighth century materials, compiled his *Life of Ninian*. Bede inserts in his *History* an incidental notice of "Nynia" within his account of Columba.[4] Bede had access to some local knowledge of Ninian's location at Whithorn in Wigtownshire through his friend Pecthelm, Anglo-Saxon bishop of that place; but between Ninian and Pecthelm three hundred years had elapsed and the Celtic character of the foundation had become a distant memory. Celtic Ninian, unlike Columba, had no Celtic biographer whose work has come down to us. But in addition to Bede, Aelred used a now lost life of eighth century date, thought to have been written first in the Irish language, and available to Aelred in Latin and English versions. He also used a document dependent on this entitled *Miracula Nynie episcopi*, which narrates miracles at the saint's tomb, and an

4. Bede, *Ecclesiastical History of the English People*, III, iv. Aelred's Life of Ninian was edited by William Metcalfe in 1889 and translated by him in *Ancient Lives of Scottish Saints* (London, 1895). Another translation is by W. F. Skene in *Historians of Scotland*, Vol. V, (Edinburgh, 1874).

eighth century poem on Ninian, still extant, but of little biographical value. Bede's statements seem designed to affirm Ninian's dutiful attachment to Rome rather than to supply data on the range and nature of his mission. He assigns to Ninian the evangelization of the "Southern Picts" and to Columba that of the "Northern Picts." These divisions of Pictland can be only conjecturally translated into geographic terms. Bede may have been thinking in terms of the map designed in the school of Ptolemy of Alexandria in which Scotland leans off eastward, so that his "southern" means "eastern" on our maps. He indicates that the two parts of Pictland are separated by a range of steep and forbidding mountains. Bede had not been among those mountains, and a geographical sense was not one of his special talents. But he may have been thinking of what was called "the Mounth," the rugged hills stretching eastward from Fort William to Aberdeen.

There is, unfortunately, no mention either in Bede or in Aelred of a place or a person among the Picts that might furnish a clue to the places he visited. Aelred undoubtedly designed his *Life* to create an expansive view of a mission to a vaguely conceived Pictish population. He uses fervid language, but offers little substance of fact. Ninian goes forth to wrest Pictland from Satan, draws throngs of old and young to belief and baptism, ordains presbyters and consecrates bishops, builds basilicas and plants monasteries, and finally returns to his foundation of Candida Casa, the White Stone House at Whithorn, to live out his days in tranquility, "perfect in sanctity and glorious in miracles." Aelred, an Englishman, brought up at the court of David I of Scotland, may well, in crediting Ninian with the appointment of bishops, have been lending support to David's important establishment of diocesan episcopacy in his realm.[5]

But it is all tantalizingly inexplicit, and efforts to clarify Ninian's mission have led in opposite directions. Ninian research has been for forty years a tournament of scholars. If Ninian's achievement was great and far-reaching, that of Columba must have been far more restricted than has usually been assumed. The ablest protagonist of a wide-ranging and vastly effective Ninian is W. Douglas Simpson. In three notable books, and other studies, Simpson has employed a body of archaeological material and, especially, evidence on church dedica-

5. David, youngest son of Queen Margaret, while often politically at strife with England, promoted a reorganization of the Church of Scotland on English lines, and like his mother opposed Celtic elements. Whithorn was not yet ecclesiastically within Scotland. See A. R. McEwen, *A History of the Church of Scotland*, 2nd ed. (1915), I, 163–173.

tions. Unlike Bede and Aelred, Simpson takes Ninian to specific places stretched over a great part of Scotland and through some areas known to have been scenes of Columba's work a century and a half later. The result is an extremely interesting network of information and argument. But most scholars remain quite unconvinced that Ninian himself labored, or directed missions, in the localities in which the dedications are found. We are familiar in America with innumerable dedications of churches, monasteries and schools to ancient and medieval saints who never knew of America's existence. We have countless Presbyterian churches which bear the name of Columba or Knox or Chalmers, men who never trod our shores. What is proved is only a wide and favorable repute and the acceptance of a spreading commemorative cult of a religious personage. This in itself is testimony of a lasting and spreading awareness of Ninian's importance in former times. One learns much from Simpson, but it is not quite what he seeks to prove.[6]

Against this Ninian-up Columba-down construction of the history, J. A. Duke in *The Columban Church*[7] defends the more traditional estimate of Columba as Scotland's chief founding saint. Father Paul Grosjean, S.J., not only combats Simpson's thesis but disallows Bede's statements that Ninian was trained in Rome and that he dedicated Candida Casa to St. Martin.[8] Nora Chadwick in a study of the Ninian sources,[9] John MacQueen in his monograph *St. Nynia,*[10] Isabel Henderson in her little volume on the Picts,[11] and A. C. Thomas in an informing chapter,[12] all from different approaches find Simpson's

6. W. Douglas Simpson, *The Historical St. Columba* (Aberdeen, 1927); *The Celtic Church in Scotland* (Aberdeen, 1935); *St. Ninian and the Origins of the Christian Church in Scotland* (Edinburgh, 1940).

7. Edinburgh, 1932, 1957.

8. Paul Grosjean, "Les Pictes apostats dans l'Epitre de Saint Patrice," *Annalecta Bollandiana*, LXXVI (1958), 354–378, using St. Patrick's allusion to "apostate Picts" in his Letter to Coroticus, 2, as his point of departure, examines the Ninian problem in some detail. He finds not only Simpson but Bede in error, holding that Ninian never was in Rome, and denying that a dedication to Martin could have occurred in 397. Here he points out what has usually been forgotten, that Bede does not say that it was Ninian who named Candida Casa after Martin. For the eighth century poem, *Miracula Nynie episcopi*, see W. Levison, "An Eighth Century Poem on St. Ninian," *Antiquity*, XIV (1940), 280–291.

9. "St. Ninian, a preliminary Study of Sources," *Transactions of the Dumfriesshire and Galloway Natural History and Antiquarian Society*, XXVII (1950), 9–53.

10. *St. Nynia; a Study of Literary and Linguistic Evidence* (Edinburgh and London, 1961).

11. *The Picts* ("Ancient Peoples and Places" series, New York, 1967).

12. "The Evidence from North Britain," in *Christianity in Britain 300–700*, ed. M. W. Barley and R. P. C. Hanson (Leicester, 1968), pp. 93–121.

argument unsupported by sound evidence. Thomas points out that Bede does not say, or imply, that Ninian was the first bishop of Whithorn, and he points to cemetery findings that suggest the earlier presence of Christians in that location. From these and other studies not much is left to affirm about Ninian beyond the fact that, near the time indicated by Bede, from his base among Britons at Whithorn he conducted a mission to some pagan Picts. A connection with Martin of Tours may not be excluded even if the alleged dedication to Martin is rejected. The visit to Britain (ca. 395) of Martin's friend Vitricius of Rouen, who like Martin was active among the Gaulish Celtic folk, may have been known to Ninian and may even have had something to do with his foundation of Whithorn. But Aelred's statement that Ninian visited Martin appears to be groundless.

What we have learned and unlearned about Ninian leaves him a shrouded figure but by no means an insignificant one. It is not forgotten that a monastic community at Whithorn claiming origin from him flourished in the century after him, harboring many an Irishman within its numerous household. The Irish affectionately called Ninian "Monenn" and often referred to the monastery as "Rosnat" from the "little cape" on which it stood on the so-called Isle of Whithorn. In the generations after Ninian a number of Irish monastic founders and bishops spent years of training at Rosnat. One of the earliest of these was St. Machaoi (d. 498), founder of Nendrum,[13] a notable monastery on an island in Strangford Lough. Another was St. Enda (d. ca. 530) whose foundation of Aranmore in the Aran Islands is said to have followed the discipline established by Ninian. Also eminent among the Irish alumni of Rosnat was Finnian of Moville, who is reported to have been taken from Nendrum, where his monastic career began, on a ship sent by the abbot of Rosnat. Contact by sea was not difficult to maintain between Nendrum and Whithorn, and Finnian's own monastery of Moville was on a shore of the same land-locked bay. It is of interest that both these men were Picts by race, from Dalaradia, the Pictish district in Ulster. Columba himself was in Moville for a time, but left after a momentous breach with Finnian. Numerous other instances of Irish contacts with Rosnat could be cited, and Ninian's name was honored by many references in Irish hagiography. His indirect influence on the upgrowth of Irish monasticism must be recognized. Apart from any claim of great service in the conversion of the

13. H. J. Lawlor, *The Monastery of St. Machoi of Nendrum* (Belfast, 1925).

Picts in Scotland, he was through Irish mediaries Columba's fore-runner.

New studies of Columba himself have not been lacking, but have added relatively little that calls for attention here. Dr. Simpson's view of him as primarily a political figure points up with exaggeration a sometimes overlooked aspect of his career. Every pioneer missionary in a pagan state has to find his way with the ruling power. Simpson himself speaks of Ninian as cooperating with Stilicho's assertion of Roman power. This is more likely to be the case where the missionary is a descendant of kings and familiar with high personages in the political scene. It is to be expected that we shall see more attention paid to his relations with Dalriada in Argylshire and with its kings Conall and Aidan who were his own cousins, as well as with Brude MacMael-chon, the powerful Pictish ruler who had his capital near Inverness. But our main dependence here remains Adomnan's *Vita*. The edition of this work by William Reeves remains valuable after a century for its massive apparatus; but the 1961 edition by A. O. and M. O. An-derson reflects more recent scholarship and uses evidence from the excavations at Iona directed by Charles Thomas.[14] The argument for restricting Columba's missionary range of activity has been associated with a new emphasis on the legends of saints who were Irish Scots and Irish-born Picts, such as Saints Buite, Moluag, Drostan and Comgall, and St. Serf, a Pict whose native place was near his monastery of Cul-ross, workers alleged to have labored in northern Scotland before, or independently of, Columba. Adomnan is not interested in informa-tion about such predecessors, although he has some references to Comgall as aide and interpreter to Columba. He tells us at some length, and with miraculous items, of Columba's visit to King Brude, that on the way he encountered and quelled the contemporary Loch Ness monster, that he preached to Picts on the Isle of Skye through an interpreter, that he and his monks made many sea journeys about the western isles, and that on his travels he conversed intimately with and consoled individuals of the common folk. The connection of Columba with St. Drostan in founding the monastery of Deer in Buchan, at the northeast shoulder of Scotland, is not attested earlier than the twelfth century. It appears now that some tidying up of the fragments of evidence on the secondary figures in the mission to the

14. Alan O. Anderson and Marjorie O. Anderson, *Adomnan's Life of St. Columba* (Edinburgh, 1961).

Picts at this period is much needed. It is fair to add that these questions do not much affect our judgment of Columba as a man. His noble stature, powerful and melodious voice, and warmth of human feeling, his love of learning and of poetry, and his achievement in establishing at Iona a lasting community of scholars which was also a missionary outpost, manned by 150 monks who had imbibed his spirit, reaching out to points within range by sea and land—these combine to make him one of the best loved and best remembered of saints. By his poems in Latin and in Old Irish he was one of the founders of Irish literature, as he was also a beginner of the art of book illumination. Though sometimes prompt and emphatic in reproof, he impressed his own monks rather with what one of them is said to have called "the true humility of Christ rooted in his soul." [15]

3. St. Patrick and the beginnings in Ireland

In the Ninian-Columba polarization we have by-passed in time the first stage of Christianity in Ireland and the still inviting issues connected with St. Patrick's labors. Among workers in this field there has been a great stir in recent decades, with much variety and some controversy, and almost surely with real progress toward clarification. It has never been supposed that the apostle Patrick was the first Christian to set foot on Irish soil; but knowledge of the first arrival of Christianity there still quite eludes us. The intimate, if sometimes hostile, relations of ancient Ireland with Britain, and its sea trade with Gaul, both reaching back into remote antiquity, make it antecedently likely that some entrance of the new religion took place as soon as it became disseminated in the frequented seaports of those trade-related lands. Among the popular stories about Cormac MacAirt, alleged high king of Ireland ca. 227–266, the reputed founder of the Tara kingship, it is said that he "turned to the adoration of God," thereby offending his court druids who by their spells caused him to choke to death on a salmon bone. His burial at Rosnaree beside Tara was regarded as instituting a new Christian burial ground. If Cormac is an historical figure, as some question, it is indeed far from incredible that from British or Gaulish captives among the "great stores of slaves and treasures" taken in his sea raids he may have become informed of, and

15. Fintan, a monk of Iona, quoted from *Acta Sanctorum*, June 9, by Lucy Menzies, *St. Columba of Iona* (Glasgow, 1949; 4th ed., 1964), p. 84.

favorable to, Christianity.[16] Patrick himself was a captive taken from Britain to Ireland with "many thousands"; and though their story in Ireland is unwritten, it is natural to suppose that such raids frequently brought numerous Christians who were not silent about their faith. Kuno Meyer found evidence that there were Gauls in Ireland in Cormac's era, not as slaves but as teachers.[17]

Prosper of Aquitaine in his Chronicle under date of 431 notes the mission of Palladius, sent by Pope Celestine *ad Scottos in Christum credentes* as their "first bishop."[18] Prosper may not have known who was the *first* bishop in Ireland, but he is likely to have known who was the bishop first appointed by a pope. His understanding that Palladius was sent to an existing flock of believers there calls for no surprise. The duration or results of Palladius' mission constitute an unsolved problem, on which much labor has been expended. It is hard to avoid belief that this Palladius is the same person as the "deacon" who is credited by Prosper under date of 429 with prompting Pope Celestine to send Germanus of Auxerre to Britain to combat Pelagianism. Whether Palladius was then a deacon at Auxerre or at Rome, he was evidently in 429 keenly interested in the campaign against Pelagianism which was a major interest of Celestine I. Is it possible that his appointment to Ireland had the same end in view? So some have thought; but we have no text for such a view, and no reliable evidence of Pelagianism in Ireland.

Nobody doubts the authenticity of Prosper's statements. But they make very strange the omission from Irish records of Palladius' name and fame. He is mentioned only rarely, and with some confusion, in Irish sources and is not celebrated at alleged church foundations. On the other hand there are several dedications to "St. Paldy" in Scotland. J. L. Gough Meissner in 1933 suggested that Palladius held that the "Scots" to whom he was sent were those of Dalriada in Argyleshire which he supposed had begun to be penetrated from Ninian's mission. Palladius then, to become acquainted with the Irish people from whom the Dalriada Scots had come, paid a "flying visit" to Ireland, and on his return to a spot north of the Wall of Antonine, and there

16. *Annals of the Kingdom of Ireland by the Four Masters* (compiled from early sources, 1632–1636, by Michael O'Clery and three associates), Vol. I, ed. J. O'Donovan (Dublin, 1851).

17. Kuno Meyer, "Gauls in Ireland," *Eriu*, IV (1910), 208. Cf. Meyer's *Learning in Ireland in the Fifth Century and the Transmission of Letters* (Dublin, 1912).

18. Migne, *Patrologia, series Latina*, LI, 595.

died. St. Patrick's consecration as bishop followed the death of Palladius and was probably at York.[19] However, it is supposed by eminent contemporary scholars that some work of conversion had taken place from activities of British missionaries in southern Ireland before the mission of Palladius, and that he came to be their bishop. It is evident that Prosper regarded his "Scots" as inhabitants of Ireland, since in his *Contra Collatorem* written after Celestine's death he credits Celestine with "keeping the Roman island (Britain) Catholic and making the barbarian island (Ireland) Christian."[20] Since Prosper's note of 431 does not mention Ireland, it may be that he thought of Palladius as commissioned to the Christian Scots wherever he might find them, and that the missionary chose an approach to Ireland by way of Dalriada whose Scottish inhabitants were at least known to Christian Roman Britons. This route to Ireland for Palladius is not adopted, however, by the more recent writers on Patrick's Irish background who are about to be mentioned, with the exception of Professor Carney.

Since Patrick's mission to Ireland apparently began in 432, one year after the appointment of Palladius as bishop, their relationship caused embarrassment to the early annalists and hagiographers. Tirechán, who wrote about 675, speaks of "Palladius who is called by his other name, Patrick," an identification that has often since been adopted, most insistently perhaps by Heinrich Zimmer in 1901.[21] In the *Martyrology of Oengus*, ca. 800, Palladius is called "the old Patrick." In 1942 T. F. O'Rahilly returned to this theme, learnedly identifying the Old Patrick with Palladius and bringing Patrick the Briton to Ireland only in 462, more than thirty years from Palladius' commission.[22] Widely varying responses to O'Rahilly's thesis have been presented, with fascinating detail, by James Carney (1961)[23] and D. A. Binchy (1962).[24] Both, however, favor a later date for the British Patrick's

19. "The Mission of Palladius," App. D. in W. A. Phillips, *History of the Church of Ireland from the Earliest Times*, 3 vols. (Oxford, 1923), I, 376–378.

20. *Contra Collatorem*, xxi, 2; Migne, *Patrologia, series Latina*, LI, 271.

21. Heinrich Zimmer, *Pelagius in Irland* (Berlin, 1901), and Zimmer's article on the Celtic church in *Realencyclopaedie für protestantische Theologie und Kirche* (1901), tr. A. Meyer, *The Celtic Church in Britain and Ireland* (London, 1902).

22. *The Two Patricks* (Dublin, 1942).

23. *The Problem of St. Patrick* (Dublin, 1961).

24. "St. Patrick and His Biographers, Ancient and Modern," *Studia Hibernica*, II (1962), 1–173. Binchy's article, "Patrick, Saint," in *Encyclopedia Britannica* (1971), presents a sharp analysis of much of the recent discussion, but may have been written before Hanson's book.

mission than that usually assigned, viz., 432, and both hold that areas of southern Ireland had been Christianized by British missionaries before Palladius came. The three writers named have brilliantly opened up new paths of interpretation and have made of J. B. Bury's once convincing biography of Patrick[25] almost a museum piece. Ludwig Bieler, in a condensed study, has some ingenious reconstructions of the Latin texts of St. Patrick's writings.[26] A stream of research papers by many hands continues to flow, in which Patrick's own acknowledged and dubious writings and the legendary materials of subsequent centuries are closely examined. One noteworthy emendation proposed by Carney would dissolve an interesting item in Bury's reconstruction of Patrick's movements after his escape from servitude. Bury in his comment on Patrick's *Confessio* 19, which in most texts contains the word *canes*, was led to the plausible conjecture that Patrick's companions on ship and overland were engaged in transporting a shipment of Irish wolf hounds to be disposed of on the Continent where these huge dogs were in demand for hunting and for the cruel sports of Roman amphitheaters. Carney utilized a manuscript that has *carne* for *canes*, meat and not dogs. Bieler, however, offers a different emendation, which saves the dogs, if not necessarily the breed. This has importance as an item in the issue of Patrick's alleged travels in Gaul and Italy. Carney finds no evidence in the *Confession* for a landing on the continent, but supposes that his escape by sea took him to Britain. He evidently hoped when he left the crew of sailors to reach his family in his former home. This view is supported from Muirchu-maccu-Mactheni's seventh century life of Patrick preserved in the *Book of Armagh*.[27] Bieler, while discarding much of the series of continental activities admitted by Bury and by such later scholars as Eoin MacNeill[28] and John A. Ryan,[29] retains a period of preparation of the missionary at Auxerre. Christine Mohrmann in a study of Patrick's Latin[30] finds in his style traces of Gallic influence; but her belief that the British church had then no competence in Latin by which he could have profited has been countered with some persua-

25. *The Life of St. Patrick* (London, 1905, 1965).

26. "Interpretationes Patricianae," *Irish Ecclesiastical Record*, CVII (1967), 1–13.

27. Albert Barry's translation and notes in *Life of St. Patrick by Muirchumaccu-Machtheni* (Dublin, 1898), may be usefully consulted.

28. *St. Patrick, Apostle of Ireland* (London, 1934; 2nd. ed. by J. A. Ryan, 1964).

29. *St. Patrick* (Dublin, 1938).

30. *The Latin of St. Patrick* (Dublin, 1961).

siveness by R. P. C. Hanson.[31] Any belief that Patrick was ever in Rome has been generally abandoned. Bury had accepted on face value the approval of Patrick's teaching by Pope Leo I in 441 ("approbatus in fide catolica") alleged in the Annals of Ulster, without the implication that he then visited Rome to be examined and approved. These annals as they stand are in a late fifteenth century recension and are at this point suspect. It seems highly unlikely that Patrick in writing or dictating his *Confession* to defend his authorization as a missionary to the Irish would have failed to claim the Pope's approval if it had been given him.

The elusiveness of the dates of Patrick's birth, mission and death continues to trouble the researchers. In the case of so great a figure, this is a distressing, almost torturing feature for historians; we may thus be sure of the continued efforts of dedicated scholars to reach certainty. Perhaps we are now nearing a consensus on the matter. The tendency is to reject not only the extremely early dating of Mario Esposito[32] who places his obit in 430, but also the late date 493 which was indicated in the sixteenth century *Chronicon Scottorum* and other late texts, and has been revived by O'Rahilly and Carney. Hanson, freshly viewing the evidence, states the case against this late date in a sentence: "One thing is virtually certain, the man who wrote the *Confession* and the *Epistle to Coroticus* could not have lived till 493." Readers of these books of Patrick will understand what is meant. Both works were obviously written late in his career, and they have reference to events that can best be associated with an earlier part of the fifth century. Hanson comes back approximately to the dates arrived at by Bury, placing Patrick's death "about 460" for Bury's 461.[33]

We are indebted to Newport J. D. White[34] and more recently to Ludwig Bieler[35] for careful editions and translations of the works of Patrick, and they have been freshly described and historically interpreted by the authors already mentioned, and by others. They are well

31. *St. Patrick, His Origins and Career* (Oxford, 1968), ch. IV.

32. "The Patrician Problem and a Possible Solution," *Irish Historical Studies*, X (1956), 129–156.

33. R. P. C. Hanson, op. cit., ch. VI.

34. Newport J. D. White, ed., *Libri Sancti Patricii*, Proceedings of the Royal Irish Academy, XXV, Sec. C (1905; and separately, London, 1918); *The Latin Writings of St. Patrick*, tr. Newport J. D. White (London, 1920).

35. *Libri Epistolarum Sancti Patricii Episcopi* (Dublin, 1961); *The Works of St. Patrick* ("Ancient Christian Writers" series, Westminster, Md., 1953). Arnold Marsh in *St. Patrick's Writings, a Modern Translation* (Dundalk, 1961), aims to use homely language consonant with Patrick's style, with interesting effect.

worthy of thoughtful study, not only for what they reveal of his missionary career but also for their luminous revelation of the man, his ideals, his dedication, his sensitivity under criticism, to some extent his methods as an evangelist. The eloquence of religious fervor breaks through the handicap of weak syntax of which he is so painfully conscious: "Ego Patricius peccator, rusticissimus et minimus omnium fidelium." A few well-chosen paragraphs from Patrick's writings would outweigh a good deal of 17th March oratory. They deserve a wider public than they have obtained.

4. *The Welsh church from Germanus to Gildas*

Problems concerning the church in post-Roman Britain have attracted attention from numerous writers, some of whom have made large use of archaeological evidence. Early in the disastrous fifth century Britain gave to the Christian West its most influential heretic, Pelagius, who drew many followers in Rome, North Africa and Palestine, and aroused the wrath of Jerome and Augustine. So attractive was his doctrine of man's natural religious endowment that through his associate Celestius he was able to obtain for a short interval the assent of Pope Zosimus. General condemnation followed, but meanwhile his doctrines were propagandized in Britain, and Germanus of Auxerre with Lupus of Troyes (the former sent by Pope Celestine, the latter apparently by a Gallic council) were the agents of its suppression there in 429. It is alleged by his biographer Constantius of Lyons (ca. 480) that Germanus, a former Roman administrator and perhaps soldier, was made the commander of a Welsh force which won the celebrated Alleluia Victory (430) against an army of Saxons and Picts. A second visit by Germanus, reported by Constantius, is now dated by Hanson, if historical, about 444–445.[36] A. W. Wade-Evans has pointed to the strong and relatively early tradition that Germanus played a notable role in Wales, where St. Illtud of Llantwit Major was his alleged disciple. A book now lost was compiled in Wales, "The Book of the Blessed Germanus," from which Wade-Evans prints excerpts made by Rhun, son of Urien, prince of Rheged (a wide area around the Solway Firth reaching to Carlisle). These paragraphs, preserved by Nennius in the *Historia Brittonum*, include one in which it is

36. Hanson, op. cit., p. 50.

claimed that Rhun, a prince who became a priest, baptized Edwin king of Northumbria at Easter eve, April 11, 627. This testimony, "possibly anterior to Bede," runs counter to Bede's well-known account in which Paulinus of the Roman mission was the baptizer.[37] This point has been discussed by Nora K. Chadwick[38] and others. Nennius preserves a tradition of the excommunication by Germanus for incest of the British prince Vortigern, with other incidents of hostility between these two. The founding of a number of monasteries is woven into the story. It is difficult to imagine such prodigious activity of Germanus in Britain, especially since this is all connected with his first mission, 429–430; but we are certainly confronted with a strong tradition of Germanus' association with the Welsh church. The passage of Rhun, apparently recorded within a century of the event, raises a serious challenge to Bede's account of Paulinus and Edwin.[39]

A major contribution to the availability of Welsh sources was the edition of the lives of Welsh saints by A. W. Wade-Evans in 1944.[40] Ten years earlier this scholar took a controversial position on the *De excidio Britanniae* of Gildas, our most important document for the sixth century, attributing its main historical sections (2–26) to an eighth century author whom he called Auctor Badonicus.[41] With all his learning and conviction, he has left other scholars unpersuaded. The most recent studies accept the unity of the work and Gildas' authorship of it. In a detailed examination of the language and style of the *De excidio*, F. Kerlouégan finds unity throughout.[42] In a companion study in the same volume W. H. Davis enhances our appreciation of Gildas as an authentic and deeply concerned witness to the deplorable conditions of his time. Davis and other scholars have called attention to Gildas' recognition, amid misdeeds of rulers and the sprawling evils of society and church, that there were some good people still, and that monks are exempted from his jeremiad.

37. *Welsh Christian Origins* (Oxford, 1934), pp. 74f.
38. Nora K. Chadwick and others, *Celt and Saxon; Studies in the Early British Border*, ch. IV, "The Conversion of Northumbria, A Comparison of Sources," esp. pp. 156–164.
39. Bede, *Ecclesiastical History*, II, xiv.
40. *Vitae Sanctorum Britanniae et Genealogiae*, ed. and tr. by A. W. Wade-Evans (Cardiff, 1944).
41. *Welsh Christian Origins* (Oxford, 1934), esp. ch. XVII, "Auctor Badonicus and the Perversion of Welsh History."
42. "Le Latin de *De Excidio Britanniae* de Gildas," in Barley and Hanson, op. cit., pp. 151–176.

5. *The Celtic church of Brittany*

In this field the old major work of Artur le Moine de la Borderie[43] is still referred to, though sometimes by way of correction. Joseph Loth's study of the emigration from Britain to Armorica (1889)[44] is also still read with respect, and it is generally held with Loth that this migration of Britons fleeing from the Anglo-Saxon invaders was on a scale sufficient to obtain for the incomers an easy mastery of most of the province. La Borderie placed the beginning of this settlement about 455, pointing out that a British bishop from Armorica, Mansuetus, attended the council of Tours in 461. Records of an earlier Christianity are slender, and largely confined to the martyr acts of the brothers of St. Donation and St. Rogation at Nantes about 268 and Beatus at Nantes about 350. Some evidence from burials has also been found. Robert Latouche has repeatedly given attention to the early Breton settlements and churches. In a volume of medieval studies of 1966[45] he has summed up much of the work of historians in this field since La Borderie, pointing to the legendary and unreliable character of the early sources—"a realm of fable." The popular story of St. Guénolé, alleged founder of Landévennec, later a thriving monastery under Irish influence, is fiction; and the story of Guénolé's parents' landing near that spot from their own boat may not be taken as credible, or as typical of early migration. This was most likely a series of landings of armed bands or clans. Other books of high value here are by René Largillière,[46] Anatole Le Bras,[47] Olivier Loyer,[48] and Nora K. Chadwick. It is beyond doubt that the founding saints of Brittany were largely from South Wales and Cornwall. Largillière has evidence that they followed rather than organized and led the early migrations, but that they led in the subsequent organization of communities. Variant views have been held on the origin and early nature of the *plou*, the local organization of the church. The word is equivalent to the Latin *plebs*, which also acquired an ecclesiastical sense. The *plou* was the parish, in the earliest period under the charge

43. *Histoire de Bretagne*, I (Rennes, 1885).
44. *L'Emigration Bretonne en Armorique* (Paris, 1889).
45. *Etudes Médiévales* (Paris, 1966).
46. *Les saints et l'organisation chrétienne primitive dans l'Armorique bretonne* (Rennes, 1925).
47. *Le Bretagne* (Paris, 1941).
48. *Les Chrétientés Celtiques* (Paris, 1965).

of a monk. Monasticism in Brittany, as in Ireland and Wales, controlled and energized the whole church. Mrs. Chadwick examining some French studies takes up the question of the language of the people after the invasion of the Britons, and agrees with La Borderie that the language of the invaders, and not that of the earlier Gaulish Celts, prevailed.[49] The Breton church and society were oriented toward Celtic Britain and in constant communication with Wales and Cornwall. Of the early monastic founders St. Brieuc, whose monastery near Tréguier was at the site of the present St. Brieuc village, came from Cardiganshire by way of Cornwall; Samson, founder of Dol, came from South Wales and had a strangely shifting career, leaving numerous foundations in Cornwall and elsewhere; Paul Aurelian, missionary in Finisterre, was the son of a Welsh chieftain. He died at the place named after him Saint-Pol-de-Léon. The second and third of these were disciples of St. Illtud at Llantwit Major. But the migration of saints was sometimes in the reverse direction. St. Padarn (Paternus) was a native of Brittany who labored in Wales and founded Llanbadarn in Radnorshire, while his father, Petranus, left his home in Brittany to pursue a life of "abstinence and good deeds" in Ireland.

Worship and usages of the church were probably wholly Celtic until Frankish pressure forced changes. In 818 Louis the Pious took measures to replace the Celtic frontal by the Roman coronal tonsure, while introducing diocesan episcopacy and other administrative changes. The Breton church long maintained virtual independence of its nominal metropolitan superior, the archbishop of Tours. A strong reaction against Frankish aggression led by the Breton chief Nomenoë (d. 851) temporarily secured the independence of Brittany with the appointment of bishops under his control, severing all ties with Tours. Later a process set in by which the church became administratively attached to the French hierarchical structure, although many special customs and observances have continued to characterize it to the present time. It may be said in summary that recent studies have done much to clarify, and to make available, the history of the Church of Brittany, showing it very definitely a member of the Celtic family.

49. *Early Brittany* (Cardiff, 1969), pp. 200–205. A contrary view was argued by F. Falc'hun in his *Histoire de la langue Bretonne* (Rennes, 1951) and supporting articles, but Kenneth H. Jackson in "The Linguistic Geography of the Breton Language," *Zeitschrift für classische Philologie*, XXVIII (1961), 272–293, and in other studies has apparently established the British origin of the Breton speech as propounded by La Borderie.

6. *The Peregrini*

The numbers and influence of the Celtic saints abroad in Europe have continued to prove a challenge to students of medieval culture, and to offer an area of research. So great are the numbers involved, that we are apt to forget the vastly greater population of monks and nuns in communities, and the considerable number of anchorites, who remained in their native countries. Olivier Loyer has remarked that Ireland became a vast monastery, and it is probably safe to say that less than ten percent of those under vows were moved "to go on pilgrimage for Christ." Indeed a few voices were raised against the practice of religious peregrination. So great a person as máel Rúain, reforming abbot of Tallaght, apparently took an adverse view of it. But we have become more aware that the flow of missionary scholars from Ireland and Britain to many parts of Europe constitutes for historians a movement of great significance, multiple in its manifestations and effects, and a great and timely stimulus to a lagging culture. It is a story full of great names, names of men who under close scrutiny seem even more great than famous. A body of research far too detailed for notice here, has continually enlarged our perspective on the whole movement, and on countless individuals within it. To use the word movement in this context is, it must be confessed, open to criticism. Nothing could be more completely individualistic. A monk, usually of mature age and learning, felt an irresistible impulse to leave his comrades and his country to serve Christ in a foreign land. We do not read of a sleepless struggle out of which a decision is reached; one became aware that he had a divine call to go. The volunteer would obtain his abbot's consent; but he could not expect a flattering send-off: Though he loved his native land and his own people, he knew that he would probably never revisit them. His life abroad would not be guided by a home committee, or encouraged by concerned correspondents. In many cases, he went forth alone. If he had qualities of leadership he would form a group of twelve companions, all prepared to go far by sea and land to some place and folk that seemed to offer opportunity. They frequently recited the command to Abraham: "Leave thy country . . . for my sake, and get thee to a country that I will show thee." One knows that an access of desire for a change of scene, or of wanderlust, may have played a part, and that during part of the period the Danish invaders were making life in Irish monasteries difficult and perilous. But the peregrini were not refugees; they were volunteers for foreign service. With all our studies, we have no very clear impression of the motivation for the individual decision. Columbanus said that he sought the salvation of many and a solitary place for himself. Amid intense activity and confrontations with the wicked in high places, he maintained in occasional retreats his piety and scholarship.

There is something about this paragon of the peregrini that tends to elude our comprehension. A tall, strong man, content to live far below our poverty level, and despise all bodily enjoyment; who ruled and taught raw recruits to Christianity and to a rigorous monastic discipline, and won their love; who preached Christ to common pagan folk in nations foreign to him; who rebuked kings and challenged popes; who led the learned world of his age in familiarity with the Latin classics, and tossed off in a gay mood an epistle in verse to a friend bidding him not suppose the metre a novelty since it was practiced by Sappho; who companioned with friendly bears and pet squirrels in the Vosges forest, and who in his seventies with younger men shouldered logs to build his new monastery on the Trebbia, must be recognized as an unusual person, even among Irishmen. Many another of the Celtic monastic diaspora was highly gifted and utterly dedicated. We are getting to know them better; but we have no comprehensive masterwork embracing the whole company. It was Ludwig Traube's work centering on the Irish influence at Peronne[50] that pioneered the new scholarly interest in the learning of the peregrini. Dom Louis Gougaud in two studies of 1908 and in his general work of 1911[51] led the way to a comprehensive understanding of the movement. The present writer in a dissertation printed in 1923[52] and in a translation of penitential texts in 1938[53] called attention to their part in the spread of the penitential literature and of private penance.

50. *Peronna Scotorum, eine Beitrag zur Uberlieferungsgeschichte und zur Palaeographie des Mittelalters* (Munich, 1900).

51. *Les Chrétientés celtiques* (Paris, 1911). Revised English edition tr. Maude Joynt, *Christianity in Celtic Lands* (London, 1932). See also his *Gaelic Pioneers of Christianity*, tr. V. Collins (Dublin, 1923).

52. *The Celtic Penitentials and their Influence on Continental Christianity* (Paris, 1923), pp. 142–160.

53. John T. McNeill and Helena H. Gamer, *Medieval Handbooks of Penance, a Trans-*

Joseph P. Fuhrmann, O.S.B., in a dissertation published in 1927,[54] provided an orderly account of the history of Irish monasteries on the Continent. He included a treatment of the network of hospices established for the Irish monks on journey to and from Rome or other centers of piety and learning. The travellers were a class of monastic tourists quite distinct from the stable and hard-working peregrini, who were "pilgrims" in the sense of being self-exiled from their homeland but were not inclined to wander. Fuhrmann also provides an account of the Schottenklöster, the Irish houses in the German area, twelve of which Innocent III in 1215 coordinated into the Schottenkongregation under the headship of the abbot of St. James of Ratisbon. Ludwig Bieler in a work both scholarly and popular[55] has described the activities of some distinguished peregrini, with useful illustrations of manuscript materials and art objects calling attention to their service in the reinvigoration of religion and culture in continental lands. Anselmo M. Tommasini, O.F.M., has studiously examined the activities of the numerous Irishmen who labored in Italy.[56] Attention is called by each of these writers to Welsh, Cornish and Breton monk missionaries wherever they appear, but everywhere it is the Irish who form the predominant element, and the others are sometimes found making their contribution as members of houses under Irish rule.

These comprehensive treatments are supplemented by numerous special studies of individual leaders and local enterprises of the peregrini, as well as editions of writings by them and about them. Only a very few of these helpful works can here be cited. St. Columbanus has attracted much attention, and G. S. M. Walker's new edition of his writings[57] should lead to fuller appreciation of his personality and talents. James F. Kenney, in his indispensable guidebook to the sources and literature of early Irish church history[58] devoted twenty pages to materials on Columban. The biographical treatments by E. Martin,[59] "George Metlake" (John Joseph Laux)[60] and Helena Con-

---

lation of the *Principal Libri Poenitentiales and Selections from Related Documents* (New York, 1938, 1967). Miss Gamer's valuable essay, "The Condition of the Texts," occupies pages 51–74.

54. *Irish Medieval Monasteries on the Continent* (Washington, D.C., 1927).
55. *Ireland, Harbinger of the Middle Ages* (London, 1963).
56. *Irish Saints in Italy*, tr. J. F. Scanlan (London, 1937).
57. *Sancti Columbani Opera* (Dublin, 1957).
58. *The Sources for the Early History of Ireland, Vol. I, Ecclesiastical* (New York, 1929).
59. *Saint Columban* (Paris, 1905).
60. *The Life and Writings of St. Columban, 542?–615* (Philadelphia, 1914).

cannon[61] and the extended treatment by Eleanor Shipley Duckett,[62] may be selected for mention here among many essays in interpretation. J. W. Clark in 1926 greatly enriched knowledge of Columban's disciple St. Gall, missionary to the Allemanni, and of the vivid life of the abbey that grew up at the site of his labor.[63] Maude Joynt's biography of St. Gall[64] contains a translation of the ninth century Life by Walafrid Strabo.

The study of other saints and scholars of this company has been productive of many special contributions. Dicuil the Geographer who in 825 produced a surprisingly original work on geography has been studied and edited anew. Here the most important work is James J. Tierney's edition with an illuminating introduction and a translation.[65] This treatise of scientific and historical importance is also laden with much curious information. It is not too much to say that the story of the missionary monks from Ireland needs to be treated on an ampler scale than it has yet been, and to be wrought into general histories of the era with a recognition proportional to its importance. When in the 830's Walafrid Strabo wrote at Reichenau his life of St. Gall the migration of Irish monks to that area was still at full tide, and he well expresses the astonishment of those who witnessed it in his reference to "the nation of the Scots to whom the *consuetudo peregrinandi* has almost become (a second) nature."[66] His western contemporary Heiric of Auxerre, dedicating a life of St. Germanus to Charles the Bald, is even more rhetorical: "Almost all Ireland, despising the sea and its perils, is transporting itself to our shores with its flock of philosophers (*cum grege philosophorum*)."[67] Even where continental churchmen and scholars became somewhat impatient with the Irish, they respected them as "philosophers" in the sense of highly trained scholars. One of these, John Scotus Eriugena, who flourished under Charles the Bald, was a philosopher in the more usual sense of that word. His *De divisione naturae* has continued to intrigue, one may perhaps say, to baffle philosophers and historians. It has been partly

61. *The Life of St. Columban* (Dublin, 1915).
62. *The Gateway to the Middle Ages* (New York, 1938). Miss Duckett's *The Wandering Saints* (London, 1959), is of interest for numerous peregrini.
63. *The Abbey of St. Gall as a Centre for Literature and Art* (Cambridge, 1926).
64. *The Life of St. Gall* (London, 1927).
65. *Dicuili liber de mensura orbis terrae*, ed. James J. Tierney, with contributions by L. Bieler (Dublin, 1967).
66. Walafrid Strabo, *Vita Galli*, ii, 46.
67. Migne, *Patrologia, series Latina*, CXXIV, 1133.

translated by C. Schwarz[68] and we have informing books about Eriugena by H. Bett[69] and Dom M. Cappuyns,[70] and a searching analysis of his thought by Giulio Bonafede.[71] The suggestion that he was a pantheist is not supported but denied by these writers. A bibliography of his writings has been compiled by I. P. Sheldon Williams and this scholar has edited, with the collaboration of Ludwig Bieler, the first book of the *De divisione naturae*.[72] Though insufficiently known and understood, Eriugena has exercised a wide influence, and it is to be expected that his rich learning and profound thought will be increasingly influential. No less famous in medieval times, through an expanding legend, was a very different kind of saint, Brendan of Clonfert, a Kerry man who accredited himself to his own generation as a monastic founder and missionary visitor to the Hebrides, of whom the *Navigatio Sancti Brendani* took shape in the ninth century and was subsequently largely circulated in various languages. Important here is Carl Semler's edition of the *Navigatio*,[73] and there are numerous books and studies, including Geoffrey Ashe's intriguing book which attempts to show an early Irish presence in America, using *inter alia* illustrations of structures resembling Irish corbelled-roof huts in North Salem, New Hampshire.[74]

There are other aspects of my subject that could be appropriately explored, notably aspects of the history of sacred art and liturgy, and the development of writing and book illumination. But I have already, perhaps, embarrassed the editor and wearied the reader by the number of these pages. In Celtic church history we are little concerned with the minutiae of theological controversies or the structures of organization and their administrators; but we find ourselves constantly in the company of original, charming and dedicated people called saints.

68. *Johannes Scottus Erigena, On the Division of Nature*, Book I (Annapolis, 1940).
69. *Johannes Scotus Erigena, A Study in Medieval Philosophy* (Cambridge, 1925).
70. Dom M. Cappuyns, *Jean Scot Erigène, sa vie, son oeuvre, sa pensée* (Louvain, 1933).
71. Giulio Bonafede, *Saggi sul pensiero di Scoto Eriugena* (Palermo, 1951).
72. "A Bibliography of the Works of Johannes Scottus Eriugena," *Journal of Ecclesiastical History*, X (1959), 198–224. *Johannis Scotti Eriugenae Periphuseon (De divisione naturae)* (Dublin, 1968).
73. *Navigatio Sancti Brendani Abbatis* (Notre Dame, Ind., 1959).
74. *Land of the West: St. Brendan's Voyage to America* (New York and London, 1962).

Part V. Teaching in the Great Tradition

Olivi and the limits of intellectual freedom

DAVID BURR

The medieval period is not ordinarily viewed as a golden age of intellectual freedom.[1] Seen in terms of the general categories from which history books are constructed, it was an Age of Faith in which individual thought was carefully limited by such external authorities as the Bible, tradition and ecclesiastical authority. Intellectual freedom could prosper only in a subsequent Age of Reason.

To be sure, twentieth century scholars have outgrown the tendency to characterize the Middle Ages as little more than an unbroken panorama of bigotry, obscurantism and persecution. Our more charitable view of the period, however much it may owe to our increased appreciation of the medieval contribution to civilization, is also due to our awareness that the modern period has managed to breed its own varieties of repression. Having seen the extent to which intellectual freedom was nurtured in Nazi Germany and Marxist-Leninist Russia—not to mention the degree of respect currently demonstrated for it in this country by many militant anticommunists on the one hand and student radicals on the other—we may well begin to suspect that in the last five centuries we have put less distance than we might have hoped between ourselves and Thomas of Torquemada. Moreover, recent discussions involving national security, pornography and a host of other problems make it clear that the question of the *limits* of intellectual freedom remains a problem for a majority of the American people. In short, while we may still grant that on the whole the modern world offers greater scope for intellectual freedom than the Middle Ages did, we are equally aware that a convincing argument for repression can be produced in any age and that the modern world continues to offer widely divergent views on the subject.

This knowledge should encourage us to expect at least some variety in the Middle Ages as well. Moreover, it should lead us to ask, not whether a particular person believed in intellectual freedom, but what limits he placed upon it and why. Once we do so, the full range of medieval opinion will become apparent, a range of opinion substantially wider than most people would probably assume.

1. Research for this essay was partially financed through a grant from the Penrose Fund of the American Philosophical Society.

The subject of this essay, Petrus Iohannis Olivi, was in many ways a child of his period. It is well known that the later thirteenth and early fourteenth centuries, which witnessed an intellectual crisis occasioned largely by the controversy concerning Aristotle, also witnessed a series of efforts to defend some degree of intellectual freedom.[2] The two phenomena are hardly unrelated, since those who argued for greater latitude often did so at least partly because they found their own views threatened by the authorities. This observation might be made of such diverse figures as Siger of Brabant, Godefroy of Fontaines, William of Ockham, and Olivi, although only the latter will concern us in this essay.

The chronology of Olivi's early difficulties is unclear. He probably entered the Franciscan order in 1259 or 1260 at the age of twelve, studied in Paris, then taught at the order school at Montpellier in the 1270's.[3] During the later 1270's one or more aspects of his teaching seem to have been questioned by the minister general, Jerome of Ascoli, but his reputation does not seem to have been harmed and it was only during the early years of the following decade that he ran into serious trouble. The outlines of the story are clear enough. In 1283 the new minister general, Bonagratia of San Giovanni in Persiceto, ordered a committee of four masters and three bachelors of theology at the University of Paris to examine Olivi's writings. In June of the same year this committee produced both a list of censured statements and a list of positive assertions to which Olivi was to subscribe as proof of his orthodoxy. The latter document, the so-called *Letter of the Seven Seals*,[4] is extant. The list of censured statements has not as yet been discovered, but its contents can be derived in large part from a later work by Olivi which we shall call the *Apology*.[5]

In the fall of 1283 Olivi was ordered to come to Avignon and assent to the *Letter of the Seven Seals*. He did so, but with some reservations, in a document which we shall call the *Response*.[6] He notes in his

2. See M. M. McLaughlin, "Paris Masters of the Thirteenth and Fourteenth Centuries and Ideas of Intellectual Freedom," *Church History*, XXIV (1955), 195–211.

3. See Valens Heynck, "Zur Datierung der Sentenzenkommentar des Petrus Johannis Olivi und Petrus de Trabibus," *Franziskanische Studien*, XXXVIII (1956), 371–398.

4. *Littera septem sigillarum*, in *Archivum franciscanum historicum*, XLVII (1954), 45–53.

5. *Responsio fratris Petri Ioannis ad aliqua dicta per quosdam magistros Parisienses de suis questionibus excerpta*, in *Archivum franciscanum historicum*, XXVIII (1935), 130–155 and XXIX (1936), 374–407.

6. *Responsio quam fecit Petrus Ioannis ad litteram magistrorum praesentatam sibi in Avinione*, in *Archivum franciscanum historicum*, XXVIII (1935), 126–130.

Apology that the order placed him in an uncomfortable position. The *Letter of the Seven Seals* touched his work only indirectly, since it was composed of twenty-two positive statements written in opposition to Olivi's views as the committee interpreted them; yet if Olivi ascribed to it he would seem to concede that his works had the heterodox meaning ascribed to them by the committee. If he refused, he would seem to deny the articles of faith contained in the *Letter of the Seven Seals*. He finally chose a middle course, "confessing some simply and absolutely, . . . others under distinction," and offering no defense at all regarding purely philosophical matters.[7]

Thus Olivi made his peace with the order, but neither he nor the order considered the case closed. Possession of his works was prohibited throughout the order and both the list of censured propositions and the *Letter of the Seven Seals* were to be read in every house of Olivi's province. Forbidden to go to Paris and clear himself, deprived of his writings as well as the censures against them, Olivi could offer no defense until 1285, when he managed to get his hands on materials which enabled him to write the *Apology*. This work is of basic importance for the subject at hand.

A second key work for the present study is harder to date. It is a letter probably written to Raymond Gaufredi and others who had written to seek clarification regarding some of the points on which Olivi was challenged.[8] Franz Ehrle, assuming that the charges to which Olivi responds in this letter represent some of the ones made against him by the Paris committee, places the letter between the *Response* and the *Apology*.[9] Joseph Koch argues instead that the letter antedates the Paris censure, reflecting an early stage in which some of Olivi's views were censured by the minister general.[10] Koch's dating seems more probable, although the question has little relevance for the present study.

Another document[11] merits mention. It is an attack by Olivi on

7. *Apology*, p. 134. Such is precisely the course followed in the *Response*.

8. It is published in a rare edition of Olivi's *Quodlibeta* (Venice: Soardum, 1509), f. 51(63)v–53(65)r, where it is described as addressed to Richard of Camliaco. For the argument in favor of Raymond Gaufredi see Gratien de Paris, "Une lettre inédite de Pierre de Jean Olivi," *Etudes Franciscaines*, XXIX (1913), 414–422. Subsequent references to this letter will simply refer to it as *Letter*.

9. "Petrus Johannis Olivi, sein Leben und seine Schriften," *Archiv für Litteratur- und Kirchengeschichte*, III (1887), 426.

10. "Die Verurteilung Olivis auf dem Konzil von Vienne und ihre Vorgeschichte," *Scholastik*, V (1930), 494–502.

11. *Impugnatio xxxvii articulorum* (hereafter *Impugnatio*), in *Quodlibeta*, f. 42r–53r.

the errors of some other scholar and seems to be the polemic against "Brother Ar" mentioned in the letter to Raymond Gaufredi.[12] It is likely that this work, along with a shorter one,[13] represents a still earlier stage in which Olivi was at odds with another scholar in his own order. Koch suggests that it was Brother Ar who denounced Olivi to the minister general, thus starting him down the road to the censures by Bonagratia and then the Paris committee.[14]

The polemic against Brother Ar is a valuable indication of how Olivi behaved when he found himself on the attack, but the *Apology* and the letter to Raymond Gaufredi are clearly the most relevant documents for our present study. In each he simultaneously does two things. On the one hand he defends himself against specific charges, citing and commenting upon articles censured by his superiors. On the other hand—and here we finally approach the subject of this essay—these works contain nothing less than a critique of the practice of censure as Olivi experienced it.

In his *Apology* Olivi characterizes the actions of the committee as "unusual."[15] He protests that not only his views but he himself has been reproved and damaged by the committee. Koch observes that Olivi is wrong in this respect, since the activity of the committee was "of a purely scientific, evaluative nature," the result of their commission from the minister general.[16] Since it is hard to see how the treatment accorded Olivi could be construed as anything *except* personally damaging, the only real question would seem to be whether it was the committee which was responsible for that treatment. Olivi clearly thinks that they were,[17] but he may be mistaken.

Olivi's *Apology* is laced with protests against the procedure followed by the committee. We have seen his objection to the use made of the *Letter of the Seven Seals*. He is also unhappy about the fact that the committee used material written by him for his own intellectual exercise and made public by other Franciscans contrary to his wishes.[18]

---

12. *Letter,* f. 52(64)r.   13. Also published in *Quodlibeta,* f. 53r-v.
14. "Verurteilung," pp. 499–502. Koch is probably right in thinking that Brother Ar is actually Arnold Galhardi. For the full range of possibilities see Gratien, op. cit., pp. 419f.
15. *Apology,* p. 132. Koch, "Verurteilung," p. 498, cites this remark as evidence that Olivi's censors were following a new technique in labeling individual articles as "error," "heretical," etc. While the context of Olivi's remark would allow such an interpretation, he would seem to have had something more in mind.
16. "Verurteilung," p. 506.   17. *Apology,* p. 130.
18. Ibid., p. 132.

He objects to the committee's excerpts, often suggesting that their brevity makes them misleading[19] and that the committee has misinterpreted them.[20] He complains that he was not allowed to appear before the committee in order to explain and defend himself.[21] He expresses his dissatisfaction with the committee's failure to provide reasons for the censures.[22]

Koch tends to feel that Olivi's protests are beside the point, missing the true function of the committee;[23] yet such an observation is itself somewhat beside the point, for the proper function of the committee is precisely the thing Olivi really calls into question. Whatever else he and the committee may disagree on, it is clear that they disagree on the committee's right to do what it did. Here we arrive at a key problem, that of the *locus* of authority. Like other men of his time, Olivi feels that some things must be believed. There is a "substance of the faith explicitly handed down to us through the Roman church" which must be accepted "with firm and explicit faith."[24] The real question is where we must turn for an authoritative definition of that faith. Olivi consistently points to the scriptures, emphasizing their absolute centrality, but he is aware that interpretation is necessary. As man stands before the Bible, to what human agencies must he turn for help in understanding its contents?

The first step toward answering this question is taken when we observe that Olivi is quite prepared to believe that man *should* turn somewhere for help. This requirement is to some extent a natural concomitant of the humility so valued by Olivi and his order. Willingness to allow one's own views to be molded by authority is clearly one manifestation of a state of soul which, *ceteris paribus*, any friar would find meritorious. In Olivi, however, this mandate is reinforced by a strongly hierarchical view of the universe particularly imbibed from Pseudo-Dionysius, whom he quotes regularly. This sense of hierarchy is sometimes explicitly applied to intellectual matters.[25]

---

19. Ibid., pp. 135, 152, 154, 400, 403. 20. Ibid., pp. 139f.
21. Ibid., pp. 132, 134.
22. Ibid., pp. 134, 390, 397. Note the similar demand for reasons in *Letter*, f. 52(64)r.
23. "Verurteilung," pp. 506f. Koch feels that the committee's list of censured opinions was "a first-rate scientific achievement," an opinion based largely upon his view of its place in the development of such documents. See his article, "Philosophische und theologische Irrtumslisten von 1270–1329," in *Melanges Mandonnet*, II, 305–329.
24. *Letter*, f. 52(64)v.
25. Thus in his *Commentary on the Song of Songs*, published in Bonelli's *Sancti Bonaventurae . . . operum . . . supplementum* (Trent: 1772), I, 147f, Olivi notes that in lower

So far there is nothing unique about Olivi's position, nor is there anything unique about the directions in which he looks for his authorities. He looks to the *sancti*, the *magistri* and the pope. Appeal to the first sort of authority is so obvious an element in his writings that it needs no documentation. His works are studded with references to Augustine, Pseudo-Dionysius and others. The second type of appeal is less common but still very important. Olivi is concerned not only with the consensus among theologians of his time, but particularly with the common view within his order. Thus in his polemic against Brother Ar he attacks some of his adversary's views by saying that they are against "the common opinion of our masters."[26] Bonaventure's authority is especially important to him, and a thorough comparison of the two will probably reveal that Olivi's debt to the Seraphic Doctor is even greater than has been imagined.

Thus the *sancti* and *magistri* are both important authorities, but Olivi is careful to place their authority in perspective. In his treatise *On the Study of Divine Letters*[27] Olivi echoes Bonaventure[28] in calling for an order whereby one moves from the Bible through the fathers to the masters. The order of march is also an order of priority. In short, there is a definite hierarchy of authority and the theologian must be careful that his allegiance to a lower authority does not cause him to depart from a higher one. Masters like Bonaventure are to be revered, but they can be wrong. When they *are* wrong, the theologian should say so in all humility. Thus in his *Questions on the Sentences* Olivi finds himself constrained to oppose Bonaventure and other Franciscan scholars on the issue of *rationes seminales*, albeit with great circumspection.[29]

In his letter to Raymond Gaufredi and in his *Apology* Olivi does explicitly recognize one indisputable authority besides the Bible. That is "the Roman church" or the pope.[30] He says very little about papal

---

grades, since one's investigation is insufficient, one must seek an answer from doctors and superiors, just as the magi sought directions in Jerusalem. For an application of Pseudo-Dionysius and hierarchy to the idea of the beatific vision, see Olivi's *Commentary on Revelation*, MS Rome, Bibliotheca Angelica 382, f. 120ra.

26. *Impugnatio*, f. 44r and passim.

27. *De studio divinarum literarum*, in *Sancti Bonaventurae . . . Operum . . . Supplementum*, II, 38.

28. Compare *Collationes in Hexaemeron*, xix, 10–15 in *Opera* (Quaracchi: College of St. Bonaventure, 1891), V, 421f.

29. *Quaestiones in secundum librum sententiarum* (Quaracchi: College of St. Bonaventure, 1922–26), I, 165. Hereafter called II *Sent*.

30. *Letter*, f. 52(64)v refers to "sacred scriptures or papal or ecclesiastical traditions."

authority in these writings and it is pointless to pursue the matter further except to note that Olivi gives the matter *ex professo* treatment elsewhere and does grant the pope supreme power in doctrinal matters, although in such a way as to leave the limits of that power open to question.[31]

In short, while Olivi does grant the existence of an authority within the church which can demand assent in doctrinal matters, it is not the same authority he was facing in the 1280's. Thus in his letter to Raymond Gaufredi he comments that, although through reverence for his order and Saint Francis he has subjected himself to the judgment of the minister general, he knows that the minister general does not have full authority in matters of the faith.[32] In his *Apology* he tells the commission:

> although I am an abominable speck of a man, not only in respect to God but also in respect to you, and although I am nothing or (if such can be said) less than nothing, nevertheless you should not demand such obedience from me or recommend that it be demanded, as if I should subject myself entirely to your opinions— however solemn and worthy of reverence they might be—as to the words of the Catholic faith or the holy scripture or to the determination of the Roman pontiff or a general council, unless it has been demonstrated that your opinion is that of the Catholic faith and sacred scripture.[33]

In other words, the committee has no right to tell Olivi what he must believe unless it can buttress its demands with convincing arguments. Otherwise it is usurping authority. One might be tempted to observe that Olivi is being naive and that he fails to see the function performed by the committee. It was, after all, 1283 when the affair occurred. We know what dissensions were splitting the scholarly community at that time, particularly in connection with the use of Aristotelian philosophy. We know the leading role taken by the Fran-

---

Apology, p. 131 appeals to "the Roman Church, . . . to whom alone it pertains to settle questions of faith." *Apology*, p. 132 mentions pope and general council as necessitating obedience.

31. For bibliography and discussion see Ludwig Hödl, *Die Lehre des Petrus Iohannis Olivi O.F.M. von der Universalgewalt des Papstes* (Munich: Max Hueber, 1958) and Michele Maccarone's introduction to the question *An romano pontifici in fide et moribus sit ab omnibus catholicis tamquam regule inerabili obediendum*, in *Rivista di Storia della Chiesa in Italia*, III (1949), 309–343.

32. *Letter*, f. 51(63)v. 33. *Apology*, pp. 131f.

ciscans in pointing to the dangers inherent in the Aristotelian movement. Olivi's contemporaries might well have commented that his attitude toward the commission did not take into account the extreme necessity of vigilence incumbent upon the leaders of his order. John Peckham expresses it well in a letter to the pope.

> Holiest father, during a recent visitation of the diocese of Lincoln, while passing through Oxford, we discovered that some of the erroneous philosophical opinions reproved ... by ... our immediate predecessor are once more held. Not wishing such errors to prosper in our time, ... we proceeded thus, ratifying our predecessor's action in a public sermon before the clergy and forbidding anyone to defend an opinion of this sort until we should see by a canonical council of the diocesan and ministers whether any of these articles could be allowed without danger. ... We write you of these things, holy father, so that ... you should know the truth of the matter, and that the holy Roman church should take notice that since the doctrine of both orders is opposed today from within by all sorts of doubtful things, and since the doctrine of both rests almost totally on philosophical dogmas, the views of the saints being discarded and in part belittled, ... the church could be in great danger in the future. For what is more necessary than that the building should fall once the columns are broken, ... what more manifest than that diversity of opinions should prepare the way for discord of souls and the cooling of love?[34]

In reality, Olivi is as aware of the dangers as Peckham would like him to be. Far from being an uncritical supporter of the newer intellectual currents, he is one of their most caustic critics. Philosophy should be viewed as the hand-maiden of religion, valuable only so long as it is oriented to the understanding of divine things.[35] When the hand-maiden becomes the mistress of the house, the scholar is guilty of idolatry. Such is precisely what Olivi thinks is happening in his own time. Aristotle is looked upon by many scholars as "the god of this world" and "the infallible measure of all truth."[36] It is he, rather than the Bible, whom the scholars follow as their ultimate authority.

Beginning in idolatry, such scholars end in a number of other

34. *Chartularium universitatis parisiensis*, I, 626f.
35. *An studere sit opus de genere suo perfectum*, in *Studi Francescani*, LXI (1964), 150ff.
36. II *Sent.*, I, 131, 479; II, 269, 482.

heresies as well, for Aristotle and the other pagan philosophers operated under severely limiting conditions when they attempted to investigate the most pressing human problems. Dependent upon sense experience as interpreted by a finite and fallen mind, they were able to accumulate a certain amount of knowledge concerning such things as grammar, logic, rhetoric and the natural sciences, but they failed to learn anything important about God or the nature and destiny of man.[37] As a result, their works are filled with such monstrous doctrines as the eternity of the world and the negation of divine and human freedom.[38] Thus one must read Aristotle with the utmost caution, constantly testing his views against reason and the faith, appropriating the true and resolutely discarding the false.

Unfortunately, Olivi feels, his contemporaries are doing nothing of the sort. Aristotelian philosophy, far from being a minor irritant, is growing apace and is destined to play a major role in the history of the church. It is, in fact, a major preparation for the Antichrist and can itself be called the heresy of the Antichrist.[39] One might expect that such a belief would offer Olivi strong incentive to sanction, at least in principle, the sort of surveillance practiced against him by the order. Certainly a little vigilence and even a little repression seem a small price to pay in order to combat the Antichrist.

Nevertheless, Olivi takes precisely the opposite tack, arguing for substantially more freedom than his order was willing to allow. This stand is closely connected with his attitude toward Aristotle. We have seen that for Olivi the Averroists' crime is essentially that of idolatry. Olivi feels that much of his philosophical work is directed against precisely such idolatry. In his letter to Raymond Gaufredi he argues that his disputed views on the nature of quantity were advanced in order that his contemporaries "should not adhere too closely to Aristotle's words as if to inerrant principles," but should realize instead that Aristotle "said without reason or discussion of contrary opinions many things which are today held as first principles, or rather as the true faith."[40] Here, in fact, lies one reason why Olivi, who professes

37. *De perlegendis philosophorum libris*, in *Antonianum*, XVI (1941), 31–44.
38. II *Sent.*, I, 96.
39. *Quodlibet* II, q. 5, f. 12v; *An status altissime paupertatis sit simpliciter melior omni statu divitiarum sive propriarum sive communium*, MS Florence, Bibliotheca Laurenziana, conv. sopp. cod. 448, f. 40rb; II *Sent.*, I, 98; *An professio paupertatis evangelice et apostoloce possit licite ad talem modum vivendi reduci, quod amodo sufficienter vivat de possessionibus et redditibus*, etc., MS Assisi, cod. 684, f. 66rb.
40. *Letter*, 52(64)r. See also *Apology*, p. 406.

to be relatively unconcerned about philosophical matters,[41] is willing to involve himself in philosophical debate at all. The dangers of Aristotelianism must be made plain to the scholarly world.

It would be naive to assume, however, that only Aristotelians can commit intellectual idolatry. The Aristotelians are guilty because they obscure the line of demarcation between Christian faith and human opinion. Anyone, no matter what his philosophical affiliation, can do as much. Here we arrive at the center of Olivi's objection to his censors in both the letter and the *Apology*. In forcing him to ascribe to their views, they are giving these views an unmerited aura of Godlike authority. They are acting as if their own fallible opinions are the Christian faith itself.

By proceeding in this manner, Olivi's censors are not only committing idolatry themselves but inviting others to do the same. In his letter, Olivi asserts that he will have no part of it. If an opinion is held by men of stature who are worthy of credance, Olivi will approach it "reverently, with a humble heart and open to discipline, but not for all the world will I adhere to it as to the Catholic faith," for "to adhere in this way to any human inventions whatsoever . . . is to venerate the words of men as if they were idols."[42] Olivi chooses to make it a matter of conscience.

> I would knowingly obey no man against those things that are of the faith. In other things I would always obey insofar as I could as long as purity of conscience was preserved; but never against purity of conscience, for even though these matters might not affect the faith I should lie for no man, especially in doctrine.[43]

The unsettled times call, not for an enforced uniformity, but for an open discussion of the issues.

41. In *Response*, p. 130, he dismisses the attack on his view of quantity by noting that since he cares little about philosophical questions of this sort he is ready to recant. In *Apology*, p. 134, he notes that on purely philosophical questions he subjected himself to the committee without argument, since he is much less concerned about such things than many people believe.

42. *Letter*, f. 52(64)v.

43. Ibid. It is unfortunate that Olivi's *ex professo* treatment of obedience in the question *An vovere alteri homini obedientiam*, etc., MS Florence, Bibliotheca Laurenziana, Cod. 448, f. 99raff. does not explicitly deal with the problem of obedience in intellectual matters. Nevertheless, the limits placed upon obedience in that question seem to allow room for the sort of argument described in this essay.

I say that it is useful to write and recite contrary opinions without stubborn approval of any particular alternative so that it will become apparent that neither is held as the faith and that neither is unshakably held; and also so that, through comparison of these opinions, the understanding of the advanced reader (as well as those upon whom it is encumbent to advance) can be exercised more fully; and finally so that we can be led to the defense and elucidation of the faith in several ways.[44]

This catalogue of the values of open discussion needs no explication except to note that it overlooks still another benefit cited elsewhere by Olivi, the investigation of hidden dangers to the faith.[45] All things considered, the values of free inquiry far outweigh the dangers involved.

In the light of these considerations, Olivi's own approach as explained in the *Apology* is quite understandable.

I have recited various opinions, asserting none of them except that sometimes I present, without responding to them, a preponderance of arguments in favor of the opinion which contradicts the one common to certain masters. Thus I seem to imply that I approve of that part more, although in most cases I say that those opinions are to be examined with caution rather than asserted. I have recited those that seemed to present truly perplexing problems which I myself could not solve and which seemed to me to be no less suitable for explaining and defending the faith than other views. On the other hand, I have been fearful that certain familiar philosophical opinions contain hidden snares and obscure, knotty dangers to the Catholic faith, and I have suspected (and still suspect) that these are henceforth to be promulgated by the sowers of error.[46]

Here one must allow for a degree of distortion occasioned by the fact that Olivi is very much on the defensive, but the passage is still a fairly good description of Olivi's *modus operandi* as seen in his *Questions on the Sentences*. There he is quite reticent about making asser-

44. *De obitu dicti fratris Petri*, in *Archivum franciscanum historicum*, XI (1918), 269. This work raises some thorny critical problems, but the passage just quoted is a good statement of Olivi's *modus operandi* and the rationale underlying it.

45. *Apology*, p. 405; *Letter*, f. 52(64)v.   46. *Apology*, p. 405.

tions which openly contradict the common opinion of the Franciscan masters. When he disagrees with them, his view is likely to be presented, not as his own, but as the opinion of an anonymous *quidam* or simply as a competing view which must be reckoned with.[47] There is no reason to dismiss entirely the widespread view that this procedure represents a prudential measure on Olivi's part. In this case both prudence and the dictates of humility probably accorded quite well with Olivi's notion of how such problems should be presented. Such questions can be left open, because what is important is not the individual's own opinion but the confrontation of views and the benefits resulting from it. This is not to say that the scholar should have no opinions on such issues. Olivi distinguishes between belief in the sense of simple opinion (*credulitas simplicis opinionis*) and belief in the sense of a faith-commitment (*credulitas fidei*).[48] The former is characterized by an openness which makes it compatible with the responsibilities of a scholar. The second obscures the distinction between Christian faith and human opinion and leads to idolatry as well as sects and schisms in which Christians oppose one another saying "I am of the party of Paul," "I of Aristotle," and "I of Thomas."[49]

One can go a bit farther and suggest that the sectarian approach is in danger of violating the very spirit which theology should serve. Olivi closes his discussion of the dangers lurking in a certain philosophical opinion by saying

> I shall develop the attack no further, but will leave it instead to the zealots of the Catholic faith. For although the philosopher-sadducees say many horrible things about our rational nature, the pharisees who zealously oppose them "do not have the zeal of God according to knowledge," as Paul says. For they oppose the sadducees in such a way that they seriously impugn the spirit of Christ.[50]

The remark reminds us that Olivi, like many other Franciscans, places heavy emphasis upon the role of the will in all aspects of human endeavor. The worth of study is to be measured not by its contribution to intellectual cognition but by its contribution to *caritas*.[51] Olivi is aware that the zealous heresy-hunter, while defending the purity of

---

47. II *Sent.*, I, 424; II, 410.
48. *Letter*, f. 52(64)v.
49. *Letter*, f. 52(64)v.
50. II *Sent.*, II, 125.
51. *An studere sit opus de genere suo perfectum*, p. 149.

Christian doctrine, may be a living repudiation of the love to which that doctrine should point.

It is one thing to espouse such ideals when one is being attacked, but quite another to observe them when one is on the offensive. We have seen that those scholastics who argued for a measure of intellectual freedom were often in the former rather than the latter situation. Thus one might be justified in wondering whether Olivi would have defended such freedom quite so enthusiastically if he had held a more popular set of opinions. There are hints that he may have been somewhat less scrupulous when someone else's ideas were at stake,[52] but on the whole his writings are strikingly lacking in references to the necessity of coercion. He is more than ready to label some opposing views heretical, a fact which might well have some bearing upon the zeal with which he would seem to have been attacked by others;[53] yet this in itself is not necessarily inconsistent with what has been said so far. As we have seen, he is in favor of an atmosphere in which various views can be examined so that both their virtues and their hidden dangers can be revealed. His writings are notably lacking in references to those coercive measures which constituted such an important element in his own time. Some scholars have reached the unwarranted conclusion that his *Questions on the Sentences* were written prior to 1277 because they combat the errors of Averroism without ever mentioning the condemnation of 1277. In reality he simply does not seem to feel that the condemnation has any important place in a scholarly investigation, and references to it are almost entirely lacking in his writings.[54] It is intriguing that his comments on the Cathari include no reference to their forceful suppression. Anyone reading the account of their demise in his *Commentary on Revelation*[55] might be led to assume that they were defeated, not by crusading armies, but

---

52. In *Impugnatio*, f. 49r he describes one of Brother Ar's views as *extirpandum* and in *Letter*, f. 52(64)v he confesses that he wanted the minister general to examine both Brother Ar's views and his own. Both statements are ambiguous, since neither constitutes an explicit call for official repression, but it is hard to imagine why Olivi would have sent a denunciation of Brother Ar's writings to the minister general if he did not expect the minister general to take some action against them.

53. *Letter*, f. 52(64)v; *Apology*, p. 400.

54. I am aware of one reference to it. In *Impugnatio*, f. 46v he comments that one of Brother Ar's views is among those condemned at Paris.

55. See especially f. 67ra–68va. Note also his complaint in ibid., f. 48rb that Christians cannot argue with Moslems because they do not allow the Christian faith to be preached in their lands.

by sound theology and the rebirth of evangelical poverty within the church. Such observations prove little by themselves, but taken together they seem to suggest a man unused to thinking about the role or possible values of coercion in religious life.

It is probably significant that this attitude accords rather well with Olivi's view of history. The problem is a complex one and cannot be treated here in anything more than cursory fashion. Let it suffice to say that in his *Commentary on Revelation* Olivi divides church history into seven periods.[56] He sees his own time as poised between the fifth and sixth periods. The fifth, beginning around the time of Charlemagne, is one of condescension to the weakness of the ordinary man, finally resulting in laxity. This laxity is not only present but increasing in Olivi's time, yet a new age of evangelical revival is already dawning. The world has seen in the person of Saint Francis a rebirth of that evangelical life which will eventually triumph. For the moment, however, it must undergo persecution at the hands of the carnal church, those elements within the visible church which will eventually reveal themselves as the followers of Antichrist. This persecution takes two major forms. On the one hand, evangelical poverty is combatted by those responsible for the corruption and luxury in the church. On the other, true Christian doctrine is attacked by the sowers of error, particularly the errors of pagan philosophy.

The most important aspect of this view for the subject at hand is the fact that things must get much worse before they get any better. The temptations in the days to come will be so subtle and seductive that even the more learned among the elect will barely avoid succumbing.[57] The carnal church will hold power and those who do not obey will be anathematized. If necessary they will be turned over to the secular arm for punishment.[58] In short, whatever the elect may expect to accomplish in the immediate future, they cannot expect to hold power. They will again have authority once the powers of darkness have been vanquished (by purely spiritual means), but it will be a different sort of authority than that exercised in the church at present. The hierarchical principle is eternally valuable,[59] but the relationship between superiors and inferiors will no longer be one of servility. Superiors will be related to inferiors as ministers and ser-

56. For an extended discussion see Raoul Manselli, *La Lectura super apocalypsim di Pietro di Giovanni Olivi* (Rome: Istituto Storico Italiano per il Medio Evo, 1955).

57. See his *Commentary on Revelation*, f. 67rb.

58. Ibid., f. 93ra. 59. Ibid., f. 120ra.

vants rather than as lords.[60] The higher the level of contemplation, the more profoundly humble one will be, not only toward God, but also toward the spiritual masters who reflect His glory. Both masters and subjects will demonstrate such humility that spiritual masters will forbid their subjects and disciples to honor them, while the latter will of course honor them all the more for their humility.[61]

One cannot conclude from these observations that Olivi considers the hierarchy of his time to be agents of the Antichrist. Any attempt to read the *Commentary on Revelation* as a veiled attack on his superiors would seem ill-advised. The fact remains, however, that Olivi's view does not encourage any great optimism regarding the role which the hierarchy can be expected to play in the immediate future. One who believes that the elect will increasingly be found among the persecuted rather than the persecutors can hardly be expected to show much enthusiasm for the prospects of officially sanctioned repressive measures. The truth will triumph, but only after much adversity and only on its own power. That power is spiritual power, which finally converts rather than constrains.

Again we must be careful not to push Olivi farther than he wishes to go in this respect. He is willing to grant that clearcut heresy is a crime worthy of punishment.[62] He is simply less sanguine than many of his superiors about the possibility of their dealing with the subtle temptations of the day in such a way that the good and true will be wholeheartedly supported, the evil and false suppressed.

We have found Olivi to be a man in whom a number of elements combined to encourage a surprising degree of sympathy for the rights and benefits of intellectual freedom. The degree of sympathy is surprising, not merely because it is found in a thirteenth-century Franciscan scholar, but because it coexists with (and even presupposes to some extent) an extreme distrust of the newer intellectual currents of that era. While the limits of this freedom are more narrowly drawn than they would later be by John Stuart Mill or even Roger Williams, they are impressive nonetheless.

---

60. Ibid., f. 110rb.   61. Ibid., f. 121d.

62. See his *Commentary on John*, MS Rome, Ottob. lat. 3302, f. 48d, or *Commentary on Matthew*, MS Padova, Antoniana 336, f. 150b.

The Genesis of the University

WILLIAM RAGSDALE CANNON

The university originated in the Middle Ages. Indeed, it came into recognizable existence as late as the thirteenth century, so that its development from the time of its inception until it reached mature form as a distinctive social institution was scarcely more than the span of two centuries. It began with the renaissance of the twelfth century. It was completed before the end of the High Middle Ages. Its birth and growth were contemporary with the Gothic cathedral and scholastic theology.

No institution is entirely without antecedents, and all institutions that continue to function and fulfill a vital role in society change with changing times. The university is no exception. Its antecedents were the academies of antiquity and the monastic and cathedral schools of the Carolingian Empire, and it has continued to develop and expand in subsequent periods of history. Nonetheless, by the end of the thirteenth century it had acquired enough accoutrements to be completely itself and therefore capable of differentiation from all other educational enterprises that had gone before it; and its basic nature was sufficiently fixed so that succeeding developments have not obliterated it but rather have sharpened its features, heightened its functions, and given it stability and permanence in the affairs of men. No other bequest of the Middle Ages has been any more apparent or quite of such general usefulness as the university.

Since the university in origin is entirely a Western phenomenon, its roots sink deep into the soil of European civilization and reach back to that legacy the Middle Ages received from Greece and Rome. The Hellenic Age (480–399 B.C.), which built the Parthenon and sired Socrates and the dramatists, had no schools. There were teachers of various types: those who taught reading and writing and perhaps even arithmetic; instructors in music; and the gymnasts who gave lessons in athletics such as boxing, wrestling, vaulting, jumping, running, discus and javelin throwing. But their instruction was altogether unorganized. Parents sent their boys to these teachers who taught them one by one. There were tutorial exercises but no classes.[1] Even the

1. K. I. Freeman, *Schools of Hellas* (London, 1907). J. P. Mehaffy, *Old Greek Education* (New York, n.d.).

Sophists and Socrates were altogether informal in their teaching.[2] They discussed about what they knew, and anyone who was interested was free to listen and to enter into debate and discussion if he had the understanding to follow the argument.

Plato and Aristotle were the real artificers of the Greek school. They gave their lessons in a fixed place and offered a prescribed educational course extending over several years. Plato, for example, bequeathed his home and gardens to Speusippus, who in turn willed them to Xenocrates. And these properties were directed to education in perpetuity. They were the nucleus of a school of some renown which lasted until its disestablishment by Justinian in A.D. 529.[3] Aristotle's establishment was independent of Plato's. He lectured in the mornings to his hand-picked disciples and in the afternoons to the general public.[4] Yet the most that can be said of Plato's Academy and Aristotle's Lyceum is that they were centers of brilliant and thought-provoking lectures and forums of intellectual discussion. The pattern of education was anything the master chose to make it.

The Alexandrines of the third century after Christ devised the grammar school which provided a standard course of study independent of the intellectual caprice of teachers and pupils.[5] Indeed, both the words "school" and "grammar" come from Alexandria. Here the mind found its training ground in the study of literature and the scientific technique of language out of which literature is produced. Secondary education owes its beginnings, not to Plato and Aristotle, but to the later Greeks of Alexandria. The fact that three European nations have derived their names for school from the two institutions Plato and Aristotle founded—the academy of Scotland, the gymnasium of Germany, and the lycee of France—is not proof that their systems of secondary education are based on the Platonic and Aristotelian models. They are derivatives of Alexandria instead of Athens, which is evidence that European secondary education is not the offspring of genius but rather of a later organization which lesser minds gave to that intellectual curiosity which genius had originally inspired.

2. Werner Jaeger, *Paideia*, English tr. Gilbert Highet (New York, 1945), I, 286–331; II, 27–76.

3. A. E. Taylor, *Plato the Man and his Work* (New York, 1936), pp. 1–10, 503–516. Jaeger, op. cit., II, 77–86.

4. Diogenes Laertius, *Lives and Opinions of the Eminent Philosophers* (London, 1853), "Aristotle," IV.

5. J. E. Sandys, *A History of Classical Scholarship* (3rd ed., Cambridge, 1921), I, 7.

Roman education, like Roman culture in general, began as an importation from Greece. There is no evidence of any schools in the days of the Republic. Education was entirely a family affair. Fathers had absolute rule over their children. They were expected to train their sons in manly physical exercises, to give them an example of civic pride, and to teach them reverence for the gods and the laws of their country. Roman literature was Greek literature adapted to a new and ever expanding environment. The same old gods were given Latin names. If Suetonius is correct, Homer's *Odyssey* was first translated into Latin by a Greek slave in 272 B.C.,[6] and conquered scholars were used throughout by the conquerors as the teachers of their children. What we know about the course of study is due to the *Institutio Oratoria*, A.D. 91, by Fabius Quintilian,[7] whose father had taught rhetoric[8] and who inherited his father's trade. It consisted of the Greek and Latin poets, and Roman youth were subjected to discipline as severe as that of a reformatory or English preparatory school of the last century.

The first endowed school we know about was established by a pupil of Quintilian, Pliny the Younger, near Como, though Quintilian himself is reputed to have made a fortune through his teaching. Evidently all his pupils came from wealthy families, and his fees were exorbitant. Instruction ceased to be left entirely to private enterprise when the Emperor Antoninus Pius (A.D. 138–161) set up a system of rhetoricians on fixed salaries throughout the provinces of the empire. Gratian decreed in A.D. 376 that "in every town which is called a metropolis, a noble professor shall be elected" and put into law a tariff whereby his salary would be paid.[9] Greece established the pattern of secondary education. Rome extended it to include primary education and gave it state support. The public school is a Roman invention. Its curriculum and method of operation, however, seem to have remained static, so that it was in the time of Augustine just about what it had been when Quintilian taught in the first century.

Charlemagne received from the pope the title of Roman Emperor, and he thought of himself as the successor of the caesars. What they had done, he believed he could do better; and in the schools he estab-

6. Chapter on grammarians and rhetoricians in *De viris illustribus*, ed. C. G. Baumgarten-Crusius (1816).

7. Marcus Fabius Quintilianus, *Institutio oratoria*, ed. Spalding, Zumpt, and Bonnell (5th ed., Meister, 1882).

8. Ibid., IX, 3.   9. *Codex Theodosianus*, XIII, 3. 11.

lished he definitely excelled any one of them and probably out distanced all of them combined. To be sure, he had already the Greek and Roman pattern of education, if not in actuality as a living institution in his midst, at least in isolated instances afforded by some of the Benedictine monasteries about him and in the example of literary and other intellectual activity still carried on in the domain of his competitor at Constantinople to the east. The only thriving and growing institution he had from antiquity was the Christian church. Even his empire was a contemporary innovation. Consequently it was to the church that he turned for the talent both to organize his schools and also to maintain them by providing teachers and courses of study. Finally it was to the church that he entrusted the responsibility for their continuance. Education throughout the whole of the Middle Ages, except for a few Jewish and Sarcenic exceptions, was in western Europe entirely an enterprise of the Christian church.

Charlemagne's guide in the field of education was Alcuin, an English cleric from York, whom he met at Parma in A.D. 781 and for whom he acquired a deep affection. Alcuin became his own personal instructor and that of the members of his family. To this man he assigned the task of designing his schools. Since Alcuin himself was a product of the episcopal school of York Minster in Britain and had as his master a disciple of the Venerable Bede, it was only natural that the content he gave to education was primarily religious.[10] There was the basic necessity of teaching the pupils grammar just as there had been in the Roman schools, but the literary content of the course of study was the writings of the Fathers, especially St. Augustine. Learning to write was for the purpose of copying manuscripts and keeping official records. Learning to read was mainly to seek edification and moral and spiritual enlightenment, for the mind-set of those times was not in temporal welfare but in eternal well being. The learned and the ignorant were alike in that both believed the end of the world to be imminent. Therefore the reason behind all study was to know and understand the content of Scripture and thereby to apprehend the way to everlasting life.

Charlemagne in A.D. 789 revived a canon of the Synod of Vaison of A.D. 529 which required priests to hold schools in their parishes. These schools were to be open to the children of serfs and freemen as well as the nobility, and the students were to be taught grammar, composition,

10. *Alcuini Vita, auctor anonymus*, ed. W. Arndt, *Monumenta Germaniae Historica: Scriptores*, ed. G. H. Perth et al., XV, i, 182ff.

chant, and the psalter.[11] Nothing delighted the emperor more than to see the son of a serf surpass in his studies the son of a nobleman, and often he would award the prize of excellence in person when the recipient was of humble birth, encouraging the lad by telling him he expected one day to see him become a bishop. Society in the Middle Ages was rigidly segregated and fiercely class conscious, so that one generally remained where he was born until he died. The single exception to this pattern was the clergy. Priests and monks came from all strata of society. Bishops frequently were of humble origin, and it was possible even for the son of a serf to rise to Peter's throne. It is to the credit of Charlemagne that from the outset he encouraged through his schools the advancement of men of all ranks by initiative, learning, and general competence in the management of the affairs of the church. He saw to it that they received ecclesiastical preferment. He decreed that every monastery and every cathedral should maintain a school for the training of the young clergy, yet until A.D. 817 outsiders were permitted to study in these schools along with the religious and secular novices. After the Council of Aachen in A.D. 817, two types of schools were established, one for monks only and the other for the secular clergy and the laity.[12]

Charlemagne under the tutelage of Alcuin of York laid the foundation in the monastic and cathedral schools on which the university was later erected. Yet the superstructure was a long time in being built, for the foundation itself was greatly impaired after Charlemagne's time though it was never entirely destroyed. The political and social upheavals which afflicted Europe in the ninth and tenth centuries disrupted the general system of education which he had organized, but particular monasteries and cathedrals were able to maintain and in some instances even strengthen the schools they had begun. His own palace school at Aachen, popular and renowned from its inception because of the pedagogical gifts of Alcuin, had only a brief career. Under Charles the Bald it experienced a burst of glory in the brilliant speculation of John Scotus Eriugena, an eccentric genius of extraordinary originality and creativity, only to burn out almost entirely in the depressing darkness of ensuing centuries. Yet here and there over Western Europe the candle of learning, though it often flickered, was

11. Etienne Baluze, *Capitularia regum francorum ab anno 742 ad annum 922*, I, 237.
12. Joly, *Traité historique des écoles épiscopales en France* (Paris, 1849), p. 144 sq. Baluze, op. cit., I, 585.

not snuffed out, so that Alcuin's educational accomplishments were never altogether lost.

The curriculum in those medieval schools was the same. In order to enable students to understand the content of the Christian religion a certain amount of general knowledge was essential. This was provided through the *Trivium* and *Quadrivium*. The *Trivium* contained the elementary disciplines of grammar, rhetoric, and dialectics; correctness, style and elegance, and logic of expression in both speech and writing. The *Quadrivium* added the more advanced studies of music, arithmetic, geometry, and astronomy. These two branches of the curriculum covered the Seven Liberal Arts, designated by Philo in antiquity[13] and established as the basic discipline in education by Martianus Capella in the fifth century.[14] It was Alcuin of York who divided the discipline into two parts, making the *Trivium* prerequisite to the *Quadrivium*.[15] The justification for the study of arithmetic and astronomy was that they provided the means for dating Easter, while music was understood as no more than the rules of plain-song and a half-mystical concept of numbers. What bearing geometry had on the understanding of Christianity is hard to say, since in the Dark Ages it consisted only of a collection of some of the propositions of Euclid without their demonstration or proof.[16] The *Trivium* linked the Middle Ages with the pagan past since classical literature provided the illustrative material of both grammar and rhetoric which had originally come out of it. The technical rules were still those that had been formulated by Donatus[17] in the fifth century and revised by Priscian in the sixth,[18] which St. Jerome had mastered at the feet of the former in order to produce the *Vulgate* and about which the grammarians of Toulouse had argued in their dispute over the vocative of ego amid the crash of empires.[19]

Oddly enough, the one subject in that curriculum, though a part of the elementary course of study, which proved to be the hinge that opened the door to higher education was logic. It became the tool of

13. Philo, *De Congressu*, ed. Mangey (Erlangen, 1788), p. 148 sq.
14. *De Nuptiis Philologiae et Mercurii*, ed. Eyssenhardt (Leipzig, 1866).
15. P. Rajna, *Studi Medievali* (1928), I, 4–36.
16. Hastings Rashdall, *The Universities of Europe in the Middle Ages*, ed. F. M. Powicke and A. B. Emden (Oxford, 1936), I, 35–36.
17. *Ars grammatica*, in H. Keil, *Grammatici Latini*, IV.
18. *Institutiones grammaticae*, ed. Hertz and Kiel, in Kiel, op. cit., II and III.
19. Virgilius Maro Grammaticus, "Epist. de Pron.," *Opera*, ed. J. Heumer (Teubner) (Leipzig, 1886), p. 123.

the theologian both to explicate and to rationalize the revelation of God to man, and it afforded the philosopher his sole means of handling the problems of nature and human nature and out of the ingredients of this world constructing a metaphysics of all time and all existence. St. Anselm used it to prove that the teachings of faith are all reasonable and thereby to establish scholasticism. It was the discipline on which the realists and the nominalists alike depended in their debates on the nature of universals. Logic alone seemed to satisfy the curious and inquiring minds of the later Dark Ages[20] and to provide a way for them to advance beyond an elementary and secondary education to a form of learning which we have come to call postgraduate or higher education.

The transition from the monastic and cathedral schools of the Carolingian pattern to the entirely new institution of the university took place in the twelfth century. The cause for this change was twofold: first, the expansion of knowledge itself beyond the confines of *Trivium* and *Quadrivium* and, secondly, the remarkable increase in the number of people interested in acquiring knowledge.

Heretofore the monastic and cathedral schools had been very small. Often one teacher sufficed to give all the instruction needed in a given place. Once a young monk learned enough to perform his hours he was intellectually content, while a brother of sharper mind found the creative outlet for his talents in stylistic elegance and exactness in copying texts on parchments. Pupils at the cathedrals learned enough to say mass and respond appropriately to the needs of their parishoners in confession and sermon. The more diligent sought expertise as clerks and teachers in order to win preferment in the management of church and state. Most of the high government officials in the Middle Ages were clergymen, and in the church itself the office of bishop attracted the ambitious. But most schools were small and routine. They seldom sought to go beyond the minimum requirements. Monte Cassino in Italy and Bec in Normandy were brilliant monastic exceptions, while Chartres, Reims, Laon, Tours, and Paris shown off and on in the light of some exceptional scholar.

Indeed, the occasion, or precipitating event, for the transition from school to university was the reputation and appeal of great teachers. These pioneering minds were the agents in the expansion of knowledge in the first place, and their ability to communicate to others what

20. H. Rashdall, op. cit., I, 39.

they knew inspired more and more people to want to acquire an education. In the twelfth century Western Europe was beginning to break loose from the shackles of feudalism; cities were emerging north of the Alps to compete with those of Italy; and the new middle class of merchants and artisans was establishing itself as a force of considerable strength and influence. At first, only daring and original young intellectuals, enamored of the discovery of Aristotle and the opening of a broad and bright new horizon of studies through philosophy, science, and the classics,[21] took advantage of these celebrated teachers and sought them out wherever they might be teaching. Anselm had attracted the intellectually curious to Bec in the eleventh century,[22] and Bernard of Chartres won quite a reputation as a pedagogue, though more in traditional lines as grammarian and rhetorician, in the early twelfth century. He taught his pupils to memorize something from their reading every day and to concentrate on great writings and to avoid what was superfluous and mediocre. It is the virtue of a scholar to be ignorant of some things.[23]

By this time the monastic schools, with rare exceptions, were attracting fewer and fewer outsiders and limiting their instruction to their own novices. The cathedral schools, especially in the cities, boasted masters of considerable reputation, and it is in them that the influx of new students generally took place.[24] There was considerable competition for pupils among the masters. One's reputation depended in no inconsiderable measure on the size of his classes. Students wandered about from school to school, testing this master's diet and that, and dropping their comments for good or ill like a gourmet whose gossip about food makes or breaks the chef who prepares it.

Abelard, who was twenty-one years old when the twelfth century began, gives us a vivid picture of what took place by describing his own migrations as a student and by giving his assessment of his various teachers. William of Champeaux welcomed the young Breton into his classes until this bright pupil began to argue with him and to prove

21. The best book on the explosion of knowledge in the twelfth century is still the old one: C. H. Haskins, *The Renaissance of the Twelfth Century*, now in paperback, Meridian Books M. 49 (New York, 1957).

22. R. W. Southern, *Saint Anselm and His Biographer* (Cambridge, 1963), ch. 2.

23. Bernard left nothing but his influence upon his pupils and their influence in turn upon those who studied under them. John of Salisbury has given us a vivid description of this pedagogy: *Ioannis Saresberiensis episcopi Carnotensis Metalogicon*, in J. P. Migne, *Patrologiae latina* (Paris, 1844–64), CXCIX, cols. 854–855.

24. C. H. Haskins, op. cit., p. 371.

superior to him in disputation. The aged Anselm of Laon, under whom he studied theology, "had a wonderful command of language but a contemptible judgment and no reasoning power." If any one went to him with a question, the answer he gave left the inquirer more puzzled than he had been before he came. Evidently Anselm got his name as a theologian from long practice rather than from ingenuity or memory. "When he lighted the fire, he filled the room with smoke, not with light." Presumably anyone could begin to teach when he felt ready and when pupils were attracted to him by his knowledge and wisdom. Abelard set up instruction in competition with William of Champeaux and carried off many of William's pupils. Indeed, for a time William withdrew from the city and substituted in his place another teacher hostile to Abelard. When this man proved wholly inadequate to his task, William returned to reinforce him against Abelard. But this had the opposite effect. What few students the poor man had, he lost them all when the master came back, and he was forced to give up teaching and retire to a monastery.[25] Abelard's brilliant intellect and his scintillating manner of speech made his classes the center of pedagogical life in France and, for that matter, in the whole of Europe, and his school was the nucleus of what later became the University of Paris. William of Champeaux and his compeers had lit the fire; Abelard and his successors fanned it into a flame.

By the first quarter of the twelfth century Paris was an international city of students. Soon each nationality got its caricature. English students were drawn as cowardly and drunken; French as proud and effeminate; Normans as charlatans and boasters; Burgundians as brutal and stupid; Bretons as fickle and extravagant; Flemings as bloodthirsty, thievish, and incendiary; Germans as choleric, gluttonous, and dirty; Lombards as covetous, malicious, and no fighters; and Romans as seditious, violent, and slanderous. No nationality seemed to think very highly of the other, yet Latin was the common denominator, and anyone who knew enough Latin to follow the lectures got into the school.

Each morning at five or six o'clock the bell of Notre Dame tolled the pupils into class. The Master's valet spread straw on the cold floor and collected fees from the pupils. The young men sat on the cold stone or clay floor, used their right knee for a desk, and took notes on a wax tablet. The master used a parchment manuscript. He wrote his

25. *Petri Abaelardi Historica Calamitatum*, Migne, op. cit., CLXXVIII, cols. 114–126.

own comments on the margin of the text he brought to explicate. Lectures and the copying and studying by the students of what had been read and explained, together with general discussion of the same, consumed almost the whole of a working day. Nights were free for leisure. Youth filled taverns and brothels and often ended the evening by breaking up the town. Students engaged in more healthful forms of recreation as well. On the huge meadow between the bridge from the left bank of the Seine to Notre Dame and what is now the Champ de Mars they played all the games the European youth of that day knew how to play.[26]

When Abelard first came to Paris to study, the student body must have numbered between four and five hundred. When he was at the height of his professorial career, that number had increased to between five and seven thousand.[27] No degrees were offered. No standards of instruction had been set. A pupil came on impulse, and he stayed until his intellectual curiosity had been satisfied. The teacher lived off the fees his pupils paid him, or, if he had won ecclesiastical preferment, on the revenues of the church.

What happened in France happened in Italy as well. The twelfth century was an outburst of intellectual enthusiasm in the South as well as the North. Yet both the base of operation and the interest pursued were different. The foundation on which the university was erected in the South was lay schools. Charlemagne's educational pattern had not prevailed in Italy. There was less need for it. The grammar schools of pagan Rome had molded the Italian method of pedagogy; and, though there is no evidence that any definite school survived the collapse of the Empire and lived into the Middle Ages, still the blueprint of what Greek and Roman education had been was never lost. The teaching of rhetoric according to the Ciceronian method by dividing it into three branches, demonstration, deliberation, and judicial, characterized Italian instruction. This had taken a practical bent in *ars dictamini* or epistolary composition, designed to enable the student to draft legal documents and to compose official letters. Cities remained intact from ancient times. There were always civic offices to discharge. In the twelfth century the great expansion of trade and commerce added a heavy demand on the supply of clerks and other knowledgeable people. The management of ecclesiastical bus-

26. Joseph McCabe, *Peter Abelard* (New York, 1901), pp. 79–81.
27. Ibid., pp. 75–77.

iness was increasingly more extensive in Italy than elsewhere. It required an educational staff of managers, or bureaucrats. In addition to speaking and writing, the Italians had never lost the Graeco-Roman interest in the science of healing. They remembered and used much of the medicine of antiquity; far more than most people of those times they retained a lively concern for the things of this world as well as peace and joy in the world to come.

Whereas William of Champeaux and Abelard had won their reputation as philosophers and had attracted their students by fascinating them with abstract speculation, the celebrated teachers of the South attained fame in practical disciplines and gathered students to prepare them to get ahead in the society in which they lived. Irnerius, a native of Bologna, was the first person we know of in the Middle Ages to lecture systematically on the *Digest* of Justinian in its entirety and to show the relevance of all its parts to the social needs of his day.[28] About A.D. 1100, he succeeded in attracting many students to his school and in reviving "the law books which had been neglected for a long time."[29] Soon thereafter a younger contemporary, Gratian, matched his labor and success in the field of canon law, so that the needs of students to equip themselves for service in both state and church were simultaneously satisfied.[30] Farther south unknown teachers were attracting students to the study of medicine in sun-kissed Salerno.

Indeed, Salerno, without question, was the oldest university, and medicine the first of the academic disciplines to be organized into a "higher faculty" beyond the level of *Trivium* and *Quadrivium*. Whereas in both Paris and Bologna celebrated teachers had begun alone and taught independently of each other, the physicians in Salerno worked together, and at the opening of the thirteenth century we find them a well-knit and cooperative company, displaying their talents through their success in curing patients of diseases and in practical preventive medicine.[31] Methodical medical instruction based on compilations of Greek and Latin works was in vogue there as early as

28. Thomas Diplovatatius, *De claris iuris consultis*, ed. H. Kantorwicz and F. Schulz (Berlin and Leipzig, 1929), I.

29. Burchard of Ursperg, *Chronica, Monumenta Germaniae Historica*, Scriptores, XXIII, 342.

30. The best edition of the *Decretum Gratiani* is Friedberg's *Corpus juris canonici de Théologie Catholique*, ed. A. Vocent, E. Mangenot, E. Amann (Paris, 1903–50), VI (1920), cols. 1727–2511.

31. *Regimen Sanitatis Salernitanum*, tr. John Harrington in verse in 1608, ed. R. F. Packard (New York, 1920).

the eleventh century. Arabic medicine, much superior to European, was introduced to the West by Constantine the African, an older contemporary of Abelard. Constantine translated the four treatises of Isaac Judaeus on Urines, Fevers, Pulses, and Diets as well as the *Pentegni* and *Viaticus*, all of which became standard texts everywhere in the thirteenth century.[32] But Salerno fell on evil times due to the interference in her affairs by Frederick II, who thought he knew enough to supervise her examinations.[33] She never developed any other discipline besides medicine, and even in this her reputation was early superseded by that of Montpellier in what is now France. Consequently she exerted no real influence on the development of the university.[34] Rather she shines alone like a single jewel of learning in the lustre of her own excellence, not as one star among many in the crown of higher education.

The two basic patterns for the organization of the university were developed almost simultaneously, yet independently of one another, in Paris and Bologna. Whereas the great demand for higher education on the part of so many had risen spontaneously in the twelfth century when hordes of students migrated over Europe in quest of gifted teachers, the satisfaction of that demand through a viable and permanent institution took place in the thirteenth century. The law of supply and demand displays itself vividly in this process. Some way had to be found, on the one hand, to provide enough competent and qualified teachers for so many pupils with various intellectual interests; and, on the other, to establish these teachers in their profession in such a way that their work would become definite and constant, unaffected in any major way by the whims and caprices of those they served. In the twelfth century students could be hood-winked and cheated by any charlatan who could persuade them he was a teacher. Likewise, teachers could be lifted to prominence and opulence by the enthusiasm of their pupils only later to be thrown down and destroyed by their disillusionment and disfavor. It was not enough to leave the transmission of knowledge in its higher form to the accident of a teacher's personal charm and communicative skill in attracting pupils and of a pupil's ability to discern the worth of a teacher and the sub-

---

32. *Chartularium Universitatis Parisiensis*, ed. Denifle and Chatelain (Paris, 1889–92; auctarium, 1894–97), I, 453.

33. K. Sudhoff, articles in *Archiv für Geschichte der Medizin* (Leipzig, 1915), ix, 348–356; (1929), xx, 51–62.

34. H. Rashdall, op. cit., I, 82.

ject matter he taught. Higher instruction had to become, to a degree at least, standardized and provided with a structure more permanent than the improvised lecture hall of some knowledgeable orator. What Charlemagne did to regulate and preserve basic education in the ninth century through his system of schools had now to be done in the thirteenth century for the new higher education which was in vogue in Western Europe.

There was in Europe in the twelfth century the guild, a voluntary association organized for the mutual aid and protection of its members. Three types are prominent: religious or benevolent, merchant, and craft guilds. Perhaps in the twelfth century the latter two were not differentiated from one another. Merchants who sold the products and artisans who made them were classified together as traders. Later, in the fourteenth century, as trade and commerce increased and became more diversified, guilds, too, became specialized, representing, not merchants and craftsmen in general, but the makers of particular products such as wood-carvers, goldsmiths, stone-masons, and others.[35] The university in its institutional beginnings was not dissimilar from the guild. This is not to imply that guilds exercised any creative or even directive role in the formation of the university. Commercial guilds were in the process of formation at the same time the university was. It is to state simply that the university itself was organized as a guild. Indeed, it was a guild in the area of education just as much as the merchant and craft guilds were in the areas of trade and the production of goods. Guilds did not exist then on a national or regional basis. They were local affairs functioning in a particular city or town where their members lived. The university association was the same. Its members carried on the educational process in a certain place such as Paris, Bologna, Salerno, Montpellier, or Oxford. They organized where they were for their own mutual aid and protection. Their guild was social, too. Therefore, it is historically accurate to say that the university itself represents a fourth type of guild in the Middle Ages.

This guild took two forms. One was an organization of students, while the other was an organization of teachers. The former arose among the law students at Bologna in Italy. The latter emerged at Paris where the teachers banded together to determine the pattern of education, methods of implementing it, and regulations governing

35. W. E. Wilda, *Das Gildenwesen im Mittelalter* (Halle, 1831); G. F. Renard, *Guilds in the Middle Ages*, tr. D. Terry, ed. G. D. H. Cole (London, 1919).

their own status and benefits. In both instances, however, the reason for such an organization was the city and the local inhabitants thereof, not the faculty and student body and the internal conditions of the emerging university.

Bologna, for example, was one of the free cities of Northern Italy, a member of the Lombard League which had won the war with the Emperor Frederick Barbarossa. Her civic affairs were run by her own citizens. The jurists of repute in that place were all citizens and therefore subject to Bolognese laws, while an increasingly large number of students were foreigners. They were left entirely unprotected, the prey of predatory merchants and landlords, individually helpless unless unitedly and corporately they could help themselves.

Paris, in contrast, was a royal city governed by the French monarchy, the most powerful in Europe, except for the imperial crown which in the struggle between them yielded to her French rival as frequently as she won first place. Though many of the students in Paris were foreigners, too, the king of France gave them a special status and guaranteed their freedom even when France was at war with their own country.[36] The teachers, also, took a special interest in them, and in exercising their own rights and privileges they were frequently prompted by some injustice which they felt had been inflicted on their students.[37] Nonetheless the reputation of the teachers was always the brightest star in the educational sky of Paris. Most of them had immigrated to Paris from elsewhere. They were a cosmopolitan lot. Therefore, they, more than the students, took advantage of the guild concept and banded themselves together for purposes of professional security and class aggrandizement. They were clever enough to include the students in their corporation, but they maintained control.

Such was not the case in Bologna. No doubt the teachers were organized in some loose way there in the twelfth century. Frederick Barbarossa in 1158 granted privileges to scholars in Lombardy, which was then his domain, permitting them to choose in case of a law suit against them whether they would have their case tried in the bishop's court or adjudicated by their own professors.[38] Since the law teachers of Bologna did not include students in their guild, the students formed

36. *Chartularium universitatis Parisiensis*, II. 75.
37. In 1229 the teachers suspended their lectures and dissolved the university organization when the soldiers savagely fell upon the students in an effort to quell a disturbance during carnival. Matthew Paris, *Chronica Majora*, ed. H. R. Luard (1872–83), III, 166–168.
38. *Monumenta Germaniae Historica: Constitutiones* (1893), I, 249.

guilds of their own. Their purpose was to care for one another as members of a fraternity, to regularize their organization by statutes and the election of efficient officers, and to assure themselves a comfortable and secure life while they were studying in a foreign and hostile city.[39] The natural bond among them was nationality, so the first student guilds were four in number, formed by the Lombards, Tuscans, Romans, and Ultramontanes, students from beyond the mountains, that is, the countries north of the Alps. This last one had fourteen national subdivisions.[40] Since the teachers were all Bologonese and ex-officio members of the large City Council, they were excluded from the guild.[41] It was to their interest to exclude a person who was not a citizen from a teaching post in law and to keep a monopoly on the new profession.

The great influx of students had brought business to Bologna. The city prospered because of them. When the students became well organized, they could put the town in jeopardy by threatening to leave it and set up their classes elsewhere. Their teachers as well as merchants and landlords were dependent upon their patronage. Thus the students through their mighty guilds set up the laws for the management of the university, elected the rectors, and determined the requirements a teacher had to meet in order to teach there. When the teachers protested the propriety of such action and won mild support from the city fathers, the students made good their threat and evacuated Bologna (1217–1220). The city became almost a ghost town for three years. Even the pope intervened in behalf of the students, and the city further capitulated by writing their demands into law. The students took complete charge of the university. They fired the teachers when they missed classes, determined the length and time of professorial lectures, disciplined obstreperous masters with corporal punishment, and even hired and fired the faculty.[42] Bologna was a student's paradise.

The chief officer of the student university was the rector, who was chosen biennially by a group of electors consisting of the ex-rectors and the councillors of the nations plus an equal number of special delegates. The choice was by ballot. The rector had to be a secular clerk, since canon law forbade the rule of a layman over a clergyman.

---

39. *Acta Nationis Germanicae Univ. Bonon.* (Berlin, 1887), pp. 4–36.
40. Ibid., p. 349.   41. H. Rashdall, op. cit., I, 158.
42. Heinrich Denifle, "Die Statuten der Juristen-Universitat Bologna," *Archiv für Literatur- und Kirchengeschichte des Mittelalters* (1887), pp. 256–323.

He must have completed five years in the study of law and to have attained the age of twenty-five. Each nation elected the councilmen, who with the rector formed the executive body of the university. It required the consent of someone who had been rector or the rector himself together with a majority of the councillors to call a special meeting of the entire student body. This body when it met was supreme. Everyone in attendance had the right to speak, and votes were taken by ballot with the use of black and white beans. Legislation proposed by the Council was submitted to the student body for ratification. Since law was the object of the existence of the University of Bologna, the management of the school was strictly by statute. The rector could not do anything independently of the adopted regulations of the student body. If a fine was fixed by law for a transgression and the rector failed to allot the fine for the transgressor, he had to pay it himself. He had no discretionary rights in dealing with either faculty or students. Whatever happened he was forced to deal with it according to law. Students took an oath to inform on faculty and on one another when they observed a violation of law. Yet the laws the students enacted regarding their own conduct were mild, and penalties for violations were light and easy. This was not true in respect to the faculty. The doctors had exact and difficult standards set for them, and the discipline imposed on them by students was severe indeed. It is not an exaggeration to say that at Bologna they were virtual slaves to their students who often behaved toward them as the Egyptian taskmasters did toward the Israelites in Mosaic times.[43]

Educational activities in Paris had got their start at the cathedral school of Notre Dame. It was only natural, therefore, that the chancellor who was titular head of the school should presume to the same position in the rising university. By action of the Third Lateran Council of 1179 he had been entrusted with the responsibility of judging the fitness of candidates for teaching and had been required to issue a license to every qualified applicant. The transition of a person from student to teacher was called inception.[44] On the one hand, this meant the beginning of his actual performance of the work of teaching. On the other hand, it meant his acceptance as colleague by his old teachers and the other members of his profession. He was given the Biretta, the little cap which was the professional badge. His former master

43. H. Rashdall, op. cit., I, 176–203.
44. *Chartularium universitatis Parisiensis*, Introduction, 12.

placed in his hands the ring and the open book and gave him a kiss and benediction. Afterwards, the new master entertained his colleagues and friends at a sumptuous banquet, gave them gifts, and formally took his place as an active member of the guild of teachers, or masters.[45] The chancellor made all this possible by issuing the license to teach, though he himself did not necessarily belong to the guild of teachers.

Innocent III recognized the guild of Parisian masters by authorizing it through a bull to elect a proctor to represent it at the papal court.[46] The strength of this body was soon exerted in an effort to emancipate itself from the excessive power the chancellor tried to exercise over it. At first through ecclesiastical means he could deprive a master of his license and its attendant professorial privileges. His legal prerogatives were such that he might well have been able to strangle the university in its infancy before it was old enough to acquire a legal status of its own. But fortunately the guild of masters found an international champion in the papacy. The pope forced the chancellor to grant the license to all candidates recommended by a majority of the masters of the faculties of theology, civil or canon law, or medicine, or by just six masters selected by the faculty of arts. Half the examining board of six was to be chosen by the masters and half by the chancellor.

As in Bologna, so in Paris, the nations made themselves apparent in their distinctiveness. There were four of them large enough to be organized: the French, the Normans, the Picards, and the English. But, whereas in Bologna, they had been guilds of students, in Paris they were subdivisions of the masters on the faculty of arts. The nations did not manifest themselves organizationally in the higher faculties of theology, law, and medicine. Since the faculty of arts predominated by sheer numbers, the head of that faculty gradually emerged as the rector of the combined university, though each of the other faculties maintained its dean and frequently voting was by faculties rather than by the university as a whole. The final authority was the general congregation of all the masters to which the rector might summons by bedel (his messenger) the various deans and their faculties. As a matter of courtesy, the rector went in person to the dean of theology to invite him and his faculty to the congregation.[47]

45. H. Rashdall, op. cit., I, 284–287.
46. *Chartularium universitatis Parisiensis*, I, 20.
47. H. Rashdall, op. cit., I, 318–334.

The thirteenth century saw completed at Paris a fourfold process which transformed an informal society of masters into a full-fledged university dominated and controlled by a legally recognized corporation of professors: (1) the adoption of fixed statutes of government, (2) active engagement as a recognized body by church and state in legal business including at times trials at courts of law, (3) the creation of a permanent executive staff of administrative officers, (4) the use of a public seal.[48] The *summum bonum* of the University of Paris was when its rector succeeded finally in superseding the bishop of Paris at the end of the academic parade and establishing thereby the solitary grandeur of his position of prominence as head of the greatest educational institution in the medieval world. The power of corporate learning had lifted a penniless master of arts, chosen by his own compeers, above cardinals, archbishops, bishops, papal nuncios, ambassadors, and the peers of France as first in rank and dignity in all affairs which took place within the university.[49]

This rank and this prestige were only official, never personal. A rector held office at first for only one month. Later his term was extended to three months. Away from his office he was nothing more than he had been before he received it. After his term was out he sank back into oblivion. He was simply the grand functionary of the general corporation of masters whose rights and privileges he personified and whose inestimable worth to society he symbolized. The general congregation which through him could make demands and could strike or move away if they were not met consisted of all the masters in residence, that is, engaged in teaching, of the four faculties of theology, medicine, law, and the arts. Masters in residence were called regents to distinguish them from other graduates who had gone elsewhere to teach or had entered other professions. A faculty or nation might delay a decision of the congregation from being executed. It could not prevent it. Since each faculty and nation possessed a separate key to the chest which contained the university seal and since all keys had to be used to open the lock, a dissident party might refuse to produce its key. Yet if it remained stubborn in its refusal, there was always the remedy of breaking the lock and freeing the seal.[50]

During the thirteenth century Bologna and Paris effected a series of

48. Ibid., 299.
49. Caesar Egassius Bulaeus (du Boulay), *Historica Universitatis Parisiensis a Carolo M. ad nostra tempora* (Paris, 1665–73), I, 269–270; IV, 585; V, 543.
50. Rashdall, op. cit., I, 398–432.

administrative officers for their respective universities, the Italian composed of students, the French of masters. But there was one area of university life in which students could not trespass. That was the area of determining who was qualified for the degree, or license to teach. Only masters could set and assess examinations. They alone could make possible the transition from the status of student to that of master. This meant that ultimately the decisive control of the university was in the hands of the faculty. Gradually the Italian student university of law became an anachronism. To be sure, it flourished and expanded throughout the thirteenth century and on into the late Middle Ages, but with the advent of modernity only the faculty type university was able to survive. The university of Paris became the prototype of higher education in the Western world.

Both the form and method of university education were completed before the end of the thirteenth century. The first account of studies required for the Master of Arts degree is that of Robert of Curzon, papal legate to Paris, in 1215.[51] It is a catalogue of books on which the student was to be examined. The medieval concept of knowledge was invariably what somebody of repute had said about some subject.[52] A man was learned if he could give information and cite the authority for that information. Grammar, logic, and psychology dominated the curriculum for the baccalaureate, supported by natural philosophy and metaphysics for the license in the arts. Moral philosophy crowned the requirements for the Master of Arts degree. The student was a student, pure and simple, until he attained the bachelor of arts. Then he began to teach some himself, under the tutelage of his master, as he progressed in his studies toward the master's degree. At Bologna this was merely an academic exercise, like simulated situations of instruction and learning in schools of education today; but at Paris a certain amount of independence in the classroom was given to the young bachelor, so that he formed a part of the teaching staff as graduate students do in our universities now.

The courses of study, following the pattern at Bologna, were divided into ordinary and cursory lectures, the differences being that ordinary lectures came in the morning and were given by regent masters, while the cursory lectures came in the afternoon and during holidays and were taught by the bachelors.

51. *Chartularium universitatis Parisiensis*, I, 20.
52. Rashdall, op. cit., I, 440.

Generally the time required of a student from his arrival at the university until he was accepted as a bachelor of arts was a year and a half. The examination of the baccalaureate took place in December. First the student had to dispute with his master in grammar and logic. Later he was examined by a committee of his own nation on the books he had read, and the schedule of the classes in which he had enrolled was carefully scrutinized to be sure that his record of attendance had been adequate. The process of qualifying for the baccalaureate was called determination, and the goal of it was wearing the bachelor's coppa and taking one's place with his compeers in the bachelor's, or student's, guild. He swore an oath of allegiance to the proctor of his nation.[53]

At Paris it took five to six more years for the student to qualify for his license. He had to have heard the lectures on all the books required by the faculty and to have attained the age of twenty. Then, he was free to present himself for the chancellor's examination.[54] If he passed it and was successful in his public disputation, then he marched in the academic procession with the bedels, the proctors, and the rector to the place of graduation, when after giving a formal lecture, he knelt before the chancellor to receive from him his license in the name of the Trinity. The ceremony ended with the apostolic benediction.

But the license to teach was not the master's degree. The degree came six months later when the licensed candidate was invited to give an inaugural lecture before his own nation. The night before he participated in vespers, a semireligious and academic exercise consisting of disputations as well as worship. He swore his oath of allegiance to the teacher's guild. The inaugural lecture itself marked his inception when he was presented with Biretta and Book and in full academic regalia took his seat along with the old masters. That night he gave the customary sumptuous banquet for masters and friends.

What took place in the education of Masters of Arts likewise took place through a different course of study in the education of doctors of medicine, theology, and law. Indeed, the baccalaureate was first introduced at Paris as a preparatory stage, not in the course of arts, but in the course of theology. After five years of study students of theology were allowed to give private lectures. If one had the master's degree in arts before matriculating in one of the three higher faculties, the time

---

53. Ibid., 450–456.
54. *Chartularium universitatis Parisiensis,* IV, 729.

demanded of him for the course of study was abbreviated. Indeed, at Paris most theological students were young Masters of Arts. Yet the degree in Art was not necessarily a prerequisite for matriculation in studies under one of the higher faculties. In theology, for example, in the early thirteenth century the course of study at Paris was eight years, five for the baccalaureate and three more for the doctorate. The candidate had to be thirty-five years of age before he could incept.[55]

Except for the provision of room and board for a few poor students in certain religious houses which later became colleges, the universities had no buildings or real property in the thirteenth century. Their assets were altogether intangible. They possessed knowledge and in rare instances wisdom as well. With these, and these alone, they added a new dimension to civilization.

55. Ibid., I, 20.

Bibliography and appendix

Ray C. Petry: a bibliography

Compiled by JOYCE L. and DONN MICHAEL FARRIS

BOOKS

Christian Eschatology and Social Thought. A Historical Essay on the Social Implications of Some Selected Aspects in Christian Eschatology to A.D. 1500. New York: Abingdon Press, 1956.

Francis of Assisi, Apostle of Poverty. Durham, N.C.: Duke University Press, 1941. Reprint: New York: AMS Press, 1964.

Editor, *A History of Christianity. Readings in the History of the Early and Medieval Church.* Englewood Cliffs, N.J.: Prentice-Hall, Inc., 1962.

The Ideal of Poverty in Francis of Assisi. Chicago: University of Chicago Libraries, 1934.

Editor, *Late Medieval Mysticism* (Vol. XIII, *Library of Christian Classics*). Philadelphia: Westminster Press, 1957.

Editor, *No Uncertain Sound. Sermons That Shaped the Pulpit Tradition.* Philadelphia: Westminster Press, 1948.

Preaching in the Great Tradition. Neglected Chapters in the History of Preaching (The Samuel A. Crozer Lectures for 1949). Philadelphia: Westminster Press, 1950.

ARTICLES

"Art and the Message of the Church," *The Duke Divinity School Bulletin*, XXVIII, no. 3 (Nov., 1963), 210–216.

"The Arts as Interpreters of Christ and the Gospels in Worship; a Testimony," *The Duke Divinity School Bulletin*, XII, no. 4 (Jan., 1948), 139–148.

"Between Two Worlds," *The Duke Divinity School Bulletin*, VIII, no. 4 (Jan., 1944), 68–74.

"Calvin's Conception of the 'communio sanctorum,'" *Church History*, V, no. 3 (Sept., 1936), 227–238.

"Christian Eschatology and Social Thought," *Theology Today*, V, no. 2 (July, 1948), 207–217.

"Christian Humanism and Reform in the Erasmian Critique of Tradition." in O. B. Hardison, ed., *Medieval and Renaissance Studies.*

Chapel Hill: The University of North Carolina Press, 1966, pp. 138–170.

"The Church and Church History," *The Duke School of Religion Bulletin*, V, no. 3 (Nov., 1940), 63–77. (Address delivered at the formal opening of the Duke School of Religion for the year 1940–41.)

"The Critical Temper and the Practice of Tradition," *The Duke Divinity School Review*, XXX, no. 2 (Spring, 1965), 83–97.

"The Eccentricity of the Clergy and the Priority of Ministry," *The Duke Divinity School Bulletin*, XXVII, no. 3 (Nov., 1962), 131–136.

"Emphasis on the Gospel and Christian Reform in Late Medieval Preaching," *Church History*, XVI, no. 2 (June, 1947), 75–91.

"Eyeless in Gaza." An Address on Theological Education delivered at the Western North Carolina Annual Conference, Asheville, N. C., on September 22, 1950. Printed and distributed by the Board of Education and the Board of Ministerial Training and Qualifications upon vote of the Annual Conference.

"Graduation Within the Christian Community," *The Duke Divinity School Bulletin*, XXIV, no. 1 (Feb., 1959), 4–9.

"The Historic University and the Divinity School: The University as the Historic Eye of the Vicarious Storm," *The Outlook*, XX, no. 7 (July–Aug., 1971), 3–17. (The second of his Carver-Barnes Memorial Lectures at Southeastern Seminary, Wake Forest, N.C., Feb., 1971).

"Medieval Eschatology and St. Francis of Assisi," *Church History*, IX, no. 1 (March, 1940), 54–69.

"Mediaeval Eschatology and Social Responsibility in Bernard of Morval's *De Contemptu Mundi*," *Speculum*, XXIV, no. 2 (April, 1949), 207–217.

"Nicholas of Cusa," *Encyclopedia Britannica*, XVI (1966), 483.

"The People's Book and Figures of Speech," *The Duke Divinity School Review*, XXIX, no. 3 (Autumn, 1964), 177–180.

"Reading, Teaching, and Research," *Brethren Life and Thought*, X, no. 2 (Spring, 1965), 7–16.

"The Reforming Critiques of Robert Grosseteste, Roger Bacon, and Ramon Lull and Their Related Impact upon Medieval Society. Historical Studies in the Critical Temper and the Practice of Tradition," in Jerald C. Brauer, ed., *Essays in Divinity, Vol. II. The Impact of the Church upon Its Culture. Reappraisals of the History of Christianity*. Chicago: University of Chicago Press, 1968, pp. 95–120.

"Research Abstracts: European Church History," *The Journal of Bible and Religion*, XVIII, no. 1 (Jan., 1950), 108–111.

"St. Francis, Society and the Ultimate Order," *The Duke School of Religion Bulletin*, IV, no. 2 (May, 1939), 29–33.

"The Social Character of Heavenly Beatitude According to the Thought of St. Thomas Aquinas," *The Thomist*, VII, no. 1 (Jan., 1944), 65–79.

"Social Responsibility and the Late Medieval Mystics," *Church History*, XXI, no. 1 (March, 1952), 3–19. (Presidential address, American Society of Church History, read in New York City, Dec. 28, 1951.)

"Some Basic Conceptions of Christian Social Thought to the Reformation," *Religion in the Making*, II, no. 2 (Jan., 1942), 120–134.

"Survey, Medieval Church History," *Church History*, XI, no. 2 (June, 1952), 146–149; XXII, no. 3 (Sept., 1953), 239–292; XXIII, no. 4 (Dec., 1954), 364–367; XXVI, no. 2 (June, 1957), 169–173.

"Three Medieval Chroniclers: Monastic Historiography and Biblical Eschatology in Hugh of St. Victor, Otto of Freising, and Ordericus Vitalis," *Church History*, XXXIV, no. 3 (Sept., 1965), 282–293.

"Unitive Reform Principles of the Late Medieval Conciliarists," *Church History*, XXXI, no. 2 (June, 1962), 164–181.

"The Yearnings of the Laity," *The Duke Divinity School Bulletin*, XXVIII, no. 1 (Feb., 1963), 3–8.

Appendix: Religious affirmations of a lay Christian

Selected and Introduced by GEORGE H. SHRIVER

Ray C. Petry is a layman who has been involved in the theological education of ministers during most of his career. This has resulted in unique opportunities as well as unusual problems. Dr. Petry himself has said: "A layman teaching church history in a Divinity School has a problem somewhat like that of Siamese twins in a traveling circus. Like theirs, his private life is doubly public. The ministry look at him as if he were a layman. The laity scrutinize him as if he were a minister." Needless to say, he overcame any such problem in a way which has led to deep appreciation by both clergy and laity. He is not ordained but he has delivered religious affirmations at many times and places. To select only several of these dozens was a difficult task, but finally three were chosen which illustrate recurring interests and commitments of his career.

Though written earliest of the affirmations presented here, the first deals with an area which has most recently engaged Petry's mind, for in "The Church and Church History" he addresses himself to the problem of the critical temper and the practice of tradition. Rejecting the highly uncritical approach as well as the myth of pure objectivity, he accepts the scholarly quest for truth. Indeed, he says that "there is no history without dynamic tradition, no tradition without unremitting practice, no practice without the nicely judged and discerning application of the critical temper." His people-centered interest is found in one of his conclusions: "One of the greatest fascinations of Christian history is the interest of real people in each other down the ages."

In the second piece Petry literally soars. I have never read a more beautiful impressionistic statement concerning the relation of Christianity and the arts. It becomes a compressed diary of what the world of Christian literature, architecture, the plastic arts, and music has meant to him personally and of his identification with this world.

The third and most recent article defines the role of the divinity school within the context of the larger university. He riddles his reader from every angle with the unexpected in his refreshing picture of the situation where teachers learn and learners teach. He suggests that "the mark of a free man is the seal of a true university" and observes that a part of his freedom is being redeemed to graciousness in the midst of a university whose genius is manifested in "corporately practiced, endless critiques." Often in this essay, Petry is seen as a "people-professor" involved in a seminar on humanity. His humanness is a delight to experience as he projects the themes of mutuality, reciprocity, and equilibrium.

One of the major purposes of education is to evoke disclosure. By means of performative language and use of the "poetic simple," Professor Petry evokes disclosure in these affirmations. Though two were written several decades ago, they also illustrate the fact that truth is not the daughter of authority but rather of time. The language in them continues to evoke disclosure and to speak cogently.

Dr. Petry once said that "he who would be a predecessor must come in last." Though these essays appear last in this *Festschrift* they are certainly written by a predecessor.

The church and church history, in classroom and parish

> *Remember, Lord, thy Church, to deliver her from all evil and to make her perfect in thy love, and to gather from the four winds her that is sanctified unto thy kingdom which thou didst prepare for her. [The Didache, x, 5]*

> *But if administrators, who prosper through those who make progress because of them, and if scholars, who advance by themselves under God by acquiring spiritual wisdom, remain in their chosen way of life, they proceed by different roads, it is true, but they travel towards one homeland and arrive at one kingdom, doing service in different capacities as Christ, the King of all, calls them. [Julianus Pomerius, The Contemplative Life, iii, 28]*

A paper of scholarly character ought, as a rule, to deal with a limited subject. This should be treated in intensive fashion with a minimum of generalization. Upon certain occasions, however, it is imperative that a broad subject of general moment be considered. Its handling may then require the bold, sweeping outlines more appropriate to a brief period of discussion. Such valid generalizations as may be most useful for subsequent reflection will then be in order. This is such an occasion.

The subject proposed for discussion this morning is "The Church and Church History." The implications of this topic cannot safely be ignored by anyone however remotely concerned with the Christian church as a factor in human experience. Least of all can those in preparation for the Christian ministry and those assisting them in that preparation afford to neglect the relationship existing between the contemporary church and its career through the centuries. Theological teachers and students, who are unconcerned with, or uninformed as to, the church's history, will serve to produce a membership severed from the fullness of its spiritual heritage. An alert faculty and

This address was delivered at the formal opening of the Duke School of Religion for the year 1940–41, and was published in the *Duke School of Religion Bulletin*, V, no. 3 (Nov., 1940), 63–77.

a ministry trained in the history of the church's weakness and strength, alike, may help to realign the current institution with its enduring purposes.

When viewed in such a connection, church history may be regarded by theological professors and students, not only as a course in academic discipline, but also as an indispensable aid to the most enlightened churchmanship. This, of course, raises the whole question as to the relationship which should exist between the study of the church's past and the active participation in its present. Many approaches have been made to the study and writing of church history. These overlap and diverge in highly confusing fashion. However, three such approaches may be singled out as fairly representative of the major lines of consideration.

The first of these exploits the church's history in a highly uncritical manner. The ostensible search for the truth about the past is more frequently a rationalization of partial data in support of established preconceptions. The facts of Christian history are often distorted in the attempt to defend subsequent traditions and dogmas held indispensable to the church's existence. History is so far subordinated to the demands of the current church as to become not merely its deferential servant but, even more, its ignominious slave. Early experiences and institutions are frequently glorified to the disparagement of all later developments. Segments of Christian thought and life are wrested from their natural contexts and set up as normative for all subsequent times. Thus the evidences for a given type of primitive church order may be dissociated from other, and not always corroborating, evidences and held to be determinative of later church organization. The desire to confirm accepted ideas and usages governs the investigation of past thought and conduct. Testimony from the past which conflicts with present conceptions is derogated, "reconstructed," or ignored. Traditions which are of doubtful authority, but replete with edifying materials, are regularly preferred to a more trustworthy, but less moralizing, history.

The sources are selected and appraised without due regard to the generally accepted methods of scholarly research. The records are "pieced" and "cut" in cinema-house fashion in order to propagandize the claims of denomination, school of interpretation, or homiletic clique. The lives of great men are not portrayed in accordance with the best probabilities as to what they were in their own day. They are, rather, depicted in keeping with later surmises as to what they ought surely to have been. The net results of this "censored" history are most detrimental to the church. Though inaugurated, often most sincerely, to keep Christian life true to its fundamental character, such a study succeeds only in obscuring the developmental nature and vital resourcefulness of historic Christianity. The artificial promptings of a static, arbitrary institutionalism even deny what has been in order to insure more fully the crystallization of the church as it has since come to be.

A second approach swings to the opposite extreme in relating Christian history and the present. Its laudable purpose is to discover the truth about the church's past, be the record what it may. The canons of scientific history are employed in what is declared to be an objective analysis of the facts and nothing but the facts. Critical acumen is brought to bear upon all available sources, which are sought out, classified, and given exposition in accordance with the most rigorous demands of scientific methodology. Interpretation is strictly limited to a statement of what the evidences proclaim when safely immunized from the contagion of the least subjectivity. Church history, which is thus regarded as but a specialized department of history, is presented ideally as a pure science. All concerns with values, edification, and lessons from the past are disciplined to the point of near-extinction. Interest in the church itself is confined to a scientist's regard for a phenomenon under observation.

The phenomenon in this case is just one of many social institutions to be studied not with a view to evaluation and constructive criticism but with the intent to secure statistical information. The not too amusing inference is sometimes drawn that the dependable church historian cannot be an active Christian. His being more than nominally such might involve sympathies with, and loyalties to, the institution being studied. This would be quite disruptive of the scholarly detachment which ought to characterize the objective scrutiny of an item in social evolution. From this viewpoint, the interest of the church historian in the church is solely that of a scientific researcher for his data. Church history's only service to the church thus becomes a most indirect one. It consists in supplying to those who are committed to church loyalty the authoritatively objective findings discoverable only by those who are not. Students of ecclesiastical history so interpreted are encouraged to pursue their subject with the scholar's devotion to pure research in itself. At the precise moment when they or their professors ask, "Of what use is this to the church and its ministerial work?" they cease to be worthy students of church history and become merely Christians.

A third approach seeks to preserve the scholarly quest for truth about the church's past without being duped by the myth of pure objectivity. It recognizes the grave danger of fabricating the story of the past out of the wishes of the present. But it also challenges the possibility and the desirability of subtracting history and the historian wholly from the realm of personal opinions, meanings, and values. After all, as a ranking church historian has said, "There are no infallible standards on which to base judgment, and all historical research is at bottom an art which, like every art, is primarily founded on the very qualities of the individual himself; but it can be developed by regular cultivation, rich experience, and ever fresh activity in various fields, until a high degree of certainty in opinion is reached."

Proponents of this third approach remind those of the second of significant factors which secular historians have already begun to consider. These scholars know that researchers in the social sciences can command no such rigid control of their data as that which isolates the laboratory experiment. They admit, in increasing numbers, that history which ignores minds, meanings, and values is hardly real history; that pure facts divorced from interpretation are something of a mirage; and that past experiences which have any meaning for the present necessarily undergo some valuative interpretation at its hands.

Thus the "New History," which has long since attained its years of maturity, definitely commits itself to an interest which extends beyond episodes and events. It is unashamedly curious about the meaning of these facts in relation to ordinary people. Human environment, attitudes, motivations, doings, ideas, and ideals are as definitely the concern of history as they are beyond the sheerly quantitative measurement of pure science. The historical process is rightly seen to include not only the more material elements such as geography and economics, but also the psychic factors, without consideration of which the record of living men cannot be even approximately known. History thus abandons atomistic and isolated approaches for a critically interpretative survey which gladly employs the findings of cooperative research in sociology, anthropology, psychology, art, archaeology, and other related fields. Scientific methodology wherever applicable is in no way compromised. However, the concern of history with man's individual and social integrity, with his mental as well as with his physical activity, goes beyond the findings of pure science into the realm of applications and values as well.

To be sure, the historian as such occupies himself properly with the consideration of human life in its natural, observable interrelations and not with metaphysical speculations as to final causes and ends. That is, he does not assume the philosopher's and theologian's task of speculating critically upon man's relation to supernatural forces and cosmic ultimates. In so far, however, as man's religious beliefs and philosophical ideas concerning the superhuman have influenced human affairs, these conceptions must be related to the whole of his social experience. Thus his standards of worth must be given interpretation even though this involve the historian's opinion, as it invariably will. In every case, events, situations, relating factors, ideas, and institutions form a part of man's discoverable record within the social environment. These, therefore, command the research effort and interpretative powers of qualified historians.

This command is, however, more often acknowledged than it is obeyed. Unfortunately, many of those who have had a wider vision of history's domain still have a pronounced astigmatism where the church and its past are concerned. Too often, they become neglectful or scornful of an institution which has dared to commit itself to ends not fully answerable to historical analysis. In violation of their own principles these secular historians veer away from a full consideration of society's most significant reagent throughout history.

Obviously, then, there is great need for men equal to the secular historian in ability and scholarly methodology, but superior to him in the interest and training necessary to relate the continuing Christian institution to its total past. Such stipulations indicate the task and requisite qualifications of that historical specialist, the church historian. But one group of church historians, so called, is too scornful or neglectful of tested methods to get valid results; another is too fearful of compromising its objectivity to give due regard to data which cannot be truly known apart from a measure of the subjective and valuative. The third approach therefore makes its claim to consideration. It applies undeviatingly the tested principles of cooperative research and the courageous interpretation, open always to scholarly criticism, which characterize the only true historical method. In addition, it accords to the church its due primacy in the history of significant institutions. There is, likewise, a frank and unapologetic interest in the church's welfare.

Secular historians, sociologists, and economists have at solemn moments admitted that social values are not entirely foreign to their interests. Church historians of the third group do not shrink from making available to the present church the implications of its past; neither do they fail to inform society of the debt which it owes to the church of that past. They challenge society to examine its present standards of value in the light of former experiences which it sustained in relation with the church.

Such Christian historians have sufficient evidence that their Christian loyalty need not impair their effectiveness as historians, and that their contribution as historians is invaluable to the progress of the present-day church. To be sure, the historian of Christianity struggles to discipline his very human tendency to read the present back into the past. He tries to be on the alert against distorting past beliefs by imposing upon them his own credo. He is not so lacking in courage, however, as to suppress at all times those personal convictions and theological speculations to which he has a perfect right as a Christian. But he does strive to make a clear distinction between what he believes theologically and what he may justifiably state historically. Thus in the words of Emerson: "If we say that God led the Israelites out of Egypt, we are making, not an historical, but a theological statement. . . . If, however, we say that faith in a divine leading was a powerful motive force in the deliverance of Israel out of Egypt, we are stating a fact . . ." With this distinction made clear, the church historian may judiciously go beyond the limits of his special field, at times, to aid in relating his subject to that unity of truth for which the Christian seeks. He is happy in the conviction that this field of study in its own right serves to aid ministers and lay people, alike, in a more effective prosecution of the church's present task.

When, therefore, church history is taught in the Divinity School of Duke and other universities like it, three things may be inferred: (1) that church history is a legitimate field of training and research in higher education; (2) that church history is indispensably a part of ministerial equipment; and (3) that, upon occasion, church and society at large may profit from the fruitful conjunction of Christian teachers and ministerial students functioning as researchers for knowledge and servants of the Gospel.

A more adequate conception of what church history as a subject of academic dignity may offer in service to the church can be gathered from its contribution in several related fields. Its services there, as already indicated, are not offered in selfish isolation, but in fullest cooperation with related, scholarly efforts. These contributions may be seen, first, in the research area and, second, in the field of everyday experience.

I

The first research contribution of church history to the church has to do with the founder of Christianity. Students of early Christian history have joined with New Testament scholars in establishing the facts of Jesus' historical career. Not only has his historicity been convincingly evidenced, but his primacy in the whole Christian movement has been impressively documented. A widening range of primary sources has been critically appraised, and the life of Jesus placed in intimate relation to the ideas and circumstances which environed him. The dangers of modeling his life and character to suit the easy reconstructions of his modernizing biographers have been soberly set forth. The need for tentativity and the scholarly weighing of conflicting evidences on moot points has been sufficiently demonstrated. Many problems such as those involving the Messianic consciousness and his eschatological thought forms have been given intensive study.

The difficulties involved in providing a trustworthy biography of Jesus have been honestly faced. Some reputable scholars have declared a true *Life of Christ* to be an impossibility. However, the true church historian has helped to establish a remarkably dependable picture of the fundamental Jesus. His historical witness is increasingly clear on issues basic to the church's life in every age. He did advocate absolute loyalty to God's Kingdom. This was yet to come in its eschatological consummation, but it laid its full demands in the present upon those pledging uncompromising allegiance to it. In the interval between the present and the future age, no "interim" pattern of behavior but the way of the ultimate Kingdom was to prevail among Christ's followers. Thus, there was an overlapping of the present and future aeons. The new "had already begun, before the old had collapsed . . ."

Christ's expectation, in faith, of the imminent new age did not, therefore, result in any paralysis of action in the social present. He demanded of himself and all true followers "a preparatory discipline in the present measured by ideals that were no whit below the standards of perfection to prevail in the coming Kingdom." Jesus was not, as certain confused interpreters have tried to make him out, a modern social reformer who hoped to make the future Kingdom out of the evolving present. He felt it his duty to show the way in which man's present must conform to the decree of God's future.

Whatever else he may have been, Jesus was a prophet unique among prophets. Whether or not he thought of himself as the Messiah is a point hotly disputed. That he did regard himself as having a singular function in the preparation for the Kingdom which God should bring in, is hardly debatable. That he advocated creative sacrificial love, not as the desperate opportunism of his day, but as the only way of eternal victory in God, is also clear. The ingenious rationalizations which are inseminated by fratricidal conflicts would have it otherwise. But even they cannot successfully portray him as resorting to violent coercion upon special occasions, so that the option of loving one's enemies might be defended as a general principle.

The Jesus whom church history presents from critically reconstructed sources is one who exacted and promised more than any "Fuehrer" before or after him. No ascetic, except in the disciplinary sense, he gave an heroic embodiment to the uncompromising ideals which he required of all unreserved disciples. He challenged all relativism and all accommodation to lesser ideals which were promulgated in the name of human weakness. "Be ye therefore perfect, even as your Father which is in heaven is perfect" may have been impossible of literal fulfillment. An attempt at its application was nonetheless requisite upon those who followed him.

The church has seen fit when its comfort is menaced to denature Christ's demands. But a great Christian and church historian, Harnack, has here interposed a grave observation. The church may feel it necessary at times to declare its independence of Christ in order to repudiate any obligation laid upon itself by less "reasonable" sayings and doings. The church historian as a historian is hardly called upon to preach. He is not forbidden to recall the disturbing judgment of numerous prophets of the Christian past. These have suggested that it may be more honest for the church to deny Christ openly, and repudiate his way of life frankly, than to label its distortions and cover its retreat with his name.

In any case, church history has helped to delineate Jesus' character and influence more clearly. It clarifies not only his earthly career but the continuing challenge which his life has issued and still issues to his church, which is *in* the world and so susceptible to the temptation to be *of* it.

II

Christian history has made a second research contribution in its study of the early church and its developing organization. Evidences as to the true character of the primitive "ecclesia" have been gathered from the writings of Christian Fathers throughout the ages. Proper attention has been given to the church as the true foundation of Christ. The arguments which represent the ecclesiastical institutions as having been founded by him at a given time and under a specific circumstance are placed in contrasting relief over against another group equally insistent. This school sees in the church a community spiritually engendered by Jesus, but never instituted as an organization separate from the Jewish religion. It is pointed out that Jesus' constructive criticisms of Jewish religious life were never other than those of a loyal Jew.

Church historians have not reached agreement as to the genuineness and historical significance of Matthew 16:18–19, in which Christ is purported to have committed his church to Peter. The most likely relation of this passage to the whole problem of the church's institutional origins has been repeatedly and intensively studied. Perhaps an increasing number of scholars find the evidence most convincing which presents the church as having both genuine continuity through Christ with its Jewish heritage and a fresh commission from him as the "New Israel."

That the perpetuation of Jesus' distinctive ideal made inevitable its institutional investment by his followers seems obvious. It is equally apparent that they came to think of the church increasingly as having a fundamental unity under a duality of aspects. As a mystical body of which Christ was the head, the church was an organism, a "communion of saints," a pneumatic association, a *koinonia*, a transcendent fellowship of all those called out of sin and the world to help make men ready for the returning Christ and God's Kingdom. As a terrestrial institution indispensable to the propagation on earth of God's will as declared in Christ, the church was an organization, an empirical society seeking to disentangle itself from its human defects and to rise triumphant over the world's evil. Mysteriously, paradoxically, but surely, this church of two natures was one in Christ. The "ecclesia" on earth, that communion outward and physical, thought of by the Protestant Reformers as the church "visible," sought, however unsuccessfully, to pattern itself after the church "invisible," the communion inner and spiritual. It was the church "organic," with its true community of saints in Christ, which the church, "organized," struggled to make more visible in itself.

Church history has made appreciable progress in ascertaining the organizational processes through which the institutional church functioned. The rapid transition from the pneumatic community of Pauline days to the highly institutionalized church of the later second century is, at least, understandable. The transcendent Kingdom was long in coming. The pragmatic considerations of economic survival, social solidarity, and propaganda facility necessitated system and functional cohesion. Organism could survive only with the aid of organization.

Church order in the early centuries has been of great interest to subsequent churchmen. Not the least concerned of these have been Christians who feel it imperative that the later church reproduce primitive forms. In this connection church history has yielded evidences which may well serve to warn as well as to inspire. Best indications are: (1) that exact and comprehensive data on early church order are not at hand and such as are available can well be viewed with critical tentativity; (2) that early church order was not of a uniform type but diverse as to areas and functionally responsive to varying needs; (3) that the instructive deduction from the history of primitive organization is hardly that some form was utilized which must be slavishly reproduced regardless of later circumstances and needs; it is rather that the early church met its problems with vigor and versatility in the light of its own requirements, as the church in every age can well afford to do; (4) that wherever, and whenever, diaconate, presbyterate, episcopate, or papacy emerged, this was in all likelihood not owing to some prescription of Christ, direct or indirect; it was more probably the recognition of agencies which were proving themselves useful in perpetuating the emphases of dominant Christian groups. That these groups may have felt their institutional procedures to be in harmony with Christ's purpose need not be denied.

The church historian scarcely needs add that the history of the church at its best reveals a ministry of forms to the spirit, an employment of organization as means to the end of true community, the subordination of static but necessary institutions to the dynamic realization of ideals.

III

In a third area the researches of church history are today serving to focus the significance of a neglected Christian heritage which is an indispensable resource of the church. The historian, alone, can adequately trace the vicissitudes of Christian community and catholicity as exemplified through the centuries. The thorough student knows how effective was the *koinonia* of the ancient church. He is both inspired and startled by that authoritarian medieval unity which put such definite restrictions upon catholicity, and which identified spiritual community with the visible, hierarchical church. The church historian knows, also, and would have others appreciate, a valuable bequest from the Protestant Reformation, which is all too often neglected. He is keenly aware, as Protestants generally are not, that the abiding tradition of Protestantism is not, as the Roman Catholic charges, a schismatic individualism. The Protestant tradition is, rather, the passion to reincarnate the true "communio sanctorum"; to realize as never before that Christian solidarity in which every man is a priest in Christ to every other; to revive the genuine catholicity of the "universitas fidelium"; to place the whole "congregation of the faithful" under the headship of Christ, one and indivisible.

Church history witnesses effectively, therefore, to the fact that a united Christendom is not the restless imagining of a decadent civilization but the enduring ideal of the church throughout history. Christian historians, Orthodox, Roman, and Protestant, have often begun their tasks by examining the claims to superiority of their respective communions. They have, not infrequently, remained to marvel at the unused resources of a Christendom which may yet some day be one church, holy, catholic, and united.

In the meantime, Roman historians survey the very real tragedies of Christian divisiveness and exploit the history of community as it is conceived and practiced under the Roman obedience. The Protestant historian puts at the disposal of churchmen in his communion the lessons of the past which show the way to greater unity and ecumenicity. The contributions which church history, in cooperation with theology, has made in laying the basis for denominational reunion and ecumenical progress can hardly have gone unappreciated. Wherever authoritative information is solicited and a sane challenge is desired as to the religious basis, the ecumenical outlook, and the constitutional principles of unitive Protestantism, the researches of church history are in demand. And when, in time, the craving becomes strong enough to confront the pagan world with an undivided Christendom, the whole cumulative record of the church's struggle for enduring community will be discoverable at church history's hands.

IV

In any survey, however brief, of church history's researches, a fourth contribution to the church should be mentioned. This has to do with worship's place in Christian history. Historical researches of the highest caliber have been concentrated on early types and evolving forms of Christian worship. That this worship has in every era of the church's greatness been the heart of its being, is plain for all to see. It is likewise clear to the student of Christianity's past that subtractions from, and additions to, primitive forms of worship have brought both undoubted glory and lamentable degeneration to the "service of God." The historian has a vantage position from which to view and analyze worship's accretions from pagan as well as from Christian sources. He can trace the distortions which have been accepted, in time, as the natural outgrowth of Christ's own will. Fortunately, the historian has, likewise, the welcome opportunity to record the healthful reaction of worship forms to the constructive criticism of genuine worshipers. The liturgical strength and weakness of the major historical communions have been indefatigably evidenced by such masters in research as Duchesne, Lietzmann, and Will. The positive elements of Orthodox, Roman, and Protestant worship have been given a most irenic treatment in the versatile writing and experience of Friedrich Heiler.

The church must also pay tribute to the many researchers of all faiths who, in whatever area of theological or sociological investigation they have labored, have employed proper historical techniques at appropriate times. The mere mention of their colossal projects would pass the limits of a lengthy paper. Of prime importance are the historical analyses and interpretation of that fraternal solidarity which is insured by "the pure preaching of the word and the right administration of the sacraments." What the church has been, and can be, when welded into the unity of a common faith, the community of sacramental grace, and the prayerful incorporation of the Gospel, has significance not only for church historians but also for those who may be guided by their disclosures. Thus, recent ecumenical conferences have wisely had recourse to the researches of church historians. These scholars have been called upon to testify anew that worship at its highest has made the church, not an esoteric band, but a community of service for the world's salvation.

The church today could, presumably, reexamine its dedication to God in an age of competing, final loyalties. Church history stands ready to review, with a minimum of bias, the record of the church in its long development as a community of worship. That record will, without question, be found to confirm Dr. J. H. Oldham's contention that "Insofar as it achieves its true and full purpose, the worship of the Church may be regarded as the most potent and fruitful form of social action."

V

This reference to social action reminds us of a fifth research contribution to the church provided by its historians. For, as church history shows, the Christian movement has not been something done in splendid isolation by a few, individualistic, leaders. It has, from the first, claimed the loyalties of the people and demanded investment in a living society. No greater service has been rendered by the Christian historian than the elucidation of social ideals and the assessment of social contributions which came as a noble by-product of the church's loyalty to the Divine. Christianity's prime dedication was made in love to God, but the inevitable concomitant of its loyalty was growing affection for all fellow men. The story of an eschatology which resulted in mounting social activity; the account of a growing band of men, women, and children adjusting themselves to environmental circumstances but never quite surrendering themselves in their function of challenging the world to something higher; the amazing career of a spiritual household which started out to save a few brands from the burning and then went on to rebuild the whole social edifice—all this and much more is the open secret of the church historian. What is more important, these are the vital statistics of our spiritual ancestry.

For, with all of its faults, Christian society in the past has been vital. It is not the church historian's business to weave his materials into sermonic form. But it is his research obligation and the ministerial student's responsible privilege to look closely at a living record which is good for innumerable sermons. For that record is the story of people cast like us in the perpetual crisis of continuing life. The church historian's examination of their thoughts and actions had an interest for him and a value for the church which is paralleled by no other type of research. What they did or neglected to do cannot, and should not, shackle our response to contemporary problems. But it may have some instructive suggestions for the meeting of such problems.

True, it may not be reassuring to know that Christians have compromised their ideals before and defended their actions as realistic; but our disappointment at their surrender in the past may throw a little light on the possible regard of the future for our own policies of convenience. On the other hand, the resourcefulness of former Christians who not only survived but thrived in the face of apparently insuperable obstacles is a portion of history which ministers and people ought to find useful at just about this time.

The everyday experiences of our Christian forefathers when clarified by, not buried under the weight of, documentary research are invariably found to be both fascinating and serviceable. They were well acquainted with menaces to the good, competing philosophies of existence, and life and death struggles, both material and spiritual. Such stimuli were surprisingly like those which make our own parish sojourns anything but placid. These predecessors of ours sometimes stretched the definition of Christian enterprise, reinterpreted their doctrines to accord with their actions, and found their souls again only in days of adversity. Facts such as these can hardly fail to arouse some interest in people who are now doing these same things.

An undergraduate some years ago paid his tribute to the social interest which Christian history may hold for modern people. He declared that it was a shock to him when he realized for the first time that even the apostles had to make a living, eat, sleep, and agonize with real problems like other fallible creatures. But he hastened to add that they certainly were more interesting to him as real people than as perfect beings remote from all ordinary experience. Such at least was his idea, though not his picturesque idiom. And I believe that he was right. One of the greatest fascinations of Christian history is the interest of real people in each other down the ages.

Some twenty years ago, a distinguished professor declared that church history would not come into its own until it was studied, written, and taught as a living, growing experience related, as all human life is, to specific environments and circumstances. Only then, out of its wealth of individual and social experiment, could the Christian past enrich the Christian present. The professor, like the student, was right. I suspect that other professors and students like these two have had something to do with the titles and contents of later textbooks, such as the recent *History of the Christian People*. In any event, it is a step in the right direction to include the everyday problems of average people in histories designed for us, their descendants.

––––––

Granted, then, that here are five great fields of research in which church history has served, and still serves, the whole church. What more does it offer of everyday use to the busy pastor and his parish? Anyone who can read a moving story or profit from its recounting can enter into the heritage of historical Christianity. From it he may derive a new sense of fellowship with those of the past who have believed in the victory of Christ over all things. In the turning pages of Christian history he may read the indisputable proof that true Christianity has been dynamic, developmental, and creative rather than static and effete. He may be interested to learn that each time the church has been urged to die peaceably and be decently buried it has stubbornly demonstrated that it is just ready to begin living more abundantly. It must surely be worth something to the average Christian to discover that no institution has so invited criticisms from within and without, and that none has so thrived upon it, as the church.

This living book of the church's past is full of tested remedies for human fear, a contagious disease widespread in our time. In this volume, also, are numerous accounts of Christianity's battle, lost through adopting the weapons of its enemies, and won through the employment of Christ's sacrificial love against brute force.

But Christian history has other ministries than that of demonstrating how to shatter the dictator's arm. It shows unerringly which men have been great and which not. It even has some hints as to what makes men great—and women too. It provides the one satisfying, synoptic view of triumphant living, not only on the part of a few spectacular leaders, but in the experience of obscure, yet victorious millions as well. In short, church history, when heard or read, provides the great primary source book of immortal Christianity. It contains the secret of the things that live and the things that die, together with a chart of the course pursued by them.

But however little the people of a pastorate review Christian history, they cannot but profit from the service of a minister richly endowed with such historical knowledge. His clearer perspective, better trained mind, and more vigorous spiritual leadership thus derived from his fraternity with the past should greatly augment his usefulness to his people. His sermons, like his life, should continue to grow and bless those committed to his care.

It has already been suggested that it is not the professor's province to leave his chair of history for the homilist's pulpit. However, there is something wrong if his ministerial students get no materials for good sermons. The fault may be his, theirs, or the responsibility of both. He and they can hardly be expected to harbor the kind of pride which filled a scientist's heart years ago when he proposed to his class the following toast: "Here's to pure mathematics and may it never be worth a ————— to anybody." The church historian is proud that the knowledge of the Christian past may be worth much to a great many. He is anxious that those in the pulpit and those in the pew may profit alike from this too little used resource.

This, of course, is not all that church history means in relation to the church, nor is it all that church history can do for teachers, ministers, and people. Some may not believe that it has done, or can do, even these things which I have claimed for it. Perhaps the fairest test to which such doubts may lead them will be the study for themselves of historic Christianity's records. They may then judge more accurately of church history's possible usefulness in their own experience and of its potential ministry, not only to the church of tomorrow, but also to that of today.

Christic and the Gospels in worship and the arts

Blessed are the dead
which die in the
Lord from hence-
forth
Yea, saith the spirit,
that they may rest
from their labors
and their works
do follow them.
[Brahms, *A German*
Requiem (op. 45,
based on *Revela-*
tion 14:13)]

The verses on the door
(of St. Denis)
are these:
Bright is the noble work,
but being nobly
bright, the work
Should brighten the minds
so that they may
travel, through the
true lights
To the True Light where
Christ is the true
door. [Abbot Suger,
On Administration,
xxvii]

Public worship is a communal experience. The confession, praise, and dedication of the individual are joined to that of others who bow before God. In Christian worship, Christ as he is revealed in the Gospels is the bond that unites and empowers his people.

Throughout the ages, this centrality of the Master in the Fourfold Evangel has been focused for worshiping Christians by the creative arts: especially literature, the plastic arts, and music. It is these which conduce to a prayerful community of spirits through the spoken and written word; the moving appeal of glass, canvas, wood, and stone; and the evocative language of instrument and song. The rich freight of spiritual imagination, thus imparted, may be communicated to the praying individual at places and times outside the worshiping community. But whatever enters the mind, heart, and soul in hours of private meditation may be reappropriated and shared in the moments of high communion. Looking inward upon himself and his prayer experience—whether in times of private devotion or corporate dedication—one may discover with something of grateful surprise how much the spirit and the work of Christ as conveyed by the Gospels have been

A Series of York Chapel meditations, Duke University Divinity School, 1947. Published in the *Duke Divinity School Bulletin*, XII no. 4 (Jan., 1948), 139–148.

mediated to him and to his fellows by the versatile imagery and the majestic vitality of the arts.

Assuming that the day of personal testimony that edifies the worshiping group is never really over for the practicing Christian, I ask the privilege of witnessing to the redeeming role of the arts as they have enriched my participation, both direct and indirect, in the society of Christian worshipers. I wish to testify as to the manner in which the historical life of Jesus and his lordship in the universe have been made worshipfully real to me: through the literary arts; through the arts of sculpture, mosaic, painting, and architecture; through the art of music.

I

The Christ who comes to physical birth and ever-expanding life in the Gospels of original language and translation is a being of heart-twisting winsomeness, shattering power, and tender unpredictability. These Gospels of literature are vibrant with a pulsing, yet restrained, sense of destiny that quietly lays hold on me—particularly when I join with others of the faith in the full commitment of worship. The Evangelists confront me with a Christ who so ferrets out my sinful inadequacy that I am reduced to despair. They envelop me with his divine-human love until I am quieted in the assurance of his having already overcome the world—and uplifted me by all-sufficient grace.

Here in the Christ of the Gospels the usual becomes misleading and impotent; the natural ways of men like myself are road-blocked, by-passed, and diverted until I walk a new path. Here the surprising, the unacceptable, and the impossible—in my eyes—are shoved aside by the processional hosts of God's possibilities. And these ways of God in Christ, so foreign to me and all men, I see best in the language of symbol and vision; with the aid of plastic arts; under the spell of organ and choir, as of drama-dispensing color and light.

Reading these Gospels, haltingly yet expectantly, in students days; reading them increasingly in my maturity with all the ebb and flow of the soul's dark night and the spirit's bright day; I have yearned ever and again for understanding associates with whom to kneel and pray.

These Gospels read in the originals baffle me, take me unaware, lift me up high, and dash me down low. In the dignified, sweeping dexterity of Jerome, they both delight and appall me. Translated and paraphrased by Bede the Venerable, they show me how far restrained allegory can lead. Launched at me like catapults by Master John Wyclif, they uncover my defenselessness, even as they point me to the church's sole head and fount of all salvation. The sonorous witchery of the King James version teaches me the language of prayer and the majesty of aspiration. Tyndal—he of the clear brain and the leonine heart—tells me whence the King James comes. Faber, translating the New Testament into French, acquaints me in his introduction with the birthright obligation of every Christian man and woman: to read the Gospel *before* worship, if he would meet Christ, the Father, and the Spirit *in* worship. And Faber, being properly source-minded, leads me to Chrysostom's *XIth Homily on St. John* for a further incentive to Gospel inculcation.

In the glorious literature of the ages are many lives of Christ, now scorned when they are not neglected. The Pseudo-Bonaventura rings with a prose-poetry that proclaims how different is the Kingdom of Christ from the Kingdom of men. Ludolph the Saxon wrote a life that challenged me to research and kept me after hours for the lessons of devotion. Renan, the literary critic, the always solvent treasurer of human riches, finds in Jesus his more than colorful match—and goes on trying to solve the mystery until, once more, I want to pray. Even Santayana, that intensifier of dark places and compromiser of light ones, cannot but fail *gloriously* at times, when confronted by the Gospel mystery.

The world's great Confessions, Testaments, and Journals have been good to me. Augustine, like myself, backs into every open cistern and avoids all the right places where God may best be found. But when he does look within, above, and beyond—lo! Christ has been there before him. Augustine understands why I do what I do, and why I do not commit myself unto God when I most clearly ought. Francis of Assisi has left such an unimpressive little *Testament*. But the plea to follow Christ and the Gospels in poverty of self-will applies to me, and not just my Roman Catholic friends in regular orders—and I know it. Woolman's *Journal* is hard on me. Very hard. It is a classic exposition of how easily God is missed and Christ is avoided by people who never stop talking long enough to wonder what they have been saying. Thomas R. Kelly's *Testament of Devotion* has to be read and reread to be made one's own. But once received, it is a part of one's life of communicating prayer—forever.

Poetry and the language of vision raise my soul aloft; purify it; and bear it home. The Psalms speak for me when I am dumb; but when wrought into the Christian book of life, they teach me to utter the praise of Christ and his Gospel. Cynewulf, in his mellifluous vision of *The Christ*, leaves open the door that leads me into the great hall of heaven. Hildegarde of Bingen, prophetess of teachers' and preachers' responsibility in an age of loosened reins and trembling lips, takes me up behind her on her Gospel charger and rides, with me, onto the very porch of the celestial mansion.

The Day of Wrath, ageless poem of impending judgment, gives voice to my fears and phrases my dependence on the mercy of the great Judge. Bernard of Cluny levels all the proud institutions of man's idolatrous Babeling. He turns my gaze upon an ultimate citizenship so intimately conjoined with the Christ that I look about me for the fellowship of Christ-serving men in the here and now. Milton towers over me until I faint; when I revive he is on his knees, before an inescapable conqueror: a death-defeating, evil-annihilating Christ.

Nurtured in the unadorned halls of free prayer, I have lived to find Christ and his Gospels in the language of unpremeditated eloquence as in the virgin womb of inviolate silence. But I have also learned to repeat in humble gratitude the mind-compelling invocations of Boethius and the swelling importunities of Chrysostom. Anselm the Scholastic, raised to the wisdom of faith committed unto God, hammers for me upon the doors and windows of the Divine dwelling-place.

Yes! The Liturgies of the Roman church have claimed a place in my heart. The worship of Eastern Catholicism, now plaintive, now nobly self-abasing, urges me on to the common Father in Christ. Luther's service, purged of Roman obfuscation and contrite with the birth cries of men, women, and children in vernacular appeal—this touches me to the core of my being. *The Book of Common Prayer* stills my proud ambitions and trains my lips in the language of supplication. *The Methodist Book of Worship* redeems the times of heart searching in all ages and places. It bids me be still and know that He—The Great I Am—is God.

To this end I read, review, and try to relive the Preached Word. Luther thunders at me, entreats me to stand up and read the Gospel like a man. He demands to know in what my justification lies. He calls me to accounting before the Shepherd Supreme for my pasturage of a teacher's flock. Origen taps me on the shoulder and reminds me that Christ the Saviour is the best source of all. Calvin thrusts upon me his peace-shattering, brain-clearing sermons on the Gospel Harmony. Bernard of Clairveaux, long before Pascal, declares unto me that the soul seeking God is always anticipated by Him. Men go out to Christ in love because he first loved them. Meister Eckhart warns that the Kingdom of God is at hand. Savanarola cries: Repent! Repent! Michel Menot fixes me with a gaze that never wanders and exacts a promise that I "cry aloud and cease not to lift up my voice like a trumpet."

But all of these with one accord lead me to the altar of worship, the heart of the Gospels, and the fellowship that is in Christ Jesus.

II

Christ and the Gospels made their appeal to me through the medium of literary art in my early boyhood. The Bible word and the message of the pulpit came to me from behind the long table—a Gospel propelled by as many as six preachers and exhorters in a single Sunday. The art of simple eloquence was theirs, on occasion. Furthermore, theirs was a free ministry—the congregation criticized them freely and paid them nothing. Some of them, reading the sacred text, made Eden's blossoms fall and the riders of the great Apocalypse thunder by for me as no one has done since.

But these men, fearing God much and the subtle insinuation of beautiful church buildings (not to mention their cost) even more, left me no heritage of beauty in worship. Relatively late in my boyhood I came to worship in sanctuaries that brought me to my knees before the glories of silence-working beauty. Then the poetic inspiration of my father's instruction on Christ and the Gospels was lifted up and transformed by God's living cohorts in blazing window, ensouled statuary, and all the history-preserving archives of tower, chancel, and nave. Then Christ and the Gospels lived anew.

Thwarted in my passion to mingle with living worshipers and deathless Christians immortalized in the church art of Europe and other lands, I have been blessed with a study of artistic reproductions that helps to make them my own. I have shared vicariously with some of you in the worship experiences which were yours in Constantinople, Rome, and Paris. Christian monuments reproduced in architectural plates, and the published outlines of fresco, painting, ivory, sarcophagus, altar, and baptistry have been my companions in private prayer and my associates in public worship. The invaluable ministrations of art historians like Morey, Enlart, Mâle, Diehl, Gonse, and many others, have delighted my mind and disciplined my soul.

Illuminated Greek manuscripts such as we have at Duke have left me humbly edified—marveling at the patient dedication of unknown hands joining these of other worshiping Christians across the vicissitudes of centuries. Here, not only, are the words of Christ in Gospel story, but also the color and movement without, that match the marching spirit within.

The art symbols of Byzantium, so often maligned for their stylized turgidity, have been for me, increasingly, tributes to Christ and the Gospels in terms of significant, selected form. In the churches of Eastern Christianity, there comes to me from across the ages—and out of dazzling colors in high-flung mosaic—the Christ enthroned in universal glory. About him are the symbols, in animal form, of the Four Gospels. Surrounding him also are the apostles, martyrs, and others of an undying company. Now the Gospel book is open as Christ the Judge intones: "Inasmuch as ye did it to the least of these my brethren ye did it unto me." Again, holding an open book, Christ the universal ruler proclaims: "I am the light of the world . . . ."

Out of the West, from the ages of catacomb, barbarian invasion, and Carolingian Revival, as from the apogee of Gothic inspiration and Christian Renaissance, have come to me a call for prayer and worship. Recently, in the Boston Public Library, I wondered soulfully on the Latin Gospels transcribed in Charlemagne's time; even as I was deeply moved by Harvard's original Gutenberg.

Across the tumultous centuries of the Early Church, and down the jostling corridors of the Middle Ages, stream the men, women, and children of whom the Gospels speak and for whom Christ gave himself in ransoming love. These are the little and the great, the wicked and the good, the conscientious ruler and the usurious exploiter, the tender mother and the wily demon, the stolid peasant and the brilliant fool; all of whom Christ knew in the Gospels and whom we know still. Into the cathedral nave, that ship of souls, they march; up over the portals, into the choir stalls they clamber; high over the doorways they strut, make faces, scream imprecations, bellow orders—and call at last in agony, even as I, upon the Christ of the Gospels. Here, in cathedral statuary, the vices and virtues take their stand. A softly fashioned, well-satisfied, maiden proclaims the virtues of chastity. Jeering at her naivete is a seasoned rake, proud of his technique, a virtuoso in petty seductions. Seeing these cinemas made throughout all our yesterdays of our own todays and tomorrows, I am reminded of the salvation these people craved and the Gospel of Christ I, too, must feed upon.

In all the windowed glories of high Gothic the children of men go sinning by; find themselves sought by a loving Christ; and sigh out their praises for the man-God. Whether I join those who live again on the panels of a baptistry, watching, as they do, the baptism of Christ; whether I trace the moving column of martyrs enrolled on catacomb walls—the effect is the same. Here go I—fearful, defeated, slain, and resurrected in my Lord.

Irony, pathos, humor, ecstasy—all are here. And they are fit companions for those who make pilgrimage on earth to the City of God. Here by the wayside sits Jabal, father of flocks. He takes the cooling breezes outside his tent. His beloved sheep pass in sprightly review. Scornful of ordinary lambs that go as one in a given direction, they amble right to left and left to right. A little dog sits disgustedly by, asking himself, no doubt: "How can one prove one's ability with affected ninnies like that?" But Jabal only smiles—so broadly that his beard is pulled apart in the middle; and the whole of heaven laughs.

Further on, the foolish virgins look very foolish—and the wise ones very wise. Down the road comes a procession of knaves, kings, badly diapered infants, and gleeful satyrs—all down from their cathedral portals, gables, and porches. They have an afternoon off for Judgment rehearsal. Just rising from the sleep of death, out of his erstwhile grave, a little fellow blinks ruefully and begins dressing in a hurry. This is his Big Day—the Judgment morn—and, flustered, as he is, he somehow knows that he is safe from the goats at Christ's left hand.

All of these are my people. Each of them is myself—one of my selves —all of them in need of communal cleansing in public worship. With them I laugh, and revile, and sin, and plead forgiveness. I scan the figures of birds eating from a dish. I, too, crave the food of eternal life. Here is a fresco of the loaves and fishes. They suit me well. They are the Gospel symbol of my Christ. Yonder is a beardless, vibrant Good Shepherd. On his broad shoulders I am already borne. However often I raise my eyes to scenes of the Great Judgment, I am not really afraid. He who will judge in his humanity, glorified, was on earth as in heaven the keeper and the doorway for his sheep.

There breaks upon me now a painting of Raphael—"The Exaltation of the Holy Sacrament." On earth as in heaven there is one mystical body—one great church. Da Vinci's "Supper" is mine to rejoice in. Here are men sitting at table breaking bread; as they did at the Love Feast in my boyhood. And with something of the profound self-examination here implied, I reexamine myself, as I sit by the side of my elders long ago. One time, I remember, the aged man who sat by me looked at my littleness and broke a double portion in Christ's name. All of the brethren broke bigger portions that evening—because of a little boy taking the first communion in memory of the Lord.

Recently there has fallen into my hands a beautifully illustrated volume. It tells in Abbot Suger's own words how he praised the Lord at St. Denis and served the king of France in the twelfth century. Here he and his brethren raised up a beautiful sanctuary. Vessels of gold and silver were not too good for the Lord. Through the portals of beauty they entered the Lord's house. Through the doorway that is Christ they turned their eyes to heaven.

In the Duke University Chapel, I often sit and think on these things—as the color mounts and the organ plays. Here in York Chapel, I muse and pray as you, my brethren, minister unto me. Together, we are one with all the hosts that have followed the Christ of the Gospel, in Beauty's way.

III

There have been times in my life when I have known sickness of the body; times, also, when I have been ill with diseases of the soul. In recent years I have sensed more and more that the Lord's most unfailing prescription for the sick soul is music. Worship devoid of instrument and song is frequently a struggle without victory—a dolorous confession of sins committed without exultant testimony of praise for sins forgiven.

My youth knew the release of burdens that comes with a concerted outpouring, by even the most untuned voices, of the heart's sincere desire. The not unfounded prejudices of my ecclesiasticating elders against castinets, clavichords, and trumpets retarded my acquaintance with versatile instruments in the symphony of spiritual resurrection. But I have learned my lesson of music's worth both the hard and the easy way. Sometimes I have starved myself, too long, away from the banquets of harmonic praise. Then I have had to be interred in the chaos of the mind before I could be raised to new life in music. Only after the Gospels have been sung and instrumented have I fully realized that in Christ there is no death—rather joy, and peace, and life. On happy occasions I have turned worshipward, down the avenues of dedicated sound, before my mind has had time to bury itself in the researcher's low-vaulted sepulcher.

Whether in times of despair or ecstasy, my spirit has been wont to traverse the aisles of Latin hymnody. Hilary of Poitiers has dissolved for me the miasmas of sickened faith by letting in the light of heavenly glories and summoning the therapy of Christ's overcoming joy. Ambrose has not only preached to my truculence of mind; he has also cleansed my rebellious spirit with disarming song. Marching in the gladsome choruses of Gregory the Great, I have been companioned by his Grand Marshal—Jesus, the inspiration of heaven's choirs and the concord-dispensing Saviour of the world.

Bishop Fortunatus, even as Erasmus, sings of a dying Christ whose cross rescues my mortality; whose crimsoned love washes out the panicky and self-annihilating defeatism of my age. The grave that yields up the body of my death is surmounted by my risen Lord. It is He—the Christ of the Gospels—whom the hymns of Bede, Peter the Venerable, and Adam of St. Victor lift upon the Cross; it is with his arising that they plunder publicly, and render triumphantly empty, all Christian tombs.

Recently, I listened raptly to the lately restored melodies of some early cantatas. The thin, piping tributes of twelfth-century music, impoverished as it was in instrumentation and voice, yet gave forth an uncompromising Gospel sound. The redemptorial themes of a Christ, slain but evermore living, gathered power and range as they commandeered the swelling voices and ecstatic strings of later centuries.

Up through the ages of polyphonic deliverance swept the Easter motets of Gombert and the dedicated arias of Kriedel—Kriedel, scorned of men but well worn on the automatic record changers of every celestial citizen. Only the little angels can sing his songs to blessed Jesu; the older angelic choruses are too throaty and the choirs of earth are too sophisticated and weary. On, up, and over the symphonic Psalmody of Heinrich Shutz and cascading through the archways of eternity swept the Whitsuntide Cantatas of Telemann. Meanwhile, the human voice pleaded—as violins, violas, and violincellos wept and rejoiced.

Once more I was caught up in the struggle of life and death that the Middle Ages handed on to Luther. For some years, now, I have been renewing my acquaintance with the singing evangelist of Wittenberg through the musical translations of Johann Sebastian Bach. And Bach has been mediated to me through the Cantatas and organ works interpreted by Albert Schweitzer. The Jesus of the Gospels for whom Schweitzer went on historical quest, and the Christ of worship whom he has joined on pilgrimage in Africa, is the Christ Jesus of Bach and the justifying Lord of Luther's faith.

The "Ein' Feste Burg" of Doctor Martin found in Psalm 46 a mighty stronghold. Clément Marot glorified this high tower in the Reformation French of Strasburg, Calvin, and Geneva. In the majestic invocation of the Psalms, sung as never before in the people's language of Scotland, France, Switzerland, Germany, England, and finally, America, I find anew the universal craving which Christ alone satisfies.

Bach, of course—blessed be his Gospel and his Lord—slays many a demon with organ blast whom Luther has only crippled and left thrashing about. When in a paroxysm of ordered passion Bach turns the music of faith on the terrors of the Psalmist and the Lucifer of the Saxon Reformer, as of his own heart—then an invincible champion appears. The "Right Man, the man of God's own choosing" enters the fray:

> Dost ask who that may be?
> Christ Jesus, it is He.

And Christ Jesus, the justifying, loving Saviour of Paul and the Gospels, is the "Right Man" throughout all of Luther's translating, preaching, and hymn writing. Yet never has Luther's Christ—"the Christ (who) lay in Death's grim prison; (and) for our sins was given"— risen more gloriously to bring us "life from heaven" than in Bach's Cantata No. 4.

When, in public worship, with full choir and organ, or with recordings heard in private meditation, I face with Bach the powers that no mortal dare oppose, I do so in the expectant surety of one who knows that:

Christ Jesus—God's only Son,
From earth hath now arisen.
He late did for our sins atone,
So death is bound in prison.

A few months ago I heard E. Power Biggs play one of the sweet-piped Bach organs. Then I realized that defeat had not come to Johann Sebastian Bach. Thwarted by his age and little men he might be—in his struggle to release the Gospel-Christ, through music, unto the re-vivifying of the church. But for him, as for all believing men, the Christ who lay in bonds of death has rended Death's dominion.

As for Schweitzer, he still peals out on the organ, as he pours balm upon the wounded, the "reverence for life" that proclaims Christ's victory.

In the joy of this revelation I turn to César Franck—"Father" Franck to me as to his handful of early disciples. For to all listening hearts he proclaims that, though our human struggle may still be in progress, the celestial festivities are already waiting upon the triumphant conclusion of our earthly witnessing. This is the Franck of faith-transforming sound; the Franck of the Gospel Beatitudes set to melodic ineffability; the Franck of the swirling affirmations and spiraling ecstasies in the "D Minor" Symphony. He and his soul-washing, light-endowing Christ make the Gospels more fully mine. When the organ in our University Chapel breaks, after him, the bread of life that Christ commissioned him to share with all worshipers, I am at peace.

My nieces, neighbors, students, and colleagues, bringing me the ministry of music in living Messianic fire take me for a season to the pinnacles of glory. And they proffer me no Satanic promotions—but only the proof that logic vainly seeks. They tell me in the language of Charles Wesley, of Palestrina, and all Christ's ministers in the holy arts:

That my Redeemer liveth
And will keep that
Which I have committed unto him
Against that Day.

The historic university and the divinity school: the university as the historic eye of the vicarious storm

I am not going to spend the time this morning talking in generalities. I have a closely prepared address which I want to follow; mainly, because I have thought about it a lot and I want you to think about it. I realize that you may not feel some of my remarks particularly relevant to the ministry that you most need at the moment. About this I am perfectly unrepentant. Sheer relevance is a very suspect commodity. Sometimes the things we ought most to say to each other may appear to have no immediate bearing on what preoccupies us. I have had students who say to me reproachfully: "Dr. Petry, I was in your course a whole term and I got hardly a single Sunday's worth of references or quotations that would do me any good." Does that sound familiar? To which I say, "Bear up, live fifty years more and you may understand."

Yes, I am chiefly concerned this morning about something that may not seem to you pertinent to your precise situation. After all, are you university people? Is this the university? Is this not, after all, a Southern Baptist Seminary related only to God and to the Convention? The answer to all of this is: "Yes and No." In a real way, there could not be people more interested than you are in the university, and in its crosslines of relationship to the seminaries, attached and detached. I am going to talk with you about some universal considerations. If we do not face these issues now, we may not have any specific gospel for anyone. This is not egotism on my own part, though I have stopped being modest beyond a certain point. If my forty years of teaching are not worth anything more than pleading with you to agree with me, then I pray to be struck out of the pulpit now.

This second lecture is announced under the title: "The Historic University and the Divinity School." Its subtitle is: "The University as the Historic Eye of the Vicarious Storm." After my introductory

The second of his Carver-Barnes Memorial Lectures on: "The Critical Temper and Practice of Tradition: The Role of the University and the Arts in the Seminary and in Church History." Delivered in Binkley Chapel, Southeastern Baptist Theological Seminary, February 24, 1971. Published in *Outlook*, July–August, 1971, pp. 3–17.

words you cannot say: "But what have we as a denominational seminary to do with the university?" A little reflection ought to show that the university and its divinity school or any other, however closely or remotely related, administratively, are the common concern of every one of us here. We have, in varying degrees, sprung from the university; directly as graduates, or indirectly through our teachers who studied there. Perhaps, by way of our academic validation for which the university has gone surety. Entirely self-contained seminaries, independent of all university contacts, have their own distinctive problems. If you think I do not know what some of those are, just try me. But university-connected institutions have their own peculiar tensions too. Sometimes, strangely enough, these stresses are not foreign to each other at all.

The thesis of this lecture is that the university, with the divinity school or seminary, is the fostering mother of the arts. It is the veritable alma mater of all the interrelated disciplines. I am thinking now of the creative arts that may be most appropriately associated with church history in the resourceful critique of our tradition. Behind me, in the organ loft, is a man who has attained real eminence in the performance as in the theory of music. He and I have talked together. Furthermore, he is going to do me the honor of listening to what I, a church historian, have to say about men whose works he has played. In performing them, he has done something I never could.

This is as it should be. Some church historians think it is their special calling to bring particularly new light from the gospel in terms of church history, just because they are church historians. I have my doubts about that. I think church historians should talk, on occasion, about some things other than church history. Musicians should be interested in church history as well as music. When church historians and musicians walk down the same paths and cannot remember whose speech comes next, perhaps the Lord leans over and says: "Good boys, Take turns." Occasionally, I have observed more historical pertinence in a musical drama or in an architectural monument than in some purportedly historical lectures. The fact that someone called them historical, or lectures, does not prove much.

But all of this is poignantly related to the contemporary confrontation of academic life generally; as to the university and to the seminary in the turbulence of much antihistorical posturing that goes on today.

In this circumstance, the university and the divinity school may well serve as the historic eye of the vicarious storm that is swirling all about us. If so, the physically unattached, but spiritually affiliated, seminary is by no means unconcerned over what goes on in Chapel Hill, at Duke, or elsewhere. It cannot be uninvolved in the encounter of those who have an animus for history with those who know that no one can be born or live without a proper sense of it. This battle is going on. There isn't a day that some student at Duke does not look at me as if to say: "Dr. Petry, of course you know, as I do, that you are outmoded. We are not interested in history any more; we will do our particular thing on our own." And with my eyes I reply: "To hear you talk, one would think you never had a navel, or an umbilical cord."

History is not only what happens to us by way of our heritage, but it is also what we deduce from this experience as significant for us and pass on to others by our thought and action. All of this spells an honest, historical critique of tradition. The university is, first and last, a *studium*. It is a *universitas*. This is a word that has been used throughout Roman and Christian history to mean anything from a volunteer fire company to an association of students. A guild, a society! That is what the university is. And it is submitted to the rigorous nurturing of mind and spirit in disciplined, dedicated concord. This fraternity gives itself, with responsible delimitation, to the critique of all corporate and personal whims. It is open to the positive protest of disturbed people and of explosive ideas. The university does not have to admit or keep anyone with mayhem in his heart or vacuity in his mind. It dares not, however, eject in anger or sustain with patronizing aplomb any individuals or groups who submit their yearnings and their frustrations to the guidance of dedicated hope; who humbly consecrate their affirmation of the human, under God, to the common good.

The university, however recreant and noble by turns in the perspective of its larger destiny, is one of the few durable institutions in the Christian era and human history. I am saying this advisedly as a historian.

The university is unique in history. It was, and is, an ever renewable society of inquiry and reflection, whether evolved by the centuries or newly brought to birth. The university can be denatured by the slightest deviation from the human, and it can be restored as often as free spirits transcend apathy and barbarism or cultivated hypocrisy. About the only hostile forces before which universities need tremble is themselves. Of course, wise men, if they are really wise, will be frightened, if not dismayed, at unbridled rebellions without and within. Only unselfish service, as well as public and private consecration, can outlast such subhuman convulsions.

Let the university be recognized forthwith as that social nexus of incarnated minds and hearts, however vulnerable, that run like nerves and blood vessels up and down the corridors of the human spirit. I can just hear some graduate student sneering and saying, "Poetry, yet." Well, a university that isn't poetry isn't a university. But a university is cerebral, first and foremost. Its business is thinking, or else it prorogues its very existence. Suppose it is to be merely a social passion, however good, or a burning sense of injustice, however justified. Then, it is not to be differentiated from a hundred other hurting sores or pressure groups. A university is a specific locus, a place, a condition, in corporate experience for transcending provincial preoccupations, however germane. It rigorously evokes and deploys the most critical concepts for the disciplining of human dedication to unconquerable ultimates. The university is for the engagement of resourceful minds with awe-inspiring abstraction. It deals endlessly with the specific universalities of untethered thought. What counts here is not facile communication of popularly applauded, common denominators. It is not enough to be satisfied with quick lunges of insight, so long as entire layers of routine research and befuddling contradiction have not even been invited. This is not the place where human beings huddle to undergo indoctrination in the quick, the simple and the good. It can no more exhaust itself with benevolent busyness, than it can immure itself in stolid unreceptivity to divine call and human need. For the university to forget the past agonizings of seeking spirits is to disembowel itself and to slide around on the slippery entrails of its own aborted tradition. The university, at heart, is a stubborn meeting of positively criticized yearnings and a shaking of human brainwaves in the test tube of historic vicariousness; a summoning of minds in solemn assembly before imponderables yet to be delivered from the more-than-human. This *studium* is a newly invited and constantly refocused society. Its genius is manifested in corporately practiced, endless critiques.

Does not a case really need to be made for critically reconstructed

university studies as being, in themselves, a form of social commitment? Many of my students think and do exactly what some little
friends did at a birthday party my wife gave years ago. They sopped up
all the liquids and had the icing off the cake in three minutes. Whereupon, a little four-year-old said to my wife, "What do we do now?"
Action has its uses and obviousness its limits. Perhaps what we *should*
do is *not* to do something *obvious*.

The university, then, is at heart a place where people can discuss
anything; but where they must listen, again, to something more than
what is immediately practical. This may be the time and the place
to use the mind with such rigorous inquiry and dedication that it will
establish itself as having a kind of social priority, both in terms of
what it is and what it leads to.

The university is, indeed, the appropriate arena for the much
vaunted search for truth. It is even more properly the well invited
vulnerability to unsought revelation. The true university sinks deep
wells for the slaking of unsatiable thirst. Never does it substitute
oversimplified clarity for life-giving complexity. Nor does it relieve
grainy abstractions with itchy banalities. It does not try to cure a
lump in the throat with a hole in the head. Such a community sows
the seedbed of truth with land mines and treasure maps, all mixed
up in hazardous confusion. You may come upon one, first, or the
other. Here, it is often quicker to wait than to hurry. Especially, is
the divinity school in a university seducible by unctuous strivings.
It often gives way: to a kind of dedicated pawing to be the first on
the scene with a pronouncement or an activity. It is all too prone to
locate oversimplified reality, to place it in a campus museum, and to
sell heaven-blessed tickets to it; or to take some ill-studied action just
to prove that it is really relevant. Yet, this is being just too sure in the
very way that people like us can least afford to be certain. Is it not a
fact that we professionals get the most trussed up and tied down by
our logic and our logistics? Take a man in Old Testament or a professor of church history. He can let himself be bound up till he is
worse than Lazarus; so that he never can be resurrected.

To cite John 8:32 at this time may be as jarring as leading off with
prayer at a college football game. But Jesus said: "If you continue in
my revelation, you will be my disciples. You will be hit by the full
impact of universal truth as it is in me, and you will be rendered
submissive to my liberating *logos*." That is a large order; and they

have not issued a complete syllabus on it yet. A university divinity school is where and how we see what we never expected, let alone wanted. We need habitual exposure to what might happen under God if we regularly sublet our wills to the uncharted *logos*.

Remaining in Christ's word is declaring ourselves answerable to his personalized, discriminating revelation of the whole cosmos. It is being disciples according to the order of expendability, not after the fashion of indispensable generalissimos. Here is submission by *alatheia*; not truth as urbane dialectic but as personalized giving from within the *koinonia*. One lends his brain to the fluctuations of the human-divine seismograph while he is still conscious. There are people who give their brains away to be disposed of on condition, after death; but for one to dedicate his to special uses while he is still alive—that is the real test. This is *theoria*, a getting a piece of contemplative action; not so much at the sit-in or the talk-out as in the blow-up of the mind, the seat of God's molecular center. Observable now is the rarefied white-heat of all action. This is that pure worship which is the unreserved concentration of being. It is the contemplative self-giving that thaws the deep-freeze of human pride and stews the garrulity out of hell. It is a seeing, a beholding, a *Schauen*, a vision. We could neither search it out nor endure it if it were not given us after a long discipleship to itself. Now behold a theory truly practical, a praxis fused of faith, hope and charity and unrevealed to cautious prudentialists. Ours is the trajectory of the worshipful gaze, freely locked in to the active-contemplative rhythm. This is the well-plotted unpredictability of God's own joyous surprises reserved for those uncalculatingly rendered up to him.

The unique role of the divinity school in a university is to mediate such worshipful freeing of the disciplined mind for intellectual and spiritual vision. This is not to demand that others capitulate to the rationale which we do not ourselves accept. It is, rather, the demonstration out of our own fearsome unbelief of the realities that transcend our feebleness. This is what frees us all—namely, discipleship in tearful awe before the infinitely logistical initiatives of the divine *logos*. And with this freedom of the Son we are truly liberated, indeed. Never is the human being in this life released from the need of study. The rigorous invocation of the Word in worship is rather the invitation to God's emancipating vision. The *studium*, then, is the handmaiden of the holy, the *arcanum* of perfect liberty. It is the insemination of true liberality.

If this is true, then, who is the true liberal? Who is the free man and free woman in our midst? Well, a false liberal is arrogantly sure of his freedom or full of unexpected demands for it. But a free man knows his limitations. He also rejoices that life is not solely a matter of definition. I do not know how long I taught before I realized that God would approve if I did not try to define everything. A university can well afford to invite reflection beyond mere definition in the direction of genuine freedom.

The purported sons of Abraham disdained slave status; they demanded the designation of free men as their due. But they demonstrated the constriction of mind and heart that rendered them unaware of their true parentage. Sin seduces people into squandering their life thrust. Not to recognize the Son is no compliment to the Father. And not to see the Father in the Son is downright insensitivity. How can people be so reckless with paternity as not to recognize fraternity?

The indubitable mark of a free inheritance is generosity of spirit, a condition of liberality. It is not just jabbering about current addictions to theological politics or social strategy. What we are and whence we have come must be up for renewal more often than that. Actually, the university is an area where liberals and pseudo-liberals freely gather. You cannot always tell who is who, either. Whose fathers and whose sons belong to whom is withheld from us. This uncertainty sometimes confuses both parents and children. An apocryphal story is told of an absent-minded church historian long ago who had fathered a large family. One day on a street car he was severely embarrassed. He kept shrugging off an overly companionable little boy who just as obstinately kept snuggling back. Sternly asked who he was, the little fellow tearfully implored, "Daddy, don't you know me?"

Unfortunately, it is not always easy to recognize one's own progeny. Nor can one always spot his true progenitor. When, actually, is the Son of Abraham, Abrahamic? That is, free rather than a slave? Jesus pressed this point very hard. Professional liberals quote the Bible, the Constitution, Thomas Jefferson, and Gertrude Stein. "A liberal is a liberal is a liberal," they say. This is a lie, thrice compounded; a heritage thrice denatured. It is the freedom for magnanimity traded for false genealogy. I am reminded of a youngster who once said to me that he lopped off all relatives beyond first cousins. The family resemblance after that was lost for him in undifferentiated humanity. But I would ask you the question: "Just how close to paternity does one have to stick to preserve real sonship and brotherliness?" One thing seems sure: a free man is one generated in the divine benevolence. He shares in the habitual interchange of endlessly reverberating generosities. Remaining in Christ's personalized disclosure of the universe graduates him ever so slowly to the eternal discipleship of the truth.

A free man may say that he was born free. That is his birthright. But he may fall into the slavery of human willfulness. He may need reorienting and reliberating. If he has associated too long with "phony" liberals, he may not even suspect that he is unfree. One may quote good sources for his own defamation. He may even boast of a paternity that is completely foreign to his acquired alienation. "Abraham exulted to know by faith that I should be," said Jesus. "You strive to kill me in the name of him who loved me. He saw and knew me in faith for the *logos* that preceded him and for the historic revelation that beckoned him on. I was before him, even as I am after him."

Now bastards are those denied the right to the family crest. The matter of fraternity, however, is not so much one of physical loins and wombs as it is of the homing instinct of true graciousness. Who can save a man who will trade inherited generosity for barren family trees? What, then, of the liberal instincts that show beyond modesty and reassure as out of our affiliation in graciousness?

An authentic university man, a true liberal, simply acts like one. Graciousness is a delicate accomplishment, however, that cannot be "faked." Try it on a youngster sometime. I know people who claim to be much interested in children, yet who make all the little, patronizing gestures that a child knows instantly to be a rejection of his true self. Try turning the flank of a four-year-old and tell me how you get along. To be genuine is the hardest thing in God's world. And to be self-consciously aware of how honest we are is actually to be hypocrites with tin-foil tails. What genuineness requires is gratitude to somebody; to a university, to a seminary, to a faculty, to a teacher, to a wife, to a friend. It is to be so glad that someone has been so much better to you than you deserve that you are completely defenseless.

This kind of man appears to the manner born, not to arrogance but to liberality. He walks through his father's house as if it were his own to share with others. A slave can only roll his eyes and warn you what not to do. But a son dares to invite you in to sit, eat, sleep and rejoice awhile.

A university is a condition of magnanimity. To be a student or a teacher there is to invite someone to larger freedom and deeper obligation. I have had students say, "Does the Dean know what is going on?" And I say, "No, God bless him, he is busy with the Lord. But this is *our* problem. We can even do something not in the curriculum. The angels will probably rip their wings and lose altitude, if we do, but it is possible."

For, if some students scream out their right to obstruct, others surely have the prerogatives of affirmative quiet in which to do their work. I understand that while I was in Oxford in 1968, some students at Duke blew the bull horn and demonstrated for twenty-four hours a day. Nobody could hear anything. Perhaps some of the things they got done were good. But one fellow said, later: "You know, I have my best thoughts when no one is screaming at me." That is strange, but it is a distinct possibility.

A free man replaces constrictions of the spirit with expansion of the heart. He freely crosses the demilitarized zone between youth and age. For him, unadvertised discipleship rules out cultivated display. The genuine liberal is free to outlive fads, whether in hairdos or vocabulary, in mini-wear or mini-minds. He scorns cherished sneers as he does *Playboy*-ese.

The liberal even nourishes a few fresh words and expressions all his own that he did not get from anyone else. He is not completely at the mercy of "identifying" or "relating" or "becoming involved" or "doing his thing." These expressions are often code words characteristic of mental exhaustion. The panhandler of relevance is seldom relevant. The free soul recoils from public gurus as a swimmer fears cramps. Genuine contemplation is not to be bottled on demand for a Frank Sinatra or an English Beatle. It is not purchasable at so many sniffs a snort. Freedom springs alert before the "trap" laid in "the trip." Clever double-talk is abominated, whether on public issues or on the twilight of the gods. For one born free or liberated at great price, cheap slogans are repulsive. Cliches are unclean. Trumped-up tolerance is unbearable.

For one truly emancipated there must be something more noble than current rhetoric. One must feel redeemed to graciousness. He can not lean in salacious fascination over the enormities of the human pit. In sociology and in psychology, we sometimes get to the place where we take notes like mad on human debasement. We feel so bad that we actually feel good, and render it all up to science. *Life* magazine, you remember, ran a series of pictures on dying people. That's *Life* for you! But this is merely simulated concern with the human— not humanity. Generosity, on the other hand, runs from the contrived spirit as a one-time "junkie" dreads readdiction. The freed man is released to the joys of God's world: to friendship and the love of men, women and children; to the visual delights of nature's seasonal glories; to the pianissimos and fortissimos of musical language; to the intriguing odors of newly-washed babies; to the hilarious delirium of birds at their bath. Have you ever watched birds taking a bath? It is a perfectly decent and wonderful sight. They don't even require clean water. I saw one sparrow simply inundate three doves out of a mudhole one day.

The mark of a free man is the seal of a true university. Theirs alike is the zest of discovery; the heart of compassion; the joining of forces with all the disinherited; the collaboration with all of those out of rapport with the tyrants of current vogue; the defending of despised castaways, be they rich or poor, middle class or *déclassé*. There are many people in the middle class economy crying to high heaven for deliverance. Some seminary students ought to develop sympathy for them!

True liberalism is never a stance out of one persuasion merely excoriating or idealizing another. The well-considered liberal will not be spared loneliness and defeat. Fame is illusory; energy fades; old friends die; the world forgets; heroes do not last; age breaks its heart; youth is frustrated; middle life yearns over both. The church sometimes seems given to complete ambivalence; now resigning itself to human feverishness, now prostrating itself in divine calm. Meanwhile, each soul must emerge into the world and depart, alone. The human being is increasingly frightened by those expanding rooms of hollow conviviality from which he shrinks into himself, unvisited. Unvisited, that is, until he gradually discerns the beckoning hand of his true freedom. Then he is subject even more inexorably to true *theoria*, to the active-contemplative mind, to the pitiless exposure of the revelation of God in Christ. The Son invites him to the awe-inspiring, beautiful intimacies of the Father's house. Daily and nightly, he is seared by the lightning of the Father's immolating love and ministered to by the Spirit's ubiquitous servantship.

He is, indeed, habitually happy who has thus mediated to him the ministry of a true seminary, a true university. Here, dedicated community is brought to personalized receptivity, and critical judgment issues in liberalizing revelation. Person and university, as well as the seminary itself, become the disciples of the living truth; and are thus set free. Now, are we, indeed, the grandchildren of that Abraham who rejoiced to see in faith Him who is our truth and our freedom.

A true university, then, is a dedicated *studium*. It is the ideal place for the exercise of genuine liberality and magnanimity. The guild of the university, as of this seminary, is the properly corporate environment for the emergence of the distinctive person. Why do so many people come out of universities looking and acting just alike? Something has gone wrong somewhere. From such an ecology of the positively critical temper as the university and the seminary ought to proceed the discerningly affirmative and negative critiques that nerve the practice of tradition. The bionomics of mind, body and spirit should be most nicely poised here. The mutual relations between social organisms and their environment can here become most creatively interpenetrating. The university may actually constitute the ganglion, the virtual nerve center, of critical reflection upon, and discriminating application of, historical vicariousness. It may induct us into a fuller practice, under God, of the humane tradition.

Is it too much to set one institution apart for research into the historic sources of what makes humanity most humane? Can we not dedicate one resource to the liberation of all those forces and motivations that draw human beings into a moving entente of free personhood? The university on which so much blame is laid, and to which so much credit is due, may be peculiarly destined to serve as the authentic parable of historic vicariousness. And by parable we mean no exclusively literary narrative, but rather that vital pod of comparative examples from which a moral and spiritual truth is drawn. By historic vicariousness, we mean the sacrificial standing of each in the other's place, and the self-realization of every one in the common heritage of all. May not each of us, both learned and less tutored, share in the university's function as the historic eye of the vicarious storm?

Aerial navigators have learned to venture boldly, if at great risk, into the very center of scrutiny in the revolving weather frenzy. Oriented to the relatively inner calm of the outward passion, they see both the history and the future of the present tempest. There are few more dramatically accurate, if admittedly analogical, similitudes than this of the university's role in our time. The university fits properly and vicariously into the very pupil of the eye of upheaval. From it must come the calm, contemporary researching into the exact nature of humanity's historic stuff.

Academic scholarship exists to ferret out and to deploy historic wisdom into the ferment of contemporary agony and ecstasy. There are those who would make of the university an existential test tube for inseminating violence; others would turn it into a cozy corner for antiquarians. It ought properly to be the risky pilot's seat in the veritable center of cosmic flux. Here what *is*, may be accurately assessed against the backdrop of what *has been*, and apropos the beckoning visage of what *is to be*. But let us not forget that our function, however far from, or close to, the university campus we are, is one of creative parable. What we are, and do, in *academia* must be seen by ourselves and others as icons or images of our historical vicariousness, as warranties of our society-wide interdependence.

The university is a good place—it may be the only one—for all disciplines to collaborate. That cannot happen at NASA; or in the United Nations. It has to be in the university center and in all of its spiritually affiliated relationships that these things can go on. Here, a church historian can actually go to the music department and say, "I want Schoenberg's opera, *Moses und Aaron*." True, someone may reply, "Aren't you a little bit out of your line?" Whereupon, I would retort: "Don't talk back to me; your line is my line and mine yours. We're both church historians on the loose." That can happen only in the university.

But what goes on most appropriately in a university worthy of the name, is not so much a series of precise experiments by exact practitioners, as it is a practicing of the humane tradition in its primary character as history and parable. And here, iconography or symbolic writing comes into true focus. The creative sciences and the fine arts, both performing and interpretive, are as inseparable as they are distinctive. Those who practice these ineffable critiques are not only poets, philosophers and theologians, but also scientists and historians, as well. Conversely stated, these exact interpreters are not only scientists and historians, but they are also musical composers and sculptors, organists and poets. Poetry has habitually given rise to science and to history, whether in Homer and Schliemann or in Schoenberg and the Hebrew Christian tradition; not to mention Jules Verne and the moon landings. Iconography, whether in Egyptian hieroglyphics, Keplerian science fiction, or musical discourse, is the prime exponent of historic parable.

If the university is to be—as I think it must—the preceptor in spiritual image-writing, or iconographic parable, how and to what end is it to proceed? At this point, I'll be so egotistical as to be perfectly modest; I'll just tell you some of the ways we are trying to go at Duke.

I think it may be instructive to say that, in the division of church history, we give large, bifocal attention in the present, to the past and to the future. We try, increasingly, to supply a dual but undichotomized content, methodology and historiography that are closely knit to the historical and to the contemporary. We also expand the role of the historical and the theological, as of the biblical and the pastoral. These fields are made to inter-sect, to inter-discipline, and to be inter-disciplined by the creative arts. Thus, in a current seminar on the Medieval Church, we are relating the councils and their problems in the Middle Ages to the "so-different" and yet "so-like" issues of ecumenical conciliarism. By no means lost on us are what the documents of Vatican II have to say. These statements treat the universal right to education; moral and religious education in the schools, especially Catholic schools; the particular function of Catholic faculties and universities; and, notably, faculties of theology.

But this range is not limited to Roman Catholics. I cannot believe my eyes at some of the wisdom in the Vatican II "good book" on the matter of how theological faculties should be able to talk with other faculties. I will say, that at Oxford, one's chances of doing this are good. If you are at a dinner or at a hightable, and if you are a church historian, you are likely to be put down by the side of a molecular physicist. That is wonderful; or terrible when you learn that he knows some church history, too; and you are not sure if you know any physics. But this is the kind of thing that will clean up hypocrites in a hurry.

Well, in any case, we consider artists, fine arts, and the sacred arts, even as Vatican II does. My students have become accustomed to the fact that a part of the source materials in the course in medieval church history may be Stravinsky and modern times. Discovering this fact, some just shake their heads and walk right into the edge of a door.

Theirs is an edifying trance—wondering what goes on here. We do not overlook the rich entries in the Latin-French edition of the Vatican II documents. These are about priests, laity, bishops, and the communion of saints. Nuns in modern dress with uncropped hair saunter through it. They, the priesthood, and the laity are a part of biblical community and political order. There are 250 pages of analytical tables and indexes. It is positively frightening. We study these things as if what went on in the Middle Ages actually had something to do with what goes on now, and vice versa. All of this experience relates the present to the historic past. We study medieval documents and events. We relate the logistics of the Crusades to present-day Israel; as to Laos and Thailand. We interfuse the eschatology of the Koran with Dr. McNeill's *History of the Cure of Souls*; also the pastoral psychology of the Duke Clinics; together with the Methodist Conferences, and some things that Baptists do. But, especially, do we see the function of the creative arts, theoretical and performing, as belonging in the historical division as much as anywhere else.

We give a lot of attention to medieval iconography. One of the ablest students this year in my seminar, The Medieval Church, was from the English department. She did a special study of medieval iconography and the role of the medieval midwife. That may seem to be "reaching for it"; but, after all, a baby has to get born. And, hard as it may be for academicians to realize, some of them are not born in the Duke Hospital, or at UNC either.

We ponder seriously the Vatican II critique of the role of universities and how you talk with people. Here we confront faculties of theology, the cultivation of the arts, and the propagation of the faith. Once in a while I have a student who says, "Ah, that's propaganda." And I say, "Yes, thank God, it is." Because if you cannot propagate, there are going to be a lot of nonexistent people going nowhere.

We labor, sometimes self-consciously and a little bit smugly, I fear, to make our point. But, again, we succeed almost without knowing it. And that is the best way to put the university right in the eye of the storm.

What else can a university do? Well, it can help us realize that pastoral care is historical, and that church history, at times, comes down to music. It can help us to let, not only graduate students, but also M.Div.'s teach the class. It is a wonderful thing to set up a schedule, to give a couple of introductory lectures, and then point out to students that, with all of their inexperience and their frustration, they will be responsible for the presentations. They will be required to see to it that historical documents speak realistically, that selection is injected, and that they then sit in judgment and appreciation of each other, as of the primary sources. Maturation and thwarted inexperience go their accustomed round. And if things get too easy, I unsheath my little scalpel too. This is wholesome. Here is the critical temper in the practice of tradition. This is the way learning and teaching ought to go. I have students who say, "I never would have believed, Dr. Petry, that this is church history." I just reply, "Keep your mouth shut and go ahead. The Lord and I already know it is. You, too, will learn to rejoice that is so." Among other things, it is very instructive that our courses in church history were designed to let in Arnold Schoenberg, and Olivier Messiaen, as well as Benjamin Britten and Le Corbusier, the architect. We act as if these were historical sources, too. And they are. This is the parable of it.

For history itself is a supreme parable, a laying out to the side of facts and events the comparative interpretations of these experiences that make facts what they event-ually are. This recreation of living parable is necessarily historical, even as it is historically vicarious.

The University of Illinois has a multi-million-dollar center for the practice of the performing arts. They have it arranged so that all the cars can be parked underneath. There is no traffic problem. No one gets tickets for being in class. Here is every aspect of operation; of musicology, of teaching music, of performing it, of putting on unbelievable things, things that the Metropolitan Museum of Art and the Metropolitan Opera would just faint dead away to contemplate. This, they study, create, and perform. This is incredibly and joyously maturating. I wish we had a center like that at Duke. But no seminary of creative enterprise, not even a small one, is left out. Not in this day. Now, electronic devices can almost scare you out of a year's growth, or inspire you to the point where you can even go out and preach the gospel to someone. There is no telling—it could happen. You may become so enthusiastic that you want to witness, to be a martyr—with blood or without.

Notes on contributors

A James B. Duke and Gurney Harris Kearns Fellow at Duke University and twice a junior fellow in the Southeastern Institute of Medieval and Renaissance Studies, H. Lawrence Bond is Professor of Medieval History at Appalachian State University in Boone, N. C. His major research interest is late medieval reform movements, and at present he is contemplating a book on Nicholas of Cusa's efforts to reform fifteenth-century theology.

David Burr received a B.A. from Oberlin College, a B.D. from Union Theological Seminary in New York City, and a Ph.D. from Duke University. Since 1966 he has been Assistant Professor of History at Virginia Polytechnic Institute and State University. He has published articles in major journals on William of Ockham, John Duns Scotus, and Peter John Olivi.

Author of eight volumes and numerous scholarly articles, William Ragsdale Cannon is presently Bishop of the United Methodist Church assigned to the Atlanta Area. He has been active in the World Council of Churches as a delegate on numerous occasions and was an observor to the Second Vatican Council. Past Professor of Church History and Dean at the Candler School of Theology, Emory University, he has also been a Visiting Professor at Garrett Biblical Institute and at Richmond College, University of London.

Donn Michael Farris is Librarian and Professor of Theological Bibliography at the Divinity School of Duke University. His wife, Joyce, is a former student of Dr. Petry and is currently engaged in graduate work in the School of Library Science at the University of North Carolina in Chapel Hill.

Educated at Davidson College, Louisville Presbyterian Seminary and Duke University, Stuart C. Henry is Professor of American Christianity at the Divinity School, Duke University. He served as a minister for twelve years before teaching in the Department of Religion at Southern Methodist University. He came to Duke University in

1959. He has published numerous articles and three books. The latest of his books is *Unvanquished Puritan: A Portrait of Lyman Beecher.*

James Jordan was educated at Furman University, the University of Strasbourg, Southeastern Baptist Theological Seminary, and Duke University. Dr. Jordan has taught at Oxford College of Emory University, Mars Hill College, and Georgia Southern College. At present he is Head of the Department of History and Geography at Georgia Southern College.

William Mallard is Professor of Church History at the Candler School of Theology, Emory University, and an ordained minister of the Virginia Conference of the United Methodist Church. Since 1969 he has been a Fellow of the Society for Religion in Higher Education. His articles have appeared in *Church History, Medievalia et Humanistica* and the *Journal of the American Academy of Religion.*

A native of Prince Edward Island with a doctorate from the University of Chicago, John T. McNeill has taught courses, published numerous articles, and written books in Church History for many years. He is Auburn Professor emeritus of Union Theological Seminary, New York City, and has lectured in the major universities and divinity schools in this country. His work in the field of his chapter includes *The Celtic Penitentials* and (with Helena H. Gamer) *Medieval Handbooks of Penance.* His book *The Celtic Churches: A History* will be published early in 1974 by the University of Chicago Press.

Since beginning his studies of medieval historiography under Ray C. Petry, Roger D. Ray has contributed several articles to journals in both Europe and America. Presently he is preparing a book-length manuscript on the Latin historiography of the Middle Ages with Professor Bernard Scholz. He has taught at Chatham College and is now Associate Professor of History at the University of Toledo. In November, 1972, he was one of thirty-six invited participants in a conference on medieval historiography sponsored by Harvard University with a grant from the National Endowment for the Humanities.

B. Maurice Ritchie was educated at Davidson College and the Duke Divinity School and is completing his doctoral dissertation at Duke

University. An ordained Methodist minister, he served for five years as Campus Minister at Appalachian State University. At present he is the Director of Admissions and Student Affairs, the Divinity School, Duke University.

With degrees from the Duke Divinity School and Duke University, Gerald H. Shinn is currently a Professor in the Philosophy and Religion Department of the University of North Carolina at Wilmington. He wrote his dissertation under the direction of Ray C. Petry with the title, "The Iconography of the Dresden Manuscript of the Sachsenspiegel in Relation to Its *Weltanschauung* and *Zeitgeist*.

George H. Shriver was educated at Stetson University, Southeastern Baptist Theological Seminary and Duke University and has also done special studies at the Ecumenical Institute, Bossey, Switzerland and the University of Geneva. Among other fellowships received, he was a Swiss-American Exchange Fellow and a junior fellow with the Southeastern Institute of Medieval and Renaissance Studies. Author of numerous articles he has also edited one volume and translated two others from French. Presently he teaches in the Department of History and Geography at Georgia Southern College.

Professor of Christian Worship at Perkins School of Theology, Southern Methodist University, James F. White previously taught at Ohio Wesleyan University and the Methodist Theological School in Ohio. He is the author of five books and numerous articles. At present he is an associate editor of *Worship* and also serves on the Worship Commission of the Consultation for Church Union.

Assistant Professor of Religion at Oberlin College, Grover A. Zinn, Jr., was educated at Rice University and Duke University and did special study at the University of Glasgow. During 1972–73 he held a National Endowment for the Humanities Younger Humanist Fellowship. In addition to Victorine mysticism, he is engaged in comparative studies of eastern and western monasticism and mysticism. He has published articles in *Church History, History of Religions*, and *Studies in Medieval Culture*.

Index